Kent Skinner's Stories

Art by Kimberly Warrick

Kent Skinner

Table of Contents 1

Table of Contents 2

Table of Contents 3

Table of Contents 4

Table of Contents 5

Tex And Amy

Art by Sarah Kiefling

I have to preface this story with the fact that it stood alone as a great story for a long time before being told to a small group of employees, including a stylist named Amy at the front desk of my former shop, Rembrandt the Salon. At this time, it got even better.

My long-time friends, Vaughn and Michelle Stockton, had a Boston Terrier named Tex. One day, he was let in from outside, unaware that there were workmen in the attic fixing the a.c. He was walking down the hall just when the ceiling opened up, and a Mexican gentleman descended from the ladder. Totally alien concept. His eyes bugged (more than usual), his back went stiff, and as he furiously barked, a turd shot out of his butt!

Fade to salon... Amy, looking confused, asked, "How did you know? Was he not wearing any clothes?" The dog, Amy. The dog.

Famous For Something

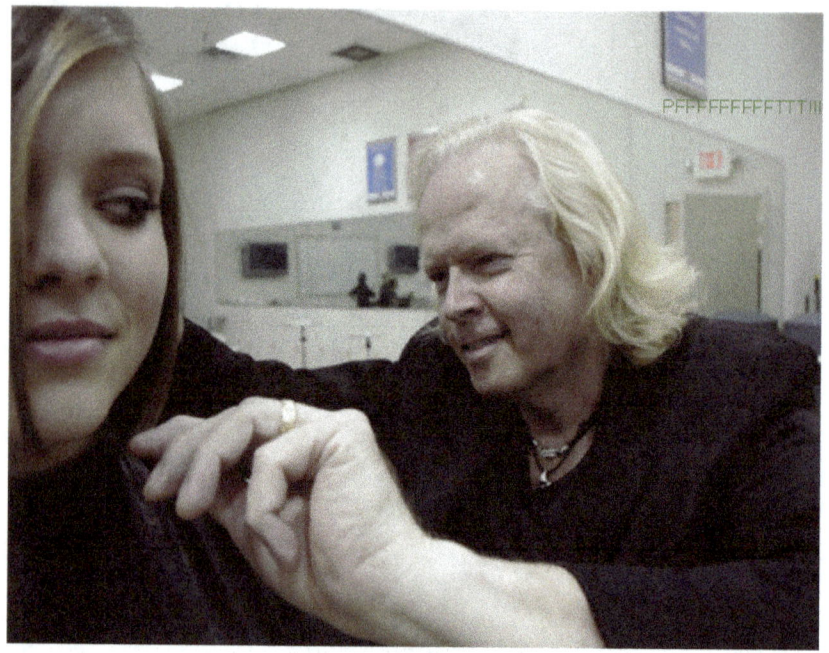

Photo by Adam Threadgill

I should probably follow with this gem.

After a long day of watching the staff of one of our California schools attempt certification in Haircutting and having missed lunch, someone grabbed me a protein smoothie, which I slammed before going on stage as the guest speaker that night. All was going well. I told stories, gave a little motivational speech, and demonstrated a very cool haircut. As I was finishing the cut, I squatted to do a last bit of refinement, and the protein shake started to talk back, and I momentarily lost control of a very important muscle. The room was all concrete and mirrors, and there was no doubt where the sound came from. After the surprise and laughs subsided (mine, too), I said, smiling, "Raise your hand if nothing like that has ever happened to you!" No one raised their hands. After they shared a couple of embarrassing stories, things progressed well. A few months later, in Las Vegas, at one of our big education conventions, a young lady came up and said, "Hi!" "Hi," I said. "Do you remember me?" "I'm sorry. Where from?" "You farted in my school!." Great. I'm famous. For Something.

Austin and Ma

Photo by Andrea Davis

This is one that confirms in me that there is some kind of cosmic sense.

When I first moved to Austin for my third year of college, I went down without a place to stay. I slept in my car for a couple of nights while I sought an affordable apartment. I found a little diner near 6th Street and Lamar, where I made my home base. Good eggs, bacon, and hash browns by a masterful cook. I would spread my newspaper and feed the payphone until I finally found my very efficient efficiency apartment near campus, The Brownlea Apartments. That's another whole chapter. A year later, my sister, Carolyn Garner, found me another little apartment. It just happened to be right behind that diner on the same driveway! O.k. Cool coincidence. Maybe. One day, my mother came to visit. She walked in with a stunned look on her face. "What?" I asked. She replied, " I used to live here! The house is gone, but it was right here on this lot!" I had no idea that she had ever lived in Austin, much less that she had lived right there. This was no accident.

Car Wash Cutie

Art by Kent Skinner

When I was in hair school, I set a goal that in five years, I would own my dream car, a Datsun 280Z. (Pre Nissan) I was closing in on year five and wasn't even close. I called in all my cheap and free haircut favors and started charging for my services. Only lost a couple that didn't really respect what I did. No big loss. Anyway, I did end up with a cool, used bronze 280Z 2+2. It was like an extended cab Z with a back seat! Great car. So, one day, I pulled into the gas station and was filling up when a pretty blonde at the next pump looked over and smiled. I smiled back and, feeling a little cocky (me?), thought, " Yeah, I'm not a bad-looking guy and I have a hot car!" I finished filling up and pulled around to the car wash, rolled down my window with the old school crank, punched in my code, and pulled forward into the tunnel. I reached for the window handle.....and it was not there! It had fallen off between punching the code and pulling in. I looked ahead, and the sprayer frame rapidly came towards me. I searched and felt frantically for the missing handle! No luck! All I could do was drive through. Totally drenched, I pulled my shirt off and dried my rock star locks and face. I looked up in my rearview mirror and guessed who was behind me in line. The blonde cutie from the pump was laughing her ass off. Lesson learned? Don't get too cocky. Something may be right around the corner, waiting to knock you down a notch or two!

Robotaco

Robotaco | Art by Kent Skinner

Another unfortunate but true story.

Years ago, I pulled up to the intercom at a fast taco place. In a monotone and robotic-sounding voice, the kid said, "May...I... Take... Your... order ?" I'm thinking, Cool. The kids were playing Jetsons and pretending to be a robot or something. So, I answer in kind. "I'd... Like... A... Beef... Burrito... And... A... Large... Coke." So I pull up to the window, and the kid isn't fooling around. He has some kind of palsy! "That'll... Be... $3...59." I shrank in my seat. There's someone ahead checking their order, a stone wall next to me, and someone behind me. Nowhere to run. I just said sheepishly, "Thanks."

It was later suggested that I should have just followed through. "May... I... Have... Some... Hot sauce?" that it might have made his day. "Maybe...they'll... Let... Me... Drive... Someday," Ouch.

Cracker Barrel

I used to travel a lot doing classes for Paul Mitchell in chain salons and might spend a week going from one city to the next and doing two or three a day. On one trip through Tennessee and Kentucky, I got hungry. When I'm hungry, I can get a little grouchy, but I usually recognize it and seek protein. I saw a Crackerbarrel ahead and thought, "Perfect. Chicken fried chicken!"

If you are familiar with the restaurant, then you know that it is behind a gift shop. I walked back and waited by the hostess stand for what seemed like 5 minutes. It probably wasn't, but it only takes 30 seconds to make or break an experience. Finally, a girl walked up and, not even making eye contact, asked flatly, "Need a table?" I was to make a wisecrack but reminded myself. "Protein, protein." She led me to a table, never looking at me or saying another word. She also made the mistake of seating me where I could watch her treat several more parties the same way. I could see them looking at each other, wondering, "What's with Miss Attitude here?" I remember thinking, " She is absolutely the wrong person for this job! Someone should say or do something." I remembered "Protein, protein." and decided to see how I felt after I got grouchy. Sure enough, I felt a little more forward-focused after I ate but decided to act anyway. I walked up to the hostess stand, reached my hand out, smiled, and asked what her name was. "Tiffany," she replied, probably thinking, "Oh crap. Is this the secret shopper?." "Tiffany, I'll bet you have a beautiful smile," I said. Then she smiled, and boy, did she have an amazing smile! I wish she had used it earlier. She said, "I called in sick today, but no one could come in, so I had to work." I then realized that I wasn't dealing with a snotty kid who hated her job but a poor, sick teenager who came to work in spite of feeling bad.

You sometimes have no idea what is going on in someone's head or heart unless you try to connect. I might have gotten her fired! As I left, I turned around and saw her greeting another party, still smiling! I don't know if I made her night or not, but I know it made mine. I still tell this story years later, though she has probably forgotten the weird guy who asked her to smile.

God Bless You!

photo by Glenna Skinner

One should be able to express oneself in one's domain.

About ten years ago, I, feeling the need, entered MY bedroom and closed the door. I entered MY bathroom and closed the doors. I entered the little toilet room and closed the door. I then made an appropriate noise for that locale. Apparently, toddler Savannah, ninja-to-be, had followed me. From outside the door, I heard her tiny voice. "God bless you!"

To this day, if I am in a public restroom and I hear someone make a similar noise, I, too, say, "God bless you!" Usually, after an awkward pause, I hear, "Thanks?"

Aussies

Art By Kent Skinner

Before I owned Rembrandt The Salon, a fellow stylist who will remain nameless unless he steps up and says, "That was me!" finally got around to watching Crocodile Dundee on VHS and...was...obsessed! Now, we all occasionally slip into a foreign accent for fun or effect, but for TWO FREAKING WEEKS, we listened to his lousy Aussie accent without shooting him. One day, I was next door eating lunch when I overheard two guys laughing and talking at the next table with what sounded like real Australian accents. I had to introduce myself and ask a huge favor. They were big rugby player-looking kind of guys and great sports. As it turned out, they were from New Zealand but close enough. About 45 minutes later, they showed up at the salon and asked for the aforementioned stylist. " What's up, guys?" he asked. "Are you_____?" they asked back. "Yes." He responded, sensing something not quite right. "We're with the Australian Anti-Defamation League, and we understand that you've been walking around talking with a bad Australian accent and makin' us look bad, and we're going to have to ask you to stop!" He started to sputter and asked nervously "Is this some kind of joke?" Unfortunately, I lost it there and cracked up, ruining the opportunity to milk it for a while longer. The fake accent disappeared for good.

The Special Shampoo

Another early pre-Rembrandt/Hair Odyssey story.

There was a newspaper article concerning some local stylist who was arrested for offering his upscale female clients a service that he called "the SPECIAL shampoo." This was a source of some amusement. The owner of our salon at the time was Richard Watts, and that day, he had a lady client in the shampoo bowl that he knew well and also knew was a good sport. He asked her if she wanted "the SPECIAL shampoo," and she said, "Sure." To her surprise and amusement, he climbed up onto the shampoo chair, straddling her, and began to shampoo her. Laughter ensued. Again, another stylist, who will remain nameless unless he responds, thought this was pretty funny and tried it on his next guest. "You want the "SPECIAL shampoo?" he asked. "I guess so," she replied. He, too, mounted the chair. Laughter did not ensue. Screaming did. She was a first-time client. I think he didn't work there much longer.

Susan and The Alien Pod

Art by Kent Skinner

One Halloween, someone left a giant gourd on our front porch. It probably measured about 3 feet long and 14 inches in diameter. It reminded me of the Bodysnatcher pods, all green and lumpy. I never figured out who put it there or why, but that would be one of the lesser weird mysteries in my life. It must have happened for this reason. I decided to take it to work, thinking there was something I could do with it. I was right. As I pulled up, Susan Jarvis, a teacher at my school, a very smart and articulate woman, was exiting her car, a white PT Cruiser. I let her get out of sight, and as luck would serve, she hadn't locked her car! I strapped the Bodysnatcher pod into her back left seat like a medium-sized kid and went to work and waited. A day went by. Nothing. Two days. Nothing. Checked the car. Still there. A week passed. Two weeks passed. Still nothing. By this time, word had gotten around, and one of her students spoiled the fun and asked her if she'd looked in her back seat recently. It was leaning on my back bumper when I came out later. Of course, it was me. Who else?

Dance Party Friday

Where else could this happen? Every Friday around 3:45 p.m. Everyone at Paul Mitchell The School stops what they're doing, the big speakers are dragged out, and for about 15 minutes, we have Dance Party Friday!

One time, someone asked, "Why don't you get out and bust a move?" I didn't reply, "Because I can't drink on the job." I said," Because my prosthetic is loose, and I'm afraid it might fall off!." Three weeks later she said "I'm mad at chu!." "Why?" I asked. She said, "You told me you had a plastic leg, and I was prayin' for you!" "Hallelujah!" I exclaimed! "It worked!"

Blind Haircut.

Art by Sarah Kiefling

My sister Barbara reminded me of this one.

One time, I had a high school kid in my chair, and he had a buddy waiting for him in the lobby. I don't remember what started it, but we decided to make his friend think that I was blind. I stared through and past him while I worked and felt around on the counter for my comb and products, knocking things over in the process. When we finished, he led me to the front counter, which I bumped into and checked him out. I said "Thanks!" and "Bye!" facing the wrong way. As he walked out, he told his friend, "My hair always looks like s---, but I feel sorry for him."

Mt Nebo

Photo by Glenna Skinner

One of my favorite places on Earth is a state park in Arkansas called Mt Nebo. I have watched countless sunrises and sunsets from her rim. I have even dedicated original music to her sunset and sunrise points, which can be found on Soundcloud under my name. It has become a soul-cleansing ritual for me to climb down the rocks and play this music at both of these spectacular daily and yet always breathtaking events whenever I am able to visit there. It's often happened that other spectators leaned over the edge and expressed their thanks. One time at sunset, I saw two eagles performing their mating ritual, circling each other, ascending, then coming together, free falling, and then breaking free to circle and climb again. This went on for a while. It was amazing! Experiences and places like this truly make me feel closer to God.

More Fish!

Art by Kent Skinner

My long-time good friend, Vaughn Stockton, and I went to lunch one day, and a fellow stylist, Robert Van Den Hull, joined us. Captain D's had an all-you-can-eat special, and Robert opted for that culinary delight. Robert is a big ol' country boy from South Dakota with a perpetual grin, an S. Dakota twang, and a good appetite. He demolished his first round of fish pretty quickly. This being his first visit, he asked, "How do you get more fish?" Vaughn, always quick on the draw, replied, "You just yell 'More fish!'" Robert looked toward the counter and yelled, "More fish!" A few people looked around at him, but there was no response from the counter. We were sideways laughing, but Rob hadn't clicked on the fact that we were messing with him and yelled louder, "MORE FISH!" Everyone looked, and we were in stitches! The counter help looked perplexed and a little concerned. "Why don't they bring me more fish?" "You're supposed to bang your fists!" He did. We're dying, tears rolling down our faces, sideways on the benches clutching our sides. He figured it out. He grinned his big goofy grin! I'll never forget the expressions on those poor girls' faces!

Laughing In Church

Art by Kent Skinner

Another uncontrollable laughter story.

We were auditioning churches. I was not paying much attention to the sermon. When a sermon becomes more about salesmanship for your particular sect than a spiritually uplifting message, you've lost me. I was doing what every hairstylist does in a public place: people-watching. Five rows up from us was an older couple, probably in their late seventies or early eighties. I looked at them just in time to see him, in an attempt to be the sweet husband that I'm sure he was, put his arm around his wife. He didn't look first, and he smacked her hard on the side of her head! She turned, stunned, and gave him the most horrified look I'd ever seen. Her hair was still wobbling from the impact. I nearly died. You know the feeling. When you can't laugh, it's ten times worse! I think Glenna may have cracked my ribs with her elbow, trying to quiet me. I don't think we are welcome at that particular house of worship.

Alligator Alley

Art Kent Skinner

A couple o' decades ago, I was on an education road trip doing salon classes and traveling in a small Ford station wagon with a sales rep we'll call..."Tammy." Well, "Tammy" was a mid-thirties ex-hippie who still had a taste for an herbal mind-altering substance that is now legal in several states. While I truthfully had lost interest in it myself, I did not deny her her herb. Nor could I have. On this particular trip, we were traveling east across Florida. "This highway is called Alligator Alley!" she informed me. "Really? So we should see alligators?" I asked. "Really! We should see lots of them!" she said. "And that's the

Everglades! She said, pointing to the foliage surrounding the highway. I replied, "Um..those are crops, Tammy." "No! That's the Everglades!" "See those lines between the plants?" I asked. "Those are furrows between the rows of crops," I corrected her. "No. That's the Everglades!" she insisted. O.k. As it turned out, not only were those NOT the Everglades, nor did we see any alligators, we were not even on the right highway! We were 60 miles north of "Alligator Alley." I rode her about that one for the rest of the trip.

A few months later, we were on the follow-up series of salon classes. The same state of mind on her part. Actually, we had to backtrack 60 miles when she left her purse at a restaurant, but his time, we really were on Alligator Alley! It was dusk, and the setting sun cast a golden hue across the landscape.... (or maybe it was 2nd hand smoke) when we came upon a large cement drainage ditch, and there were easily 2 dozen alligators in it! "Pull over!! Pull over!!!" "No! No!" "Pull over!! It's fine!" She pulled over. "Be careful!" She pleaded! "I will!" I assured her. I opened the door, and what I could see on the shoulder that she couldn't was a 4 ft strip of tire tread by my foot. I leaned over and grabbed it and jumped about, flailing it over my head and screaming, "AAAGGH!!!, AAAAAGH!!!" There was a change of undergarments on "Tammy's" agenda after that.

Border Check

Art by Kent Skinner

Another salon education trip was to South Texas, where I visited and did classes for a large chain. Having a free afternoon, I went across the border and did some Christmas shopping. I bought a piece of coconut from a street vendor and nibbled on it on my trip back to Texas. At the border, the guard asked me if I had brought any fruits or vegetables back, and I said, "Well, just this piece of coconut." And popped it into my mouth. "PULL OVER TO STATION 28!!" he suggested firmly. I complied. I hadn't considered how a long-haired American in a rental station wagon orally disposing of a chunk of white substance might look.

At station 28, they went through all of my bags several times, and one cop kept saying, "I know it's here! I can smell it!" I knew there was nothing to find and just went along with it. They got a drug-sniffing dog up on the table, and he, too, went through all of my bags. Suddenly, he lunged, snarling, and plunged his big head into one of the bags. He emerged shaking an open bag of...Cheetos, scattering them everywhere! After the laughter died down, it dawned on me what the cop must have been smelling. I said, "I know what it is... smell my hair." "What??" "I know it's weird. Just smell my hair." He did. "THATS what I'm smelling," he said.

I had been putting a little patchouli oil in my styling product and thus had a subtle herbal air about me. All was well and ended well. Moral: be aware of your olfactory effect on others and preclude snarfing at the border.

I Kilt It

Art by Kent Skinner

There is a GREAT movie that came out years ago starring Liam Neeson and Jessica Lange called Rob Roy. Watch it. Rob Roy McGregor was a legendary real-life Scottish Robin Hood-type character, and Skinner was part of the McGregor clan. I tell you this in a lame attempt to justify this next part.

O.k. I have a kilt. Yes, a kilt. It was given to me by fellow Scot David Armstrong. It's a heavy black canvas non-bifurcated garment made by Utilikilt and has lots of snaps, straps, and zippers. It's a really macho skir...I mean, kilt. Very rock star.

Anyway, being in a business where being noticed can be a good thing, I wore it to The

Gathering. No, not that one, the Paul Mitchell one in Las Vegas. It's a huge annual educational event with thousands of hair people, and, yes,

I was noticed. Lots of compliments, contacts, and conversations. Now, the good part. When I got home from said event, my wife Glenna asked me, "Why is there makeup on the inside of your kilt?.".........I had no answer! In spite of the legends you may have heard about hairdressers, there truly was NO reason for there to be makeup on my kilt at all, much less inside it! "I...don't...know!" I said. Then, thank God, it dawned on me. I had used aerosol spray tan on my ghostly white legs. Whew!

Ever wonder what goes through the dry cleaners' minds? No, they've probably seen it all.

Special

Six or seven years ago, I was at the aforementioned Paul Mitchell Gathering and was enjoying a glass of wine with my friend Kevin Michaels and a couple of fellow National Educators that I recognized but didn't know well. One of the ladies said, "You probably don't remember this, but five years ago, you sat down at our table, turned to me, and asked me, "What makes you special?" She was right. I had no recollection of this. I wouldn't put it past me, but nope. She said, "I popped off with something stupid like "I'm special 'cause I'm special." She continued, "You know how you think later about what you wish you had said? Well, I went home and thought about it. I actually made a list of reasons why I'm special. I even got a little pissed off about it. "Damn it! I'm special because..." You didn't have any idea, but I was going through a bad period and was really down on myself. I was suffering from really low self-esteem, and you didn't know it, but you gave me the nudge I needed to pull my head out!"

Wow. I truly had no idea. I don't even remember sitting by her. I probably sat down and asked, "What's on the special?"

Anyway, you never really know what's going on with people until they share, and sometimes, it doesn't take much to help someone.

Pirates

Art by Kent Skinner

So, one day at the front desk of Rembrandt The Salon, Melinda brought up the subject of the big deal at the time, "Riverdance." Again, Vaughn, the instigator, asked her, "Did you know that Irish step dancing was invented by a pirate with no arms?" "Really?" she asked. "Really!"

The next morning she showed up pissed and embarrassed. She had gone to a big party and shared that bit of fascinating trivia with the whole group. "I can't believe you told me that! " she said. We replied, "We can't believe you believed us!"

Picture a step-dancing pirate with two hooks protruding from his shoulders. "Arrrrr maties! This is fun!" By the way, September 19 is, in fact, National Talk Like A Pirate Day. Spread the word

Tripping In Mexico

Three or four years ago, the founder and dean of the Paul Mitchell schools, Winn Claybaugh, invited the Paul Mitchell Advanced Academy teams, school owners, and friends to go to Puerta Villarta and enjoy themselves for a week. We stayed in a really beautiful villa up on the hillside overlooking the ocean, had margaritas, watched sunsets, bonded, basked, baked, and burned. One afternoon, I walked into town alone, listening to some great music on my iPod, and while looking at the spectacular view and not watching my feet, I stepped into a pothole. Doh! I went down hard, scuffing my knees and wrists pretty bad. An American couple ran over and offered assistance. "We're staying right here. Come in and get cleaned up." I declined gratefully, stating that I was ok. I was more embarrassed than hurt. I cleaned off with my water bottle and moved on. Just as I replaced the earbuds, the song "Tubthumping" by Chumbawumba came on! You know, "I get knocked down, but I get up again. You're never gonna keep me down!...."

I couldn't help but grin as I proceeded on my adventure!

Atlanta

Nearly every time I have visited Atlanta, it has been an adventure. On one of my early salon chain education trips, I had a night off and saw that The Pretenders were playing at The Roxy. Cool! I drove down, and while standing in the drink line, I heard my name. "Kent!!" I looked around, and there was one of my former Rembrandt friends/customers, Cindy Furlong. I don't think I'd be outing her here by describing her as a little tough guy lesbian. Back here in Dallas, she and her former partner were Cindy and Cindi, if I recall correctly. Cindy reminded me of a typical 15-year-old boy, and Cindi was a real girly girl with 80s hair. Both of them measured under 5 feet tall. Not that any of that matters. Just painting a picture. Anyway, I spent the evening sitting with Cindy and her girlfriends, enjoying the concert, and joining them later at one of their hangouts, wondering if I was going to get my ass kicked. No, no problem. It was all cool. As it turned out, Cindy had gone to hair school and was now a working stylist! Anyway...on my next visit to Atlanta, my buddy Max Droz and I were attending a Paul Mitchell training, and typically, neither of us had brought our agendas. We had no idea where we were going. I assured him that we would very likely see some of our cohorts at the airport, but if all else failed, we could call Judy Froelich, our Dallas coordinator, when we landed in Atlanta. Nope. Nobody. We were looking around when an older black gentleman said, "Y'all needin' transportation?" We said, "We're looking for our friends." He said, "Who y'all with?" We said, "Paul Mitchell." He said, " Oh, I have been takin' people there all day." "Great!" We said and followed him to his van. We climbed in, and as I boarded, I clobbered my head on the door. Ouch. So we headed out of the airport, and he looked back and asked, "So, y'all with

Johnson and Johnson, huh?"

(Pause.......) "Uh...no....where are you taking us?" I asked emphatically. "To the Howard Johnson," he replied. "I know, THAT'S not it! Get me to a phone!" (These were just pre-fliptop phone days.) So he got me to an outdoor payphone. It was 43 degrees and drizzling. Not going to work. I made him take us to the nearest hotel and used their phone to try and find out where the hell we were going. After calling several likely hotels, I sheepishly called Judy and admitted our *dumbness*. So we finally made it to the hotel an hour later, missed the pre-training hair jam, and got to our rooms. It's not over. I try my door, but something is keeping the door from opening. I see through the crack, and there is a towel on the floor. "Hello?" Nobody's there. I push harder, and something gives. You know the hydraulic thing at the top of the door that eases it shut? Mine is loose, and I have just shoved it through the sheetrock into the room next door. Panic ensues, not from me but from next door. I called the front desk, explained the intrusion, and said that regardless of the issues and the towel on the floor, the bed was clean, I was tired, and I was just going to stay. They were nice enough to comp the room for the night.

The next day, I called little Cindy to see what she was up to that night, but she had plans with her lesbian bowling club. O.k. Fine. I went down to the lobby and saw one of my mentors, a very smart and intimidating Tommy Callahan (V.P. of education for Paul Mitchell), in the lobby, and because he remembered the long leather coat he had complimented me on earlier, he asked if I'd like to join him and several other hotshots for barbecue that evening. I was not a big barbecue fan, but how could I refuse? I dragged Max along, and we sat amongst the elder gods and listened to some amazing and hilarious tales and ate some damned good barbecue. I remember listening to their stories and envying their being part of these legends at one point. Who should walk in but Little Cindy and her lesbian bowling club? I invited them to join us, and she, being a hairstylist, eagerly joined us and basked in the greatness at our table. It dawned on me that although I was sitting among earlier legends, we were part of a new wave with legends of our own to forge. From where I stand now, decades later, I eagerly anticipate and joyfully watch new legends being born! I have the best job in the world! . On my NEXT trip to Atlanta, I was determined to get to my hotel without any more craziness. I caught a real licensed cab this time, and I told him I wanted to go to the Peachtree Hilton. He asked, "Is that the Peachtree Hilton or the Hilton on Peachtree?" Frustrated and with a half whimper, I replied, "I..don't know........." Then my smart side kicked in. "Take me to the closest one, and we'll see." We arrived at the nearest one, and I asked him to wait while I ran in and verified. I stood at the desk for a minute before looking around and seeing a group of people dressed in black sitting in the bar and waving at me. I walked over and said, "So, I'm in the right place!" They said, "You're in the right place!" "Great! Order me a Bombay and tonic. I'll be right back!" I went outside and let my cab driver go. I rejoined the group in black and took a sip of my drink. Then I realized that I didn't know any of these people! Young hip people all dressed in black and partying...hairdressers, right? Nope. It seems that Bon Jovi was staying in the hotel, and they assumed that I, with my rock star locks and dressed in black, was part of the entourage! Crap! Wrong hotel again! I called another cab, and an hour and a half later, I was in my bed.

Mic Mishap

Main Stage – IBS 1996

Photo by Andrea Davis

One of my favorite moments as a platform artist was being asked on Main Stage at the International Beauty Show by Stephanie Kocielski to demonstrate a One Finger Twist, a collection technique that I might have seen once. Faked it til I made it. All was well, but this story actually took place later that day. I was on the smaller stage demonstrating a collection cut, and some woman of undetermined national origin kept saying, "I want jus to cut my hairs!" I thanked her, telling her that I had all of my models. "No, jus don understand. I want jus to cut my hairs!" Yes, thank you, but I have all of my models!" "No, I really jus wan jus to cut my hairs!" "Maybe I can get someone to cut it for you." "No, I wan juuus!"

I walked backstage and said, "Will someone please get this woman the f--- outa my face...ace...ace...ace?."..... It echoed through the hall or maybe in my mind. My headset mic was still on! I peeked out, and she was gone.

This happened again once at the school when a guest artist left the stage to answer the call of nature and forgot to turn off his lapel microphone. When he returned, I said, "You look a little flushed!"

Europe Stories

It was one of many to come, suggested by my nieces Rebecca and Bethany Lodge. Rebecca went on a trip to Europe and asked me to share some stories. I spent hours with a cassette recorder and loved every minute of it. I don't know if the tapes still exist. For that matter, I don't know if cassette players still exist!

Two days after graduating from high school, I landed in London, the beginning of my real education. I backpacked through Britain and Europe for 2 1/2 months with a Britrail and a Eurail pass that allowed prepaid or inexpensive access to almost any train and youth hostel and student hostel memberships that usually provided a roof over my head. I learned and experienced so much during that short time. I probably learned more about myself and the world around me than I did in 5 &1/2 years of college. There were lonely times, times of great camaraderie, survival stories, funny pranks, spiritual growth, and goofy awkwardness. Hey, I was 18. I may not tell these in exact order and may have to elaborate (make stuff up) to supplement faulty wiring upstairs. Some names will be changed to protect the narrative. Why let a little truth get in the way of a good story?

Just to help me remember some of the stories worth telling, in no particular order:

- The Woods
- The Buchanans
- I like Yanks
- Pants in the closet
- Paris and the rail strike
- The magic ring
- Marseille and Gareault Var
- Carmen and the smelly soccer team

- Miss Portugal

- Tortilla and a Coke

- Sick in Barcelona, and my guardian angels

- The station floor of Lyon

- "F--- you!" in Monaco

- Asian Woman and the Peach Pit

- "You did it! Didn't you?"

- Wendy, the good little witch

- Singing for my supper in Rome

- Standing guard in Napoli

- Switzerland, Germany Austria

- Oslo and the Kon Tiki

- Amsterdam!

- Lowenbrau

- The Rhine boat and homeward bound.

Hmmm. I know I'll think of many more and will plug them in as we go. Some of these will be combined, and some will probably be forgotten. If one intrigues you, it may get told before its time. That's cool with me. That's all for tonight. Much to come!

Braum's

A couple of months ago, I took the kids to Braums for the first time ever...I know, child neglect. Turn me in. Of course, they were excited. I was hesitant because of a couple of experiences a long time ago with fuzzy "No, that's just black from the pan" "No, it's not. It's fuzzy from lack of refrigeration!" apple pie and the time they ran our fries through a prematurely cooled down fryer, then a cook who had spent 3 minutes arguing with her boyfriend on the phone before acknowledging us hand-delivered them, her arms and apron covered in various syrups making her look like one of the background Walking Dead extras... Ok. I digress. This is actually an uplifting story. Stay with me. So we were standing in line, and I noticed an older, heavyset woman with very short "I don't give a crap anymore" hair...sorry, the hairdresser in me never sleeps...sitting, eating alone, and I thought I recognized her as the crossing guard lady from my kid's elementary school. This woman was out there rain or shine, sweltering or freezing, scowling and blowing her whistle if you looked like you were going more than 20mph whether you were or not. Yes, tweeted more than once. Sorry. I had a fast-looking car. Anyway, I digress again. I approached her and said, "Hi, my name is Kent. What's your name?" She said, "They call me Miss Peggy." "Were you the crossing guard at Groves Elementary?" "Why yes, I am!" I said, "It's nice to meet you. Thank you for looking out for my kids!." She said, "It was my pleasure!" I went back to the counter a minute or two later, bought a gift card for her, and asked that they give it to her after we left. The manager said, " Miss Peggy? We love her! She's in here almost every day." She even matched the gift card herself. Well, Miss Peggy started to leave before us, so we scrambled out to the car and escaped any "Aw, you shouldn't a." Stuff. Again, this isn't a "What a nice thing I did." story. It's a "What a great lesson for my kids" story and a " How good it made someone, including ME, feel!" story. I believe in the "Pay it forward " concept. Anyway, I don't know if it made her day or not. It certainly made mine.

Oh yeah. No fuzzy pie or cold zombie fries. Thanks Braums. I love your eggnog.

Short and Curlies

Speaking of hotel nightmares.....we were, weren't we? Oh yeah, a couple of stories ago...again, one of those many PM education trips ago, I was near Houston and didn't have a reservation but needed to sleep, so I pulled into a half-decent by reputation anyway, motel.

There was a young girl and a guy at the front desk who seemed to be her boyfriend. I got my key and went to my room. No doorknobs. Ok. Back to the office. "Room looks great. Do you have one with doorknobs?"

"Oh! I'm sorry!" she said. And ran another key for me. This room did indeed have doorknobs...but no light bulbs. "Room looks great.....in the dark. Do you have any light bulbs?" Her boyfriend ran over with light bulbs. Still polite, I said, "Thanks." I went out for dinner, returned, and discovered that I had left my key in the room. Once again, I returned to the office and shared my challenge. Just to make it a little sweeter, I lost a dollar in the Coke machine and bothered her for that, too. Alright, fed, back in my room with knobs and light bulbs. I was tired from driving and had also recently pulled a muscle in my back, so a hot bath sounded great. I pulled the shower curtain back and.....(scary Psycho music, woop! woop!)....the tub was filled with short curly hairs. Now, I didn't really care which end they came from. A bath was out of the question and has continued to be at hotels since. I was too tired to complain again, I thought. "I'll rinse the tub out and just shower in the morning." I kicked back on the bed and flipped channels for a few minutes, and then another thought struck me. "If the tub was dirty....." I pulled back the sheets. The bed was also full of short, curly hair. I grabbed the phone. " I would like a clean room with light bulbs, doorknobs, a clean bathtub, and a bed WITHOUT SHORT CURLY HAIRS IN IT! And send your boyfriend to come and move my bags because my BACK HURTS!" The next room was fine. No hair, yes bulbs, yes knobs, FINE! The next morning, when I checked out, there was a Middle Eastern gentleman working the desk. I related my experience to him, and he responded loudly, "NUT MY

FAULT!!! NUT MY FAULT!!! HEVING CONSTRUCTION!! NUT MY FAULT!!"

I told him I wasn't after anything but just thought he'd like to know. "NUT MY FAULT!!!" Another prime example of above-and-beyond customer service!

Missing Tolkien

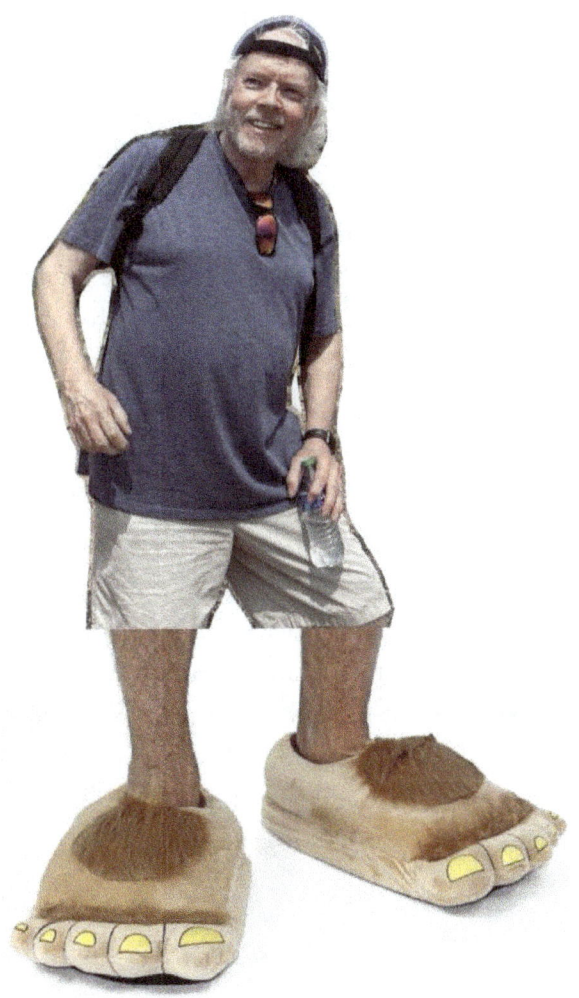

Art by Kent Skinner

Ok, one of my backpacking through Europe stories.

As some of you know, I am a lifelong Tolkien fan. I was turned on to Lord Of The Rings by a kid in our 50-mile hike through the mountains of New Mexico at Philmont at the tender age of 13. His name was Lane Houston, as I recall, and he later became an award-winning physicist.

Every night around the campfire, he would tell parts of the story very well. It was the perfect environment for my imagination to open up and live.

I later read The Hobbit and The Lord Of The Rings a couple of times. I have friends who have read them multiple times. At 17 years old, I wrote music to some of the poetry. I know, super nerd. Decades later, I recorded it without permission. You can listen to it on Soundcloud if you wish. I'm pretty proud of it. Anyway, I was pretty proud of it then too, and while traveling through England, I showed up unannounced at his home in Dorset with hopes of performing my Middle Earth Medley (Lord of the Rings Medley on Soundcloud). As you can probably guess, this didn't happen. The very polite guard at the gate said that even if he could let me in, Professor Tolkien was basically mentally living in Middle Earth, and I'd be wasting my time. He was trying to complete The Silmarillion but kept writing and rewriting and would probably never finish it. He was correct. Professor T's son tied it all together after his death in 1973. So there's my brush with literary greatness. So close, but...

Before the Peter Jackson movies came out, I dreamed that I was at the theater, seeing them and sitting, afraid that I would hear the songs that I had worked on put to different music. The songs were there, and it was MY music. I awoke thinking, "I've BEEN RIPPED OFF!" When the movies came out, I was relieved that none of the poems I had set to music were in them. Whew.

She Was Breathing

Art by Kent Skinner

Surprise surprise. I come from a long line of practical and sometimes not-so-practical jokers. I will tell some of my dad's and his friends's stories at some point.

I mentioned living at the Brownlea apartments in Austin in a previous story. I'll just say that it had once previously been a dormitory and had been converted into VERY efficient efficiency apartments. I shared a bathroom with a total stranger who became a lifelong friend, Delton Childress. Delton was a quiet, introverted, chain-smoking anthropology major. We allowed each other access to each other's apartments. I had a fridge, and he had a phone. We also had a few street people who discovered how to get on the roof and camp out. One cold night, I had, perhaps foolishly, let a couple named Lisa and Wiley sleep on my beanbags and luckily suffered no loss. I should also mention that being an art major and always a bit eccentric in my decorative taste, I owned a life-sized Christmas elf. One day, a couple of weeks later, I heard that Wiley had gotten stabbed and was in the hospital. So far, this doesn't sound much like the setup for a practical joke. Anyway, my wicked streak kicked in, and I went over to Delton's, tucked the aforementioned elf into his bed, and arranged a pillow under the covers so that it looked like someone was sleeping there. I went to class, and when I got home, I went over to check on the elf. Still tucked. Suddenly, Delton arrived. "What's up?" he asked and went to the sink and rattled some dishes. "Shhh! Keep it down!" I said. "You have company." He looked suspicious and then asked, "Who is it?" I responded, "Do you remember the people I let sleep on my floor a couple of weeks ago? Well, that was the guy that got stabbed. Lisa came to my door distraught and tired, so I let her lie down on your bed because mine was covered in laundry." "Well, o.k. But how long is she going to be? I have a bunch of homework to do." I told him to bring his books over and study in my apartment. He did. He camped out on the beanbags and studied. I fell asleep, and when I awoke the next morning, I thought, "Oh boy, well, this has gone too far." and decided to sneak over and remove the elf. Delton was awake and said, " C'mon Skinner. I gotta go to class." I went next door and, talking to Lisa the elf, said, "Oh good! You're up! Tell Wiley I hope he's o.k.." I put the elf out in the hall and retrieved it a few minutes later. Later that day, the wicked streak reappeared. I picked up the elf and knocked on Delton's door. "Yeah?" "I want to introduce you to someone. Delton, this is Lisa. Lisa, this is Delton." He responded. "No.....no...she was breathing! At first, I thought...but then I looked...and she was breathing!" To this day, he will not admit that I got him. P.S. Wiley has fully recovered and is now a Republican congressman. OK. I made that part up.

Ralph vs. Tor

Art by Kent Skinner

So, a couple more practical jokes. My buddy and Jack B. Quick bass player, Ralph Fahrbach, rented my guest bedroom for awhile while he was between wives. One of my ongoing passions is Halloween costumes and masks. A frequent recurring actor in Ed Wood's B movies was Tor Johnson, and I happened to have a Tor Johnson mask. I think this character was from "Plan 9 From Outer Space." It was a full-head mask of a bald, blank-eyed, and grimacing space zombie. One day, while Ralph was out, I rigged a dummy with the Tor Johnson mask, and I hung it from the light fixture in his closet with a string attached to its torso and the doorknob so that it would lunge towards him when he opened the door.

Later that afternoon, I was on the phone when Ralph came home. I was leaving an important message when I heard Ralph scream "SWEETJESUSHOLYJESUS!!!!!!!!." I completely lost it in the middle of leaving my very important message, whatever it was. Apparently, he had pulled the door with enough force to rip the fixture out and shatter the bulb, so in addition to a space zombie leaping out at him, it happened amid a shower of glass and sparks! Sometimes, things just work out better than you can plan!

Bruce's Van

Bruce McRoberts, the keyboardist and mastermind behind Jack B. Quick, had a bad habit of leaving his van unlocked. One night, at about 2:30 a.m., after a long night of moving band equipment, playing all night, and moving said equipment again, I saw his van full of keyboards, speakers, and amps at the U Totem near our houses. I had to pull over and check the van. Not only was it unlocked, it was running! I had no choice! Demons made me climb into his van and move it around to the side of the building. I waited across the parking lot, leaning on a gas pump. Bruce came out, and it was not just a classic double take but an actual triple take! You know that sound that the coyote makes as he hovers over the edge of the cliff before plummeting? Something like "oggityoggityoggity"? I am pretty sure I heard Bruce's head do that. I started laughing, and it all came to a crashing close. This and the previous Ralph and Tor Johnson stories lead up to the next one.

Ralph and Bruce's Revenge

After driving from San Antonio to Dallas and returning from visiting my mother for Christmas, my girlfriend and I walked into my house and turned on the lights to see that my TV and stereo were missing! "Aw crap!" I exclaimed. And began looking around the room for anything else not there. The living room was a mess, and the couch was upside down. Well, that probably had nothing to do with anything. Anyway, I called 911, and in the middle of reporting a robbery, my girlfriend came into the room and said, "It's all here." "What?"

"It's all here in the back bedroom." "Never mind!" said I. Good one, Ralph and Bruce!

Bachelor Party

First, you have to understand that the 70s were a much different time. Done? O.k. Fast Forward." Keep your finger on that button. O.k. Stop. Rewind. New millennium.

My bachelor party began at Bone Daddies, a BBQ restaurant. We were seated at a long table, and of course, I sat at the head of the table where I could keep an eye on my friends and make sure they all behaved like gentlemen. After a couple of libations, I noticed that our pretty, young waitress very strongly resembled a girl that, many years before, my long-time friend Bruce and I had both had a thing for. Well, Bruce had actually...had an encounter..just once...at a party...in a back room (hey, it was the 70s), and I believe he never saw her again. When our waitress came down to my end of the table, I said, "See the guy on the left at the end of the table? Next time you are down there, ask them if they know your mom, and when they ask what her name is, tell them it's L--- C----. If they ask how old you are, you are 21." She agreed. A few minutes later, I saw but could not hear the exchange. Bruce stared, and I watched his jaw slowly drop. He was doing math. Later, on the way out, I saw him give her a card and say, " Tell your mother that I'd really like to speak to her." The night went on, and a few hours and a few brain cells later, I remembered how I had left poor Bruce. I explained and apologized. He said, "No, that was a good one!" He later claimed that the card had MY number on it! It didn't.

Bryan and The Black Shadow

This one goes back to one of my favorite jobs, though I will freely admit that I was not mature enough to be responsible for 100-plus kids on a daily basis. I was a camp counselor and eventually director at a YMCA day camp, Camp Kiwanis on Bachman Lake. Too many stories...

There was a little guy named Bryan Anthony Meeks who was always in some kind of trouble but was also the subject of a lifetime's worth of stories. Sometimes, he went by Bryan, sometimes by Anthony. I also served as a bus driver, another whole page or two of stories. Every once in a while, we would have a sleepover, although not all the kids could stay. I made my run to the Downtown YMCA with the South Dallas kids who weren't able to do the sleepover, and as it turned out, Bryan (or Anthony, whichever it was that day) was supposed to have stayed at the camp.

Side note: I must have been a counselor at the time because of the next exchange. My group, the 10-12-year-olds (Lord help me), had found, on one of our hikes, a foot-long steel bar that weighed several pounds and, for whatever reason, would fight over who got to carry it. Well, it slowed them down and gave me some kind of reward system.

Anyway, on our trip downtown, Anthony (or Bryan) remembered that he was supposed to spend the night at the camp sleepover. No problem. We'll just go back. En route, he asked, " Why do you carry that steel bar?" "Oh, I don't know," I replied. He asked, "Fo hitting folks?" "Yeah." "Bad folks?" "Yeah." I added, "Have you ever heard of the Black Shadow?" "Yeah!" "Well, I'm the Black Shadow!" He asked, "You the Black Shadow?" "I'm the Black Shadow!" Pause........ "You got a cape?" "Yes." "You got a mask?" Yes." "Can I see?" "OK," I said. As it happened, I was in desperate need of my V.A. check and was expecting it in the mail, so I stopped by my apartment on the way back to the camp, leaving him on the bus. (I'd probably get fired today). It was there, and I grabbed the cape that I had worn in my high school senior play in the role of... yes, "The Black Shadow," a wannabe highwayman in Tom Jones. "Where's your mask?" he asked. "At the dry cleaners," I replied. He was totally impressed. "Can I tell somebody?" he asked. "No, absolutely no. It's our little secret!" It worked. For a couple of summers, we had our little secret. One day, after getting in some kind of trouble, I had him helping me with my Mr Fix it routine, and I had him holding a ladder for me while I changed a bulb on a 30-foot pole. "I'm gonna tell everyone that you the Black Shadow." "Go ahead. See who they believe!" I said, hiding my laugh. He didn't. I would love to have been there a year or three later when he realized...."Hey....wait a minute...." I'd love to know where life has taken him.

Update: Bryan, his 2 brothers, and I are Facebook friends.

The Birds

Art by Kent Skinner

I still consider myself sort of an athlete. (Back in my hippie days, that was sacrilege.) I do tie a black cloth belt around my waist and proudly and incredulously wear it several times a week, and I am surrounded by people who are WAY, WAY better than me. Including my wife, Glenna. (Word Champion in TKD and former national and state champ in powerlifting) Anyway, there was a time when I spent a huge amount of time on my state-of-the-art at the time Cannondale 12-speed bicycle. I rode in a couple of centuries. (100 mile rides) including the often lethal Hotter Than Hell 100, some 100ks, and some 50ks. So, anyway, the intro to this story has somehow overshadowed the simpler and cooler story I set out to tell. On one of my training rides, I was on the last stretch of about a 35-mile ride out by what is now Firewheel Shopping Mall. I was riding west into the sunset on Naaman School Road just east of 78. On my left was, at the time, a new housing development, and on my right was the open countryside where the mall is now. Imagine if you were a bug, where would you congregate? The first street light after open country! If you were a bird, where would you hang out? Right! So I was riding west, as I said, and I noticed a dark cloud sprawling across the road ahead of me. It was birds. An almost solid mass of birds! I rode right into it, not knowing what to expect. Shades of Alfred Hitchcock! It was denser than any scene I saw in that movie. It was actually dark in there! The birds spread out a little bit, creating a dome of space that was maybe 12 feet in diameter. The cacophony of bird sounds and the flutter of wings in total surround sound was overwhelming! The whole experience might have lasted 8 seconds, but it felt like an hour! I emerged unpooped upon, every cell of my body tingling! "WOW!!! WOW!!!!WOW!!!" I screamed!

Anyway, it was a sensation I could not do justice to with words. I just reread this story, and the voice in my head was Frazier Crane. Weird.

Tow Story

One evening, when I lived in Austin, my girlfriend and I exited the place we had gone to hear some live music (What? In Austin?) only to find her car gone. Upon looking more closely, we found the NO PARKING sign at ground level in the brush by the out-of-business restaurant where we had parked. I got the phone number, and we walked back to 21st College House, the student co-op we lived in. I called and was told that we had to wait until the morning to pick it up. Grrr. So, the next morning, we drove all the way across town in my old beat-up 65 Dodge Van to the tow yard. Her car was parked alongside the portable building. I pulled up next to it, and a man came running outside yelling, "You move that van around front!!" I said, "This is her car, and here's your money." He yelled again, "You move that van around front!!!" I repeated myself. "This is her car. Here's your money!" "MOVE THAT VAN!!" I moved it ten feet from the side to the front of the building and backed up to the window. I went in and dropped the cash on the counter. "SIGN THESE PAPERS!!" he suggested. I told my lady friend to get in her car, and I got in my van. He came after us with his dogs chasing and barking. He tried to hold the chain link gate, but I kept moving, and he jumped back. We escaped without signing anything but minus 50 dollars. Hey, we were poor college students. We got home, and I was still fuming. I called the tow yard. He answered, "Ace Towing. Can I help you?" I said, "Yeah, this is Bill Filbert down at Filbert Automotive, and I got a lady who needs a big red truck moved outa her driveway. My driver's down with the flu, and I thought you guys might want it." "Well, thank ya, good buddy!" he said. I said, "You'll recognize it. It's a big red GMC truck with a ladder and hoses on the back." I then gave him the address of the fire station around the block from the co-op. I don't know if he drove all the way across town to tow that big GMC with the ladder and hoses on the back or not, but I'll bet he did. Revenge is sweet.

The Beatles

Art by Sara Kiefling

When I was in 5th grade, The Beatles hit America. Now, every generation has had its iconic music stars, but Beatlemania was nuts! Media manipulation was in its formative years, and their machine did a phenomenal job. We saw them as good boys having a good time and devoured their music. At the time, it was mostly catchy pop songs and remade R&B tunes that we were hearing for the first time and loving. Many of us also felt a need to form camps. A lot of us thought that you could be The Beach Boys fans or The Beatles fans (soon after, The Rolling Stones became a third option). Later, we realized that it was all good. Anyway, my lifelong brother from another mother, Vaughn Stockton, made the infinitely regrettable decision to sell me his Beatles ticket for $5! Today, I don't know a greater Beatles fan (in any incarnation) than Vaughn. The concert was at Memorial Auditorium in downtown Dallas. A venue that had been swallowed by the Dallas Convention Center but was a multi-use facility with nothing more than a house sound system that was probably adequate for basketball games. They didn't know what they were in for. My dad dropped me off a couple of blocks from Memorial Auditorium with the agreement that I would meet him at that spot at 8:30. Can you imagine doing that now with a 10-year-old?

Anyway, I found my seat and waited. Every once in a while, a Beatle would pop out and run around the outer aisle, chased by a mob of screaming teenage girls. Insanity. The opening act, Cilia Black (sp?), hadn't left the stage by 8:30. I ran out and met my dad and explained the situation. I ran back and got there in time to see The Beatles, the band that would change music forever. I said, "see." The aforementioned sound system was grossly inadequate to override the cacophony of screaming girls. I could barely hear what they were playing, but in retrospect, it was really more about the experience than their performance. I recently saw a T-shirt that said, " I MAY BE OLD, BUT I GOT TO SEE ALL THE GOOD BANDS!" I did.

K&G

Photo by Glenna Skinner

I did a girl named Karen's hair once for a photoshoot, and she sent a friend in who had long, dark, wavy hair, assuring her that I could be trusted with it. This girl would come in infrequently, and I would lecture her gently but unsuccessfully about the importance of maintaining such glorious hair. While I admit to being attracted to her, I also felt that we were on different wavelengths, so I opted to just enjoy her from a short distance. Her name was Glenna. I saw her through some tough times, became her confidant, and might have jumped had I ever been given the right signals. At some point, she sent me pictures of herself in articles about powerlifting, which had become her passion. She eventually became a state and national women's powerlifting champion. On one of my trips through east Texas, I crashed on her futon, still harboring a crush but still not getting the vibe. Years, a few relationships, and many haircuts and conversations later, she showed up with a current boyfriend at a couple of my gigs with Max Droz and Marc Mydill at the Windale Tavern. One night, she showed up alone. I walked her out to her jeep, gave her a kiss, and said, "We should talk." A couple of weeks later, she called me and asked, "Are you ready to talk?." We did. We eased out of our no-future relationships and began seeing each other. A little over a year later, I bought her a very cool ring. Just a ring, mind you, but a cool ring…and I lost it! After doing a fair bit of soul-searching and deciding that I needed to make this more permanent, I found the missing ring! Well, I didn't want it to be upstaged by the diamond I had bought since, so I gave it to her. "Surprise! Cool ring! Sorry I lost it!" A week or two later, I took her to dinner at one of our favorite restaurants, Queen of Sheba and at one point, she said something like "If you ever buy me more jewelry, I hope you don't lose it again!" I said "Well, I guess I'd better go ahead and give you this then." I reached into my pocket, dropped to one knee and asked "Will you marry me?."........................silence.... She looked confused. "Did you say something?" I replied. " I SAID, "Will you MARRY me?" I can, at times, be soft-spoken, but I really think the air was sucked out of the room momentarily. I've heard that happens sometimes. Anyway, obviously, she said yes. 23 years and two amazing kids later, we're still at it.

p.s. A couple of years later, The Dallas Morning News featured us in their True Romance column, and I participated in a show of solidarity with one of the Paul Mitchell school teachers who was going through chemo and had my typically long hair buzzed off. It wasn't completely gone, but it was way shorter than Glenna had ever seen it. She reacted in shock, "Oh my god! The newspaper is taking our picture on Friday!" "Well, guess what? This is how I look right now!" We went to press with my new do.

Ma and MacDonalds

Art by Kent Skinner

Back in the 70s, there was a story in Time magazine about McDonald's, how the most nutritional part of a Big Mac was the bun that the McDonald's corporation overall used more energy in a year than 5 major cities, including Detroit, did in two years. I was never a fan of their food anyway, so I sort of boycotted them for over 20 years. I say "sort of" because I crumbled on one memorable occasion. I was doing a Christmas Holiday Hair show for Paul Mitchell with about 75 hairstylists attending. Before the show, I needed to run by Walmart and pick up some bobby pins and ponytail holders. I realized that I was starving and wobbly and HAD to eat something quickly before showtime. There was a McDonalds right there. I had seen a commercial (and did it again recently) where they showed someone cracking an egg over a round form on a big restaurant griddle. " How bad could that be?" I asked myself. Well, first they couldn't break my 5 dollar bill so I had to wait for change. Then, that girl couldn't cook, so I waited for the other girl, who I saw open the fridge and remove a carton labeled "EGG PRODUCT." Mm, Yum!

I did eat it, and I will admit that it tasted really good. About an hour later, I was standing on stage sharing some very cool styling techniques when my stomach started talking to me. I couldn't understand the words, but they had a lot of "g"s, "r"s and "l"s in them. Maybe a couple of "b"s too. I realized that I needed to leave the stage very quickly. "Talk amongst yourselves!" I said to my audience and beelined it to the bathroom just in time. Yes, I turned off my microphone this time. Sorry, Ronald. There will be no more Micky Ds for this kid. Ever.

A few years ago, when my mother was in her final weeks, she hadn't been able to eat at all, but one morning, she told me that she saw an Egg McMuffin in a commercial and thought that she might be able to eat one. Boycott be damned, I was going to feed her whatever her heart desired. I drove to the nearest McDonalds and pulled up to the intercom. "Yes, please, I'd like an Egg McMuffin, please, "I said. The girl on the other end said, "We don't make them after 10:30." I explained that my dying mother was requesting one and the circumstances. I'm sure the girl had her mind on her master's thesis or something and wasn't paying attention. "I'm sorry, sir, but we can't make them after 10:30." I saw red. "Well, my mother and I, thank you very much!" I said as I peeled out, quite pissed. Then I slammed on my brakes and said to myself, " No! This is b.s.!." I pulled up front, got out, and went in and asked for the manager. I explained the situation, and he was extremely nice. He said that they use a special grill for the Egg McMuffins and that it was cooled off but that he would do his best to make my mother the best Egg McMuffin that he could. He did and would not take any money. I got it home, still hot, and my mom managed to get most of it down. One kind act = redemption in my eyes for McD's!

Change Is Good

Back in the eighties, before I joined up as an educator for Paul Mitchell, I was at a hair show with the owner and stylists from the salon that I eventually bought. When I attended a show, I always wanted to leave with something new and, to some degree, be entertained. I had always wanted to be a platform artist, but that was yet to come. I don't remember his name, but they announced that _____ from Atlanta was going to be up next, sharing some razor-cutting techniques. An older lady (older than us and probably younger than we are now) sitting behind us leaned forward and said proudly, " I've been a stylist since the 50s, and I've been doing razor cuts for thirty years!" "Really!" I probably said, thinking something like, " Well, thanks for sharing, total stranger lady!" The artist came out, and the story he told was that he was sitting on the toilet one day...(thanks for THAT visual), and he picked up his wife's Bic razor and thought, " I wonder if I could cut hair with this!" He used her cuticle nippers to cut the guard off and opened the blade. Those of you who are in my industry know that if you've ever been to a hair show, one of the first things you see upon entering is the merchant area, basically a flea market of beauty and hair paraphernalia that you may get excited about for a moment and most of which will eventually end up in a box in your garage. Well, the artist, _____... (Maybe Gary, somebody?) found and bought what looked like a bicycle glove with open fingertips and brushed bristles similar to a Denman brush built into the remaining glove fingers. So, he attended to his model. He pulled all of her hair straight up and, in one whack with a large pair of scissors, cut it straight across. He did the same straight back and straight out at the sides. He then got after it with his glove and Bic razor, flailing away at her hair. Hair was flying through the air, and the result was that messy bedroom hair that epitomized the eighties. The audience was impressed. Lots of "Wow!" and "OhmiGOD!!" I looked back, and the older stylist who had been "doing razor cuts since the 50s" was stomping out. She was pissed.

I guess she thought that her time had come back around and that she was going to be patted on the back and validated for what she already knew. That didn't happen. Now, we weren't all going to go out and get gloves and Bic razors, but it was cool to see someone stepping outside of the box, and it was fun! I had an epiphany. I vowed that I would never be that lady, the "veteran hairstylist" who thinks he/ she knows it all. I've heard one of my mentors, Winn Claybaugh, say, "If you stop learning, you stop growing. If you stop growing, it means you died! There's a lot of people that still show up and punch the clock every morning that died a long time ago!"

I vowed to be a perpetual student and keep my mind open to Change! It's one thing you can count on. As my friend J.C Mahan in Oklahoma says and has it hanging over the door to his salon, "Change is good! Change is my friend!"

The Pendant

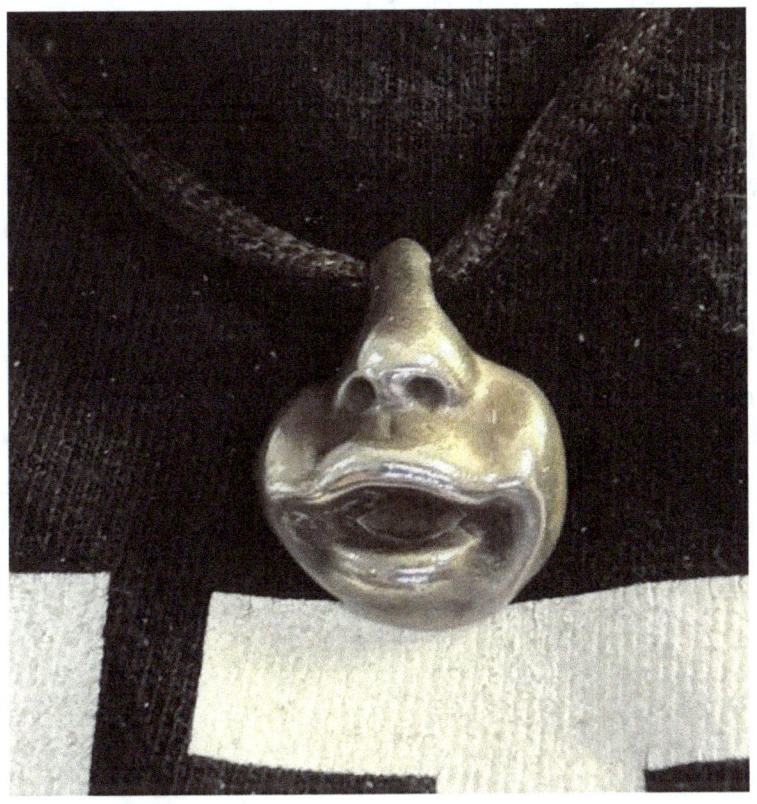

Art by Kent Skinner

I still wear this pendant (actually, one of its offspring). I made the original brass ones in the metalworking class at U.T. Austin. They made a small stir, so I made several and gave them to special friends. Over the years, I have made more and given them to people who have impacted my life. One time, years ago, I was cutting a new client's hair, and he asked, "Where did you get that?" I replied, "I made it." He said, "I have one!" We could not trace the path it had taken to him. Someone must have lost or given or hocked it or something. Two weeks later, my girlfriend and I were looking at a Foleys catalog, and I commented on a model that resembled a little girl who attended Camp Kiwanis that I had heard had become a model but probably was not this girl. The next morning, I got a phone call at the salon. " You probably don't remember me, but I used to go to Camp Kiwanis..." I got goosebumps. "I know who this is." "This is Kris Collins." I replied, astonished, "I was talking about you LAST NIGHT." Kris was one of my favorite kids, a little free spirit who had the roam of the camp because, I found out later, she had been telling people for a couple of years that I was her dad! Anyway, she had gone to lunch with some friends at work, saw the pendant hanging from the rearview mirror, and asked, "Where did you get this?" He told her about the conversation we had while he got his haircut, and she said," I've been trying to find him for 20 years!" Anyway, long story short (too late!), we reconnected. Lost track again for a while, but she showed up at a Poor David's Pub Christmas Party benefitting the Parkland Hospital Children's Burn Victim Camp. We played, and we have reconnected. Note: some of the quotes and probably the facts, though not deliberately, may have been modified in the interest of storytelling.

Honeymoon Hair

Early on in my career as a Paul Mitchell National Educator, I was assisting Jeanne Braa and Robert Cromeans in a Dallas show. People think that it's all fun and glamorous, but there is a lot of work going on backstage and pre-show! For instance, spending an hour and a half crimping Kizzy Gonzales's hip-length hair to prepare her for a 5-minute do. There are also a lot of hurry-ups and waiting and a lot of camaraderie. One of the stylists from a salon where I had done classes dared me to do something "different" with my hair for the show. At the time, my hair was about shoulder blade length, blonde, and naturally curly, ala Robert Plant. Jeanne was wearing her traditionally short platinum hair with some fun dreadlocked "mall bang" extensions. Very cool. Between the adrenaline, the caffeine, and the aforementioned backstage bonding, I decided that it would be funny to pull my locks up into a ponytail over my forehead, sort of poking fun at Jeanne's look. "Do it!! Do it!!" my backstage cohorts pleaded. I did. I walked out on stage to assist an astonished Jeanne Braa. "What is this?" she asked with a clenched smile. "It's Honeymoon Hair!" I answered. (A term we used for a quick takedown updo.) I pulled out my ponytail and shook it out. Robert was almost doubled over. The audience loved it.

Jeanne didn't. Later backstage, I got a little coaching on types of humor and their appropriate use.

Lesson learned.

It wasn't over. The next night onstage, Jeanne said to the audience, "You know? I had this little fantasy of giving Kent a chin-length bob!............. Would you let me cut your hair?" I responded with my own clenched teeth, "Sure!" "Well, we'll see if we have time."

"Crap, oh crap, oh crap, oh crap!" I thought. "Please, Lord, no time, no time, no time!" I prayed. I called my girlfriend and said, "Jeanne wants to give me a chin-length bob!"

GF says," But that's for young hunky-looking guys." "Oh THANKS!! Guess what? I'm getting a haircut!!" Says I. The show rolled on with me still praying. At the very end, when I thought I was home, free Jeanne remembered. "Oh yes! We were going to cut Kent's hair!" I submitted and smiled while I saw the locks fall and heard them splat on the stage. I was still unsure if it was directly tied to the previous night's shenanigans or not, and it is always an honor to get a haircut from the likes of Jeanne Braa, but either way, I was not ready to go surfer, dude.

We got well beyond that adventure. I assisted both Jeanne and Robert on several more occasions. No pranks. Lessons learned. Respect your mentors, and discretion is the greater part of valor.

A few years ago, I accidentally butt-dialed Jeanne while shopping for a treadmill. "Hello?...Hello?" Imagine hearing the voice of one of your heroes emanating from your shorts! She understood and asked me to partner with her in a charity event. Of course!

Jack B. Quick's Gig From Hell.

Photo from video by Michael David Pyeatt treated by Kent Skinner

Jack B. Quick was a valiant effort to perpetuate the drama and musical virtuosity (and fun) of the Progressive / Art Rock movement of the '70s, '80s, and '90s amid the rising tide of other forms resisting such. We performed all original music and played on concert stages and in all the coolest venues in Deep Ellum, Oak Cliff, Lower Greenville, and... more than a few dives. Fond memories, good stories, and a strong sense of fellowship ensued. Here is one of many, some untellable, stories.

One small venue in Deep Ellum that we played several times was called Loose Change. To load our equipment in, we had to enter through the back of the club, take an immediate left, climb a flight of stairs, turn 180 degrees, and enter a skinny hall leading to the stage above the bar. (See above picture). Understand that before any of this, we had disassembled our own and joint equipment, loaded up vehicles, and transported such to an aforementioned club, which is standard procedure for any band. We assembled our equipment, sound checked, performed all night and reversed this process every gig. Also, standard procedure.

For a long time, we had a string of great performances and receptions, including praise in the press and a small following. Occasionally, we would have a weak night and feel a little deflated, but we loved what we were playing and believed in the group mission. After a while, the tides began to turn in the local music scene, and sometimes the reception got a little iffy. This was one of those nights. Playing intelligent music to a drunk crowd can go a couple of directions. "YOU SUCK!!" came a voice from the front of the stage. "What?.......carry on." said the voice in my head. We did. "YOU SUCK!!!" it came again. Distracting, to say the least. We carried on, and as I recall, we gave a good performance with passionate, dramatic, and often whimsical music resplendent with whirling irons, rain sticks, and sexual innuendo. After the show, I was talking with Ralph Fahrbach, our terrific bass player, and happened to gesture, pointing towards the rear of the club, when I locked eyes with the moron who had been yelling at us. He looked like "DOH!" and slinked away out the back, thinking I had been pointing at him. As always, we loaded out, drove home, unloaded, and set back up for rehearsals.

A couple of weeks later, we were playing there again, and while in the bathroom, some guy said, "Man! You guys are Great!!" I thanked him and said, " A couple of weeks ago, there was some a--hole yelling " YOU SUCK" at us." Just then, the punk who had yelled at us stepped out of the toilet stall with a cast and sling on his arm. I said, "As a matter of fact, that's the a--hole!" He tried to skulk away, but I stopped him and asked, "What was your problem?" " I dunno. I was just f---in' with you." I lit into him. "YOU load all that equipment up and haul it down and drag it upstairs and play all night and tear it down and haul it home and have some drunk a-hole yell "YOU SUCK!" at you all night and see how YOU feel!" He said he was sorry. I honestly don't know how his arm got broken, but I wonder if he pissed someone else off that night. Maybe he thought it was us. I'll bet he learned to curb his tongue from all that.

If you are curious about the music that we made, find me or Ned Nefarious on Soundcloud for a taste.

Mother Blues and The Love Machine

Art by Kent Skinner

My buddy Charlie Pittman, fellow Camp Kiwanis counselor, and I were out one Saturday night, and we decided to run into the local rock club Mother Blues and see if a couple of lady friends might be there. We couldn't have been in there more than 5 or 10 minutes. I was driving a total chick magnet vehicle, a 65 Dodge YMCA camp van w 100 thousand plus miles on it, green shag carpet in the back, a see-through floor (rust), and a Craig slide mount 8 track tape deck. When we got back to the van (no luck with the chicks), the slide-mounted deck had slid. Someone had stolen it. Various curse words were uttered when Charlie said, "Look!." There was a pair of glasses on the console. We went across the parking lot and waited for a few minutes, and sure enough, some idiot stumbled up to my van and climbed in. Charlie and I ran over like Starsky and Hutch, and I threw the door open, dragged the guy out, and pushed him up against the side of the van. "Wow, man!.....I thought that this was my van!" the totally wasted perp exclaimed. Seeing how high this guy was, Charlie said, "I think he might be telling the truth!" "Show me your van!" I demanded. We walked two doors down to Gerties, MB's sister club, and he tried to get into a panel truck, but it was locked and looked nothing like my love machine. He finally admitted that it was not his truck, and we headed back to Ma Blues. Suddenly, an El Camino pulled up, and the driver, not realizing that I was holding his friend by the scruff, reached out and offered a handshake. " Name's Duncan!" he said. I shook his hand, still holding his pal. Meanwhile, Charlie was lifting the tarp off of the back of the pickup and held my tape deck aloft. "Here it is," Charlie said triumphantly. They then got a clue as to what was happening and sped off, leaving their friend. The police were already out front because young Einstein had also left his WALLET in somebody else's car! We walked up front, switched custody, and spoke briefly with the cops.

Two days later, I came to work, and everyone was saying, "You're a hero!" "Huh?" The Dallas Morning News had published a story about it. Something like.."A series of Lemmon Avenue car burglaries came to a close Saturday when Kent Skinner of 2460 Bachman Blvd and companion (Charlie didn't get his name in) caught... blah blah blah." I never spoke to the newspaper, but they quoted me as saying, "GIVE ME BACK MY TAPE DECK!!" and the hapless crook replying meekly (their words), "O.K. Sure."

Fortunately for me, the newspaper had transposed the numbers in my address, and it took the guy's lawyer two months to find me and ask me to please not press charges. The guy had a previous marijuana arrest and could not get bail. I figured two months was good enough for me. I said, acting *real* tough, "OK, but you tell your client that if he ever sees me, he'd better turn and walk away. If he sees me in a club, he'd better leave!" Like I would even recognize him. They agreed, and I got a story to tell in addition to a few months (if that) more of pleasure listening to that pinnacle of high fidelity in my intergalactic pleasure ship!

Haircuts For The Homeless

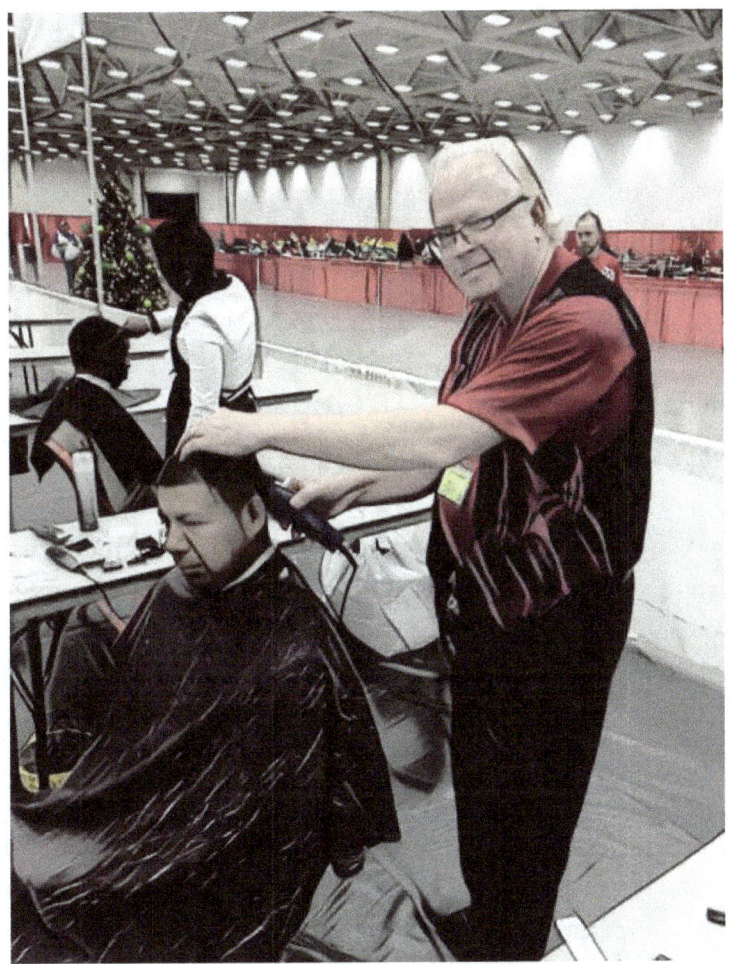

Art by Kent Skinner

Every year, our school is asked to do free haircuts for the homeless at a HUGE event called Operation Kindness. It is held at the Dallas Convention Center, where literally thousands of homeless people are bussed in and given food, shoes, clothing, haircuts, counseling, an opportunity to call family, and, if desired, religious guidance. We typically bring 15 or 20 student volunteers, and once the coordinators start feeding us people, we don't stop for hours. There are families, individuals, veterans, couples, etc. You name it, we see and serve it. My first time, I remember thinking perhaps naively that it would be a steady flow of happy and grateful people, and there were plenty. I also realized that although down on their luck, many of them still showed that they still had their pride and were pretty particular about how they wanted their hair. Some of our volunteers had hardly cut anyone at all yet at school but wanted to help. They sure got their trial by fire! " Kent!!! What's a bald fade?!!!" The last time I went, we were done and packing up. At some point, the coordinators have to close the line down and say, "I'm sorry." Well, one guy managed to slip on through the exit and, with a panicked look and tone, said, "I HAVE TO GET A HAIRCUT!! I have a job interview tomorrow!"

I said ok and asked him to have a seat. I still had not packed all my tools up, so I started cutting his hair for him. It appeared that his hair had not been washed in weeks. He was quite obviously mentally challenged and started sharing a mixed-up dialogue concerning his apparently domineering deceased mother and auto parts. He was not making much sense. Suddenly, out of the blue, his tone changed, and he said, "You cut my hair two years ago!" I stepped around and looked at him. He was right. I had cut his hair before. I hadn't been able to volunteer the previous year, but I did remember him because he vaguely reminded me of an old friend. Through the fog, he remembered a simple, ten-minute kind act and the person who, by chance, had done it. I tell my students that they are superheroes because they will have the opportunity to touch people's lives and will sometimes help change their lives for the better. Sometimes it's a simple haircut. Sometimes, it's a touch or a smile or an open ear. I was a little astonished to hear that this guy remembered that haircut. I hope he is okay, and I'll look for him this year. If I don't see him, I'll pray that it's for a good reason. Maybe he got that job.

Lionel

Let me begin by saying that "Lionel" is not my absolute favorite client. I will say that he is one of my most intelligent and outspoken clients. He is not the guest that we see in my books and say, "Oh boy!!! Lionel is here!" In fact, I have to be sure who has an appointment before and after him. Once he arrives at the salon, chances are very good that he will launch into whatever topic, usually news-related, that he is fascinated with this month and won't stop talking to whoever will listen until his hair is cut and dried, he is rebooked, and possibly he has been redirected towards the door. Let me say, in his defense, he is a good soul. He is kind, generous, lonely and needs human interaction... and a new deodorant. He is a retired lawyer, a staunch Democrat, and a practicing Buddhist. In the past, I would listen with a grain of salt to his stories of being a psychological counselor, drug abuse counselor, or being involved with special forces and politicians, and so forth. One time, the subject came up, and I asked him where he went to high school, and he responded, "Lake Highlands." I realized that he was about my cousin's age and asked him if he knew him. "Oh yeah. We played basketball together. " He told me of a basketball game in high school when he got the ball in the last minute and, from the far side of the court, sank one in and won the up-until-then-tied game. Ok, add salt. Sometime later, I remembered and asked my cousin, " Did you know a guy named Lionel in high school." He said, "Yeah, there was this weird kid I played basketball with. One game we were in the last few minutes and from across the entire court......." Wow.

No salt is needed. This story was already properly seasoned!

Lionel had been through a very rough divorce. His wife had literally lost her mind. He was so much in love with her, and it was very, very hard on him. One night, after listening to him for months and offering whatever insight or support that I could during his haircut appointments, he told me that I was his best friend.

Wow. I was honored and sad. He told me that I was one of the only reasons that he had not ended his life! Double wow! I would flinch when I saw his name on the books, and I was his best friend. Is I one of his reasons for living? I cut his hair once a month!

Whatever time you have for a person in need, however much you can give without giving too much may be just enough for that person. Sometimes, it's lending an ear, or maybe it's the stinky hug at the end of a haircut, but that's a superpower! A willing, open ear, a smile, eye contact, or a touch can help someone change their life, maybe even save it!

I will always be there for my "best friend" Lionel.

Gerald and the Chelsea Hotel

Art by Kent Skinner

There is an incredible hotel in New York City called The Hotel Chelsea. It was home to Bob Dylan, William S. Burroughs, and Dylan Thomas, and it is where Sid Vicious and his girlfriend Nancy ended their lives. It is not open to the public anymore, but Glenna and I spent a few nights there a few years ago. It is, of course, said to be haunted. I saw an elderly woman with long white hair and dressed in white glide to her room next door. We hadn't seen her before and didn't see her again. Probably just a long-time resident who cared not to interact with tourists. Anyway, there was a 9 or 10-story rectangular stairwell with unending amazing artwork lining every wall all the way to the top. It also was a great natural reverb/ echo chamber. One night, Glenna and I sat on the steps and sang and played my guitar to an appreciative passing audience. Another night, while admiring the fantastic artwork on the eighth or ninth floor, we heard two kids, I'm guessing we're 8 or 9, talking a couple of floors below. " Hey Gerald! Did you know this hotel is haunted?" "Really? Naw...!" I waited a minute and leaned over the edge and, in a loud, drawn-out stage whisper, said, "Geeeeeerrrrraaaaaalllllld!" It echoed down the stairwell.

Panic ensued. "Oh, my gawwwwd!" They yelled, running! Maybe they'll read this someday. I hope not. Now they have a story too.

Runs With Scissors

Art by Kent Skinner

I have a couple of black T-shirts that say "RUNS WITH SCISSORS." I had them made years ago with the idea of giving them to my salon assistants when they graduated to the floor. Anyway, I was wearing one when we were hosting Paul Mitchell Artistic Director Robert Cromeans and the current Director, Stephanie Kocielski, and assisting them in a crazy hair show at Billy Bobs in Fort Worth, of all places. So, Robert notices my shirt and says, "Runs with scissors?" I responded jokingly, "It's my Indian name." Ha ha funny. My assistant said, "No, Kent's Indian name is "Drops Many Combs." Ha ha, funnier and true. Robert's assistant said, "Robert's Indian name is "Makes Twins Cry" Ha ha, funniest." Apparently, there was an issue with a couple of models in a previous show.

4 or 5 months later, at the Signature Gathering at Robert's ARC booth, his tables are covered with "I RUN WITH SCISSORS" gear. Whaaaaaat? I saw him later and questioned him, "I Run With Scissors?" He replied, "Yeah, my boy Kelly (Cardenas, I assume) was wearing this shirt..." I shook my head. "That was YOU!" He realized. He invited me up on stage and acknowledged that I was the inspiration for his entering the t-shirt market... and presented me with... a t-shirt.

I burned a little bit from that for a while but came to the understanding that we seek and find inspiration from everywhere, and I can't say that I've never learned something and created something better. It's called doing your research. So he made a million bucks... Never mind.

A few years later, he posted a picture of his Hummer floating in the Mississippi River flood. I posted, "I SWIM WITH SCISSORS!" This time, I want half.

My Time

Today, sitting in on a theory class in one of our schools, the instructor asked the class if anyone had read the chapter. A student replied, "Got stuff to do!." It reminded me of an epiphany I had back in college at U.T. I had managed to coast along in my studio classes, relying on my existing talent. Now, there is a difference between talent and ability. In my opinion, talent represents your potential, and ability is the result of exercising that talent. One of my instructors had suggested that I needed to spend more time outside of class in the studio. I responded with

"But that's MY time." He looked a little astonished and said, "What do you mean YOUR time? Why are you here?" I had nothing. He was right. It was a part of my life to be devoted to learning and improving. A lot of money had been invested in my education, and as talented as I was or thought I was, I had a LOT of room to grow. Many people grow comfortable with the parameters and perimeters of their lives. What they've always done is their reality. Some continue to think and act the same way they thought and behaved in high school. REMINDER! We are perpetual students. There is a lot of room in the warehouse of your mind for skills and information. Some of it you will never need. Some of it will surprise you when the need arises, and it will be there. Soak it all in. You don't have to agree with something to understand it. End of rant.

Twins

Art by Kent Skinner

Here's an odd one that I'm prompted to tell whenever I see or hear about twins. Every twin, or mom or dad of twins, has heard a million twin stories, but this one is worthy of burdening them with. A few doors down from our house on Nashwood lived a family with three kids. At least one of them, "Lisa," was adopted and knew it. She was more of a friend to my younger sister, Barby, than me. One day, as an adult, she was walking through Valley View Mall and was astonished to see herself walking her way. Both of them stopped and gawked for a moment before speaking. As it turned out, they both knew they had been adopted but had no idea that they had an identical sister. We've all heard stories of twins growing up separately and having similar tastes or hairstyles. Not only were they coloring their hair the same and wearing it in similar styles, but here's the kicker: both of their adopted parents had named them "Lisa"! All of their lives, they had experienced weird situations like someone saying, "How did you enjoy the concert?" " I wasn't there." "But we spoke.....Lisa, right?" "Yes, but..." and the like. She must have often thought, "Am I crazy?" Anyway, our "Lisa" was excited. She had found a sister! Unfortunately, it was not a fairytale. Her sister was uncomfortable with the sudden reality shift and did not want to pursue an expanded family. She was happy with her status quo, and to my knowledge, nothing more came of it. One can hope that sometime over the years, she may have had a change of heart.

Scars

In my business, you get to see a lot of strange things going on in and on people's heads. I have asked clients politely, after knowing them for a while, how they got their hidden scars. One woman had a thin U-shaped line from about a half inch behind the hairline all the way to the back corners of her parietal bone. I asked her if she had had brain surgery or something. She replied, " No, when I was a child, I was playing on the playground, and the swing came back at me and hit me right in the top of my head and literally scalped me!" After the willies subsided and my guts un-squinched, she continued, " They flopped it back into place and sewed me up good as new!" Oh my God! That is one lucky woman. No brain damage or skull fracture, just a thin pink line hidden in her hair, unnoticeable to anyone without a reason to be digging around in there. 1/2 inch lower and... never mind. Wow.

Scar tale #2: A high school girl in my chair had a crescent-shaped scar on the right side of the back of her head. I inquired, "Do you mind me asking how you got this scar?" "Oh, not at all. One time? At cheerleader camp?" Not really. It was a cheerleader competition. "I was just coming out of the bathroom when I heard them announce that the Raisinettes (or whatever they were called) were up, so I ran down and got into formation and started doing our routine am. Ned, then I realized that I didn't know any of the girls and I was doing something totally different from them, and I cost them the competition!" Different schools have the same team name and colors. Doh! I said, "Wow! That's pretty amazing, but how did you get the scar?" She replied, "One of them threw a can of hairspray at me!"

Dog Doody College

Photo by Kent Skinner

There are so many good stories from my miserable days in beauty school. I had just graduated from the University Of Texas Austin with my bachelor of fine arts and was teetering on the edge of the real world, knowing that I did not want to be a commercial artist (remember, pre-computer, hand lettering, etc...) I had thought I wanted to be Darren Stevens, but the Elizabeth Montgomerys were nowhere to be found. Really, I had gotten my share of people with no imagination dictating the parameters of my creative output. That's another story. I had 9 months of V.A. money left over and needed to use it now or never. My good friend Vaughn Stockton was doing hair and supporting his family well and suggested that I try it. I wasn't at all sure about this, but it takes 9 months to get your license, so I figured I'd do that until I got famous as a rock star. Still working on that part. Anyway, I fell in with some brilliant people (and a few not so muc) and grew to enjoy and eventually excel in the hair business. But...this story is about Vogue Beauty College. (No relation to Vogue Magazine) Kip Cavin (above left) used to answer the phone "Dog Doody College" just to see if anyone noticed or reacted. I was one of the only people who had gone to college and/or finished high school, so it was a bit of a culture shock, and it was assumed that I should be the one to fix the door, hook up speakers, set up the slide projector or read from our 1938 copyrighted textbook. Only the school director, Mr Ken, had ever worked in a salon. He was a sour-faced but very nice old queen. One day, my mother called the school and asked for me. "Dog Doody College, may I help you?" Anyway, whoever answered the phone thought that she wanted Ken rather than Kent. Mr Ken answered in his most colorful lisp, "Thith ith Mr Ken! May I help you?" My mom, still not getting it, said, "My! Don't you sound ProFETHional!" "Why THANK you!" He replied sincerely. She then realized that she had the wrong person. No, Ma, no major lifestyle changes here.

There was a great authentic Tex-Mex place about five minutes from the school with an excellent Carne Guisada and cold beer. I'm not saying that I did anything unwise or unprofessional, but I'm just saying... So, one day, we got back from lunch, and I immediately got a ticket. My first haircut! It was an old lady that wanted a cut and a roller set. I begged my instructor, Elvia. Nope. Had to do it. The cut went fine. The roller set (the only one I ever did in school) was probably passable. There was a nasty temporary colored rinse that most of our elderly clients asked for that would stain the hair until the next weekly shampoo. They had strange names like, I swear to God, Frivolous Fawn, Pretty Beaver, and the one I had to use on this lady, Black Rage. I kid you not. I finished combing her out, my hands stained with Black Rage when she pulled out a wig and stretched it over my hard work and expected me to fix it too! I just walked away, and the beauty industry almost lost me. Elvia rescued me.

One more for now. One day, I cut a lady's hair, and then she said she wanted a manicure, too. I said, "O.K., let me find one of the girls to do it." She said, "No, I want YOU to do it!" Elvia was standing right there and nodded her head. Crap! O.k. So I set up at this little table and did the only manicure I've ever done besides the one I had to do at State Board. In addition to having to do something that I had no love for on a creepy, somewhat older lady, she started playing footsie with me (Aaaauuuh!), and her two middle fingers, on one hand, had been pulled off in a skiing accident (Aaaauuuh!) and had been reattached but were nonfunctional and a bit gnarly. "Pull on them thangs and see if you can straighten them out!" (Aaauuugh!). I believe that I developed an engram that day and, to this day, cannot stomach the thought of doing a manicure or, much less, a pedicure, even on my wife!

The Magic Ring

I said I would get back to my backpacking through Europe stories eventually. The 60s and 70s (and I suppose every decade) were full of people rebelling and seeking their unique identities. I met a young lady named Wendy in England who claimed to be a witch. Who knows? Here is our story. It really doesn't amount to much, but the important element is that she gave me a stone ring and said that it was magic. When I asked what it was for, she said that I would know when it was time. We parted ways, never expecting to meet again when I headed north to Scotland (another story) and eventually headed south again. I hitchhiked to Dover in hopes of crossing to France. Apparently, everyone else and their dogs had the same plan because I found myself in the middle of a long string of hopeful hitchers, and their dogs were also heading east. It seemed that everybody had some kind of attention-grabbing gimmick but me. One guy was dressed in his full Scottish regalia, complete with kilt and bagpipes. Another bearded fellow wore a long white robe and carried a cross. I had nothing but an army jacket, a beret, and my guitar. I assumed that I would stand for hours before someone stopped for me. I was pleasantly wrong. An old white Citroen passed all those ahead of me. The driver stopped and said, "Hop in!" I did and got a ride all the way to Dover. As I got settled, I fumbled in my pocket and felt the "magic" ring and realized that it had broken into two pieces! The driver never explained why he stopped for me with a dozen or so other people in either direction around me other than to say, "Ye look like an honest fellow!" Wendy said that I would know when the time came, and I guess that was it. Although our paths were not expected to cross again, I ran into her climbing out of some ruins in Herculaneum a month or so later. I told her about the ride and the broken ring. Oddly enough, she had no recollection of even giving it to me. - duh Duh duh Duh duh duh duh duh! (Twilight Zone music!)

My Run In With Santa's Helper

Picture me in my rock star wannabe days. I never really left that phase, but anyway, black leather jacket, long hair, black hat, and Oakleys, looking very much like the part of the biker I wasn't. I was on the last leg of my Christmas shopping several years ago and was braving the Richardson Square Mall traffic. I had circled the parking lot forever when I saw a spot come open two rows south of me. I zipped around and arrived at exactly the same nanosecond as another guy in a minivan. We paused for just a second, deciding which of us was going to be the nice guy when a little red Toyota shot in between us and snagged the space. I suppose all's fair in love and parking, but we both sat there surprised and mouthed the same word, "Really?" He shrugged and pulled away, shaking his head. I probably should have, too, but I was frustrated. I waited for a few seconds and was going to ask if she didn't see us there. She sat in her car, looking down, avoiding eye contact. I decided that it wasn't worth a confrontation and pulled away. I soon found a parking spot three rows over. I wrote on a card, "And a Merry Christmas to you!" and put it on her window and let it go. Maybe forty-five minutes later, I was pausing in the middle of the mall at a loss. "Grandma. What to get for Grandma?" I thought, staring into space. I then realized that I had locked eyes with one of Santa's elves. I recognized the bleached blond hair and black roots. It was the woman from the parking lot! Her eyes got wide when she recognized me, the scary-haired black leather guy she stole the parking spot from! I mentioned earlier that I had gotten over it. I smiled and mouthed the words "Merry Christmas." Life is short.

Paris part one

Art by Kent Skinner

I left off on my way to Dover. There's not much to tell about the trip there. I saw the white cliffs. No way not to. Very impressive! I caught a hovercraft to France. It was amazing in concept and appearance. The whole ship rises up as air fills the bottom of the craft. It was supposed to be a very smooth ride. Yeah, well, not so much. My first case of seasickness! On the boat, I met up with a couple of guys from the States who were also backpacking through Europe. I remember one's name being Pete Champion. We got lucky and managed to catch one of the only trains running due to a rail strike. I think it was on that train ride to Paris, where we were seated in different cabins. Pete and his friend were in the cabin ahead, and I was facing the rear of the train in mine. Across from me, facing the front, was a nice Asian lady who was dozing. Pete had a bag of fruit with him in the next cabin and was apparently enjoying some of it on this ride. There not being a trash receptacle, the window must have seemed a logical means of disposal for Pete's mostly consumed peach pit. As the nice Asian lady across from me started to nod again, the peach pit came flying in the window and smacked her right in the face! She woke up screaming, thinking that I or someone in our cabin had thrown it. It was hard for us to convince her as she didn't speak English. She finally calmed down, and the rest of the trip was uneventful. Needless to say, Paris was incredible. I saw all of the requisite tourist sites, The Louvre, Arc de Triomphe, Eiffel Tower, etc., all spectacular. I saw street artists, drank strong coffee, and was beset upon by would-be con men. One guy walking by as Pete took a picture of the Arc insisted that we pay him for letting us take his picture. Not speaking French, I can only guess what Pete said to him, but it included an aggressive gesture involving his left hand and an upright right forearm and fist.

On my last day in Paris, we had lunch at a restaurant that was supposedly frequented by Americans. Being a little homesick, I longed to have a Coca-Cola, hopefully with ice. Ice was not a common thing in drinks, apparently. I did not know the French word for ice, so I attempted to pantomime it. "Uhhhh...ICE!... ICE!" I made a small square shape with my fingers and pointed at my Coke. "Ice...ICE!" The waiter seemed oblivious to my request and shrugged. "ice.....never mind." I resigned myself to room-temperature soda. I glanced back at the waiter talking to his co-workers, and he was mimicking my lame pantomime, making small squares and pointing to an imaginary drink. They laughed. I fumed. Oh well, c'est la vie.

Key Largo and Katrina

One year, Glenna and I went to Florida with the intention of doing some scuba diving before I attended what Paul Mitchell used to call "Hair Camp" in Miami. After visiting Key West, we stopped in Key Largo so as to patronize the dive operation owned by one of my client's grandfathers. As it turned out, he had passed away, and I had to deal with a new owner. He asked me when we had dived last. I replied, " About a year or a year and a half." He responded was it a year or a year and a half?" I replied, "I guess a year and a half." He wouldn't take us out unless we did a refresher course. I said, "Come on, I've been diving for ten years." He wouldn't budge. Fine. We found another place that would take us out.

So, we went out. The water was so shallow that, at one point, we weren't sure where the boat was, so I stood up and stuck my head out of the water to see. Yes, that's shallow. In fact, it was so shallow that while we were out, the harbor master closed down our harbor, and they had to take us to another and ply us with drinks to keep us patient while we waited for taxis to get us back to our cars. We finally made it back, and probably due to one more Colorado Bulldog than I needed, I managed to lock the keys to our rental car in the trunk. An hour later, the rental company got a locksmith out, and we were able to head north to Miami, where we were to spend the night, fly Glenna home, and I was to attend Hair Camp. Glenna's flight was at 8:30 a.m. I somehow talked American Airlines into changing her flight to a slightly later time without charging me extra. 9:45 is just a little bit better than 8:30, but not much. We got into Miami around 3:15 a.m. The next surprise for Glenna was that we were sharing a "suite" with Max Droz and his wife. "Suite" means a fold-out couch in the living room. Horrible bed, but what the heck, we were only on it for three hours! We got up and took Glenna to the airport, where her suitcase was self-destructed, and she had to buy a new one. Not happy.

Anyway, after returning to Dallas, I decided to email my buddy Ralph whom I hadn't been in touch with for months, and relayed the sad saga of our crappy vacation. Upon hitting "send," I immediately got a message. I assumed it was one of those bounced-back emails saying that the recipient wasn't valid or something. It wasn't. It was Ralph coincidentally and simultaneously emailing me to catch me up on their rough night sleeping on the floor at the hospital with their daughter Katrina, who was born with a lot of physical problems and needed more surgery. Suddenly, my "Wah Wah! My vacation sucked" situation seemed pretty trivial. Things could be a lot tougher. Thank you, Ralph, for the much-needed reality check!

Btw, Katrina is almost 30 now and is pretty remarkable!

Alabaster and The Brownlea

I wrote previously about searching for an apartment in Austin when I first lived there. The result of that search was a year at the Brownlea Apartments. The Brownlea had once been a low-end dormitory but had eventually been reborn as efficiency apartments. Very efficient ones with cinder block walls, outdoor carpet, linoleum "kitchen" floor, and, in some units, a refrigerator. Oh, and a narrow bathroom with toilet and shower that you shared with your next-door neighbor. I was lucky and gained a distant but lifelong friend, Delton, whom I mentioned in an earlier story. I remember the apartment being about 20 feet deep and 10 feet wide. The first 12 feet comprised the living room with the previously mentioned indoor /outdoor carpet (think miniature golf but brown), and the last 8 feet were the kitchen, which had a built-in table and bookshelves. The only thing separating my living area from Delton's was a sheet of Masonite with more shelves on either side supporting it. Not much sound or light insulation. The cinder block walls allowed me to shoot the formidable water bugs (or giant roaches) with my BB pistol without any danger of damaging anything. I did discover that it took at least 2 bbs to bring one down. The other inhabitants that I remember consisted of Cindy, the stripper with a heart of gold and a black stripe down the middle of her bleached blonde hair ("It's natural! That's how it grows!"), Carey Newton is a former ROTC cadet turned hippie, a non-gender specific fellow down the hall, and a short-lived sort of girlfriend situation downstairs. Oh yeah, and someone named Wolfgang with a screamer girlfriend.

"OHH! WOLFgang!!!" was often heard loudly through several walls and became a long-running joke.

That is my only memory of him.

Heart of gold Cindy told me that the club she danced at was looking to expand their horizons, and she got me a gig playing guitar and singing...to an audience that didn't want their horizons expanded. "Hey! You know any Lynn Anderson? You LOOK like Lynn Anderson!" I played one set, packed up, and slunk home.

While I was living at the Brownlea, management of the premises was awarded to some outpatients from the state mental hospital. I'm not joking. Two couples and 5 dogs shared one of these love nests. One of the women was fond of wearing Christmas tinsel in her hair because it looked purty. People had a tendency to pay their rent on time so as to have as little contact as possible. I remember a note on their door announcing, "Dog For Sale. $26 or $39."

I shared this magic castle with my own sweet mutt, Alabaster, a blonde Lab/Cocker/Beagle mix with hair the same color as mine. Quite the pair we were. There was and has never been a more devoted dog in my life. We saw hard and good times together. She went where I went, to the dismay and joy of many. I would take her to class and tell her to "Stay!" and she would be waiting for me when I came out, thrilled that I hadn't abandoned her. Once, when it was wet and cold, she came into the Art Dept Building and must have wandered up and down four floors of hallways until she found me in my painting class. She was so glad to find me! She would also sit outside the auditorium and howl whenever the music theory teacher shared something on the piano. She definitely had more friends on the U.T. campus than I did. Someone borrowed her denim bandana and embroidered her initials on it, but I never found out who it was. I got several rides while hitchhiking because they recognized her. Not me, but her. Often, I would play with her in the narrow hall of the Brownlea and jump up as she ran towards me and catch myself on either side, my feet and hands holding me a couple of feet above her. "Well, hello, Spider-Man!" one of my neighbors said, stepping out of his apartment and seeing me suspended. Times were tight. I was living off of a small V.A. check, and I would share half of whatever food I could afford with Alabaster. I'm sure she would have done the same for me. Well, maybe not. I came home one day to find that she had jumped up on the bed, climbed on the table, onto the TV. I got hold of the pecan pie on the top shelf that my Ma had sent me. She didn't share. Well, anyway, she was eventually poisoned by a cruel landlord, I'm fairly sure. His Kharma eventually caught up with him when the house collapsed and was torn down, leaving him with unfulfilled dreams and a vacant lot. It's a different story, and enough sad stuff.

During that hunger period, I overheard a couple of sorority girls in one of my classes complaining about their last night's dinner. In my malnourished, lightheaded state of mind, I kind of lost it. "I've been living on rice and soy sauce for 2 weeks, and you're complaining about your steaks?!!" The next day, they showed up with a bag of groceries, which I humbly accepted. We all apologized and became friends. Worlds bridged.

Back to the Brownlea. As I mentioned before, the walls were not very soundproof, and I discovered that I could climb the jutting stones in the wall out back and access the roof. I'd tie a rope to my guitar case, climb the wall, and practice my guitar where no one would be bothered. The same neighbor came out one night as I was halfway up the wall and again remarked, "Well, hello, Spider-Man!" Some local homeless "street people" discovered the secret access and became nightly fixtures until one of them rolled off the roof in his sleep. He was so wasted and wobbly that he only suffered a sore neck.

Some of us at the Brownlea took to decorating each other's note boards on our doors, leaving joke messages, requests to turn the music down, drawings, etc. I dreamed up a character named Chastity Flash, a sexy space pirate (picture Gamora from Guardians of the Galaxy) traveled the universe in a giant robot called The Intergalactic Destructo Duck. She adorned several doors, and I soon found myself in competition for her affections. Carey, the ex-cadet, challenged me to a duel on the roof. We faced off with paper bags of cylindrical paper airplanes that I called "wingless wonders." I'm sad to say that Carey was the victor. I hope they are still happy and that the giant metal duck didn't fly too close to the sun or something.

Anyway, more Brownlea stories are bound to resurface. If you enjoyed these, let me know, and more will surely follow.

Peace and Pizza

Art by Kent Skinner

One jammed-packed day at Rembrandt, The Salon, I found that I had about 20 minutes to cram some lunch in. Such is the life of the busy hairstylist. What may have been the first or one of the first CiCi's Pizza joints had opened a couple of doors down, so I hustled down there and grabbed a few slices. I was seated near the front of the restaurant, and I could see a couple of little girls who appeared to be 9 or 10 years old sitting near the buffet line, enjoying themselves and their pizza.

Then, a couple of guys who looked like they may have been construction workers came in and sat in the middle. One of them had a sack lunch and only ordered tea. While the other man went up to load his plate, Joe, the owner, and a very nice guy came out and greeted guests.

"Everything o.k.?" he asked Tea Man. Tea Man looked annoyed. "Yeah. What of it?" he asked. "Just making sure that everything is alright! Enjoy!" said Joe, and he walked away. Tea man's friend returned from the buffet and sat down. Tea man said loudly, "That m-----f----- came over here and accused me of eating his f---in pizza!" Which he did not. "He continued, "I told him I wouldn't eat his G-D------ pizza if he paid me!" which he also didn't say. I sat there surprised and thinking, "I just wanted to come and relax for a minute and grab a bite, not get in the middle of someone else's crap!"

Before I could decide whether to put my 2 cents in and maybe get my own head bitten off, Tea Man went up to refill his glass. As he passed the two girls, one of them made a serious face and said, "You think you're smart!" He stopped, stunned. "What??" She said, "You think you're tough!"

He had nothing. He shut up and got his tea. I sat up front, clenched my fist, and said a silent "YES!" And a child will lead them.

Strange Day

Art by Zane Skinner

I won't swear that all of these happened on the same day. They all did, in fact, happen, but if not all, then most of them did occur on the same weird day several years ago.

I woke up. I pulled my socks and shoes on and then realized that I hadn't put my pants on yet. It was probably an omen. Fixed that. Stumbled to the kitchen and grabbed the basket from the coffeemaker, opened the freezer and filled it with ice...and...asked myself..."What the hell am I doing?." I dumped it out and made the coffee. Have you ever poured cereal into a bowl, added milk, and saw little brown specks and just for a split second thought, "Bugs!" and then, of course, realized that it was just a little dark bit of cereal? I did that and proceeded to eat my cereal. I then noticed that those little dark specks were indeed ants! O.K. Not poison. Protein supplement. Yeah. That's it.

So, all that did happen one morning. Here's where I'm not sure if I have combined two stories or not. Whatever. Here's the rest that may or may not have happened on that same day. Glenna and I had several errands to run. We pulled into the parking lot at Fryes Electronics and saw an open parking place on our right. I pulled in and apparently didn't notice someone in the other lane who had intended to ignore the parking spot right next to her and was going to cross over to my side and park in the spot that I now occupied. Had I seen her, I wouldn't have snatched the spot. She went ballistic and started cussing me out. After a few ill-chosen words, we went on into the store. We waited by the door a minute to make sure that she got parked and didn't key my car or something. She had made several passes by the front door, ignoring other open spots, when suddenly alarms went off, and security guards chased down a teenage boy and caught him by the door. She took off! Apparently, she was his getaway ride! We finished shopping and decided to have Mexican food for lunch, and we went to one of our favorite places. Timing is everything. I decided to stand up to go to the restroom just as our waitress was approaching with a tray of large tumblers of tea and water. Tumblers and water went airborne, and contrary to Glenna's remembrance (she says she didn't even get wet), I recall a reenactment of that scene from Flashdance with Jennifer Beale sitting in a chair, getting drenched with her head leaning back and...well o.k. I may have fantasized about that part. Anyway, we never saw our waitress again. They mopped up the mess, and by the way, four tumblers of liquid will cover quite a large area.

We got outside to our car, and the events so far caught up to us. We started laughing so hard that tears rolled down our faces. Alas, we weren't done.

We stopped by the grocery store and went to the deli. The man asked, "Can I help you?" and I responded. "Yes, thanks. I'd like...." At the far end of the counter, a guy who had apparently been there before us grabbed his cart and stormed off! "I'm sorry! I didn't see you!" I said. He yelled, "Never Mind!" and took off. Having pissed two people off in one day, you'd think that I'd be a little more careful and aware of things around me.

We pushed our cart into the express lane and then noticed that we had 12 items in the 10-item lane.

"You're not going to make us go to a different lane, are you?" I asked. She said, "No! That's o.k.." I said

"Thank you! We really just wanted to be in your lane because of your beautiful smile!" She said, "Thankth! And grinned a big toothless grin! Doh! I would almost bet you that it had to have been a full moon that night. Anyway, life is strange, and some days it's just weird.

Two Jackets

Jacket #1: Years ago, maybe in the mid-eighties, I went on vacation to California. We landed in San Francisco, and to our surprise, it was chilly. It was June! We got her a jacket, and I decided to wait until we got to Sausalito to check out a little mom-and-pop leather shop I'd seen on a previous trip. As it turned out, there was a very nice textured black leather jacket, just my size, on the sale rack for $150. Maybe it was just wishful thinking or my formerly cocky(er) frame of mind having rock star delusions, but the counter girl seemed very flustered and nervous. We have probably all been in those shoes around someone we were attracted to. Or, more likely, she might have had gas. Who knows? Anyway, we were well on our way heading north to a small oceanside town called Gualala before it occurred to me that I didn't recall her running my credit card or my having signed for it. I figured that she had probably run the card, and it would go through anyway. Hours later, we arrived in Gualala and checked Into our bed and breakfast. It was unmemorable, but the view of the Pacific Ocean was spectacular. Around sunset, we were walking along the cliffs when I heard a cry for help. I looked over the edge and saw a woman lying on the rocks below. She had probably stepped on the bushy grass growing from the irregular edge of the cliff, thinking that it was solid and fallen. She had broken her arm badly and was pretty banged up. She was also in shock and was more upset about her broken fingernails than her arm. Another hiker looked down at us and climbed down to help. I remembered an old Boy Scout trick and took my new jacket off, zipped it up and ran two long pieces of driftwood through the sleeves, making a decent stretcher. We got her up the cliff just in time for every emergency vehicle in Gualala and the nearby towns to arrive and take her away. We slipped away in the mayhem and continued on our vacation. The jacket was unharmed. As it turned out, my credit card was never charged, and I had no way to contact them. Believe me or not, the next time I was in Sausalito, I went by the leather shop to make my indeliberate heist good, and they were gone. Surprise, surprise if they were giving away jackets! I did feel bad about it, but I'd like to think that it was supposed to happen that way. I hope the girl did not get fired over it. I got many years of joy from that special jacket.

Jacket #2: A couple of years ago, Glenna's mother gave us tickets to see Les Miserables at the State Fair Music Hall. It was one of those shows where you had to be seated by showtime, or you had to wait for intermission to get in. We were running late and got there with just enough time to get in if we hurried across the parking lot. I was wearing a cool Marc Ecco jacket that, again, I had bought off a sale rack. I did pay for this one. Suddenly, we saw an older woman go down hard on the concrete ahead of us. We ran over to see if she was alright. She wasn't. She was conscious but hurt. I pulled my jacket off, rolled it up, and put it under her head. Someone called an ambulance, and they soon came and helped her. I picked up my new jacket and saw that it was soaked through with blood. A Music Hall manager of some sort took us inside to see if they could somehow save the jacket in their laundry facility. It wasn't realistic. It was also well after showtime. He did, however, take us to the box office and exchanged our nosebleed section tickets for 10th-row center seats for the following week! I never heard from the woman. I hope she recovered and was able to see the amazing performance we saw. Anyway, I suppose the moral of these stories is that good follows good.

Sparkly Vision

Maybe we all have undiscovered superpowers! I have long suspected that mine is the ability to slow down any supermarket line that I enter. I'm not sure how I'll use it for the betterment of mankind. Another one is Sparkly Vision. I see shiny things. You know the rays that surround raindrops on your windshield? I get a small version of that from most shiny objects. I understand that it is partly due to astigmatism. Several times at work, when someone has lost an earring or something, someone will say, "Get Kent. He sees shiny things." In fact, once, while I was telling one of my diamond stories, I caught a glint from the floor by the shampoo bowls, stopped, and went over to see. There were two very small stones that turned out to be cubic zirconias. It's not valuable, but it's still pretty.

Anyway, the earliest incident took place in my childhood home on Thanksgiving. We were eating in the "dining" room that we rarely dined in when my sister noticed a stone missing from my mother's cherished sapphire ring. "Oh no!" exclaimed my mother. Everyone glanced around, and about eight feet away, I caught the glint of the small purple stone resting in our blue and green shag carpet. We couldn't believe it. What were the chances that it had just happened and someone immediately noticed it gone?

Or that someone would spot it in a shag carpet?

On one of my trips to The Long Island school, I was staying in a nice hotel and had a floor to myself for a few days. The only minor issue was the toaster in the breakfast area, which was not functioning well. I said it was a minor issue. On my third morning, there was an Irish fellow ahead of me having the same trouble with the toaster. I said, "I've been here for three days, and I haven't gotten my muffin brown yet." He winked and said, "Sounds like a personal problem!" I cracked up. "I'll repeat this," I said. Later, waiting for my elevator to go down, I remembered that funny exchange and laughed to myself, nodding. Because of the momentary angle of my head, I caught that familiar glint in the shadows. My elevator was arriving, and I thought, "It's right after Halloween, and it's probably a sequin or something." In a fraction of a second, I remembered finding the sapphire in the carpet and decided to check it out. It looked like a small diamond. I reported it to the front desk, and the manager said that I was the only person that had stayed on that floor in a couple of weeks and that no one had mentioned it. He said, "Keep it." He figured that it would probably disappear if he took it and didn't want the responsibility. I never heard back from the hotel.

Anyway, it was a long way to arrive at this. There are diamonds all around us. You don't need special eyes to see them. Sometimes, they are not even diamonds yet. Every new class that starts and every tour of our school that I speak to, I try to look for that sparkle. Which nuggets will turn out to be diamonds? It's one of my favorite parts of my job, and I greatly appreciate those people who saw that glint in me.

THE RETURN OF KENT SKINNER'S STORIES!

Foreward:

If by chance you have read my Kent Skinner's Stories Facebook page or my previous volume, you know that I have a propensity for telling long assed stories. All of them are true to my best recollection. Some are funny. Some are life lessons. Some are tributes.

Some are embarrassing. Probably, some are meaningful only to the participants. Some of the characters names have been altered so as to not offend or because I haven't gotten permission to use them.

You can't help but accumulate a few tales in 63 years, and if you don't share them, they, like all things, will eventually vanish into the ether, so here is my stab at immortality!

Enjoy!

Scotland, England, and Pants In The Bathroom

I've written some about my adventures in England and Europe, but a couple of memories come to mind that I haven't shared. I initially landed in London two days after graduating from high school with my guitar and backpack with no plans beyond wearing a money belt under my clothes with traveler's checks, my passport, Eurail Pass, Britrail Pass, Youth Hostel membership card, and a little memo pad with phone numbers and addresses of family friends (most of whom I had never met) and a letter from a family in France that" from "Aqualung," "Stand Up," and "This Was" continually played in my head hiking through London and everywhere else, to tell the truth. There was no name for it yet, but I have a great MP3 player in my head. My next stop was in Lincoln, a picturesque town a couple hours north of London, where the family of a fellow, Robin Wood, who had stayed with us in Dallas for a summer, would welcome me for a few days. I was introduced to proper tea with milk, rutabaga, and other very British epicurean delights. Little Vanessa, who was maybe 8, loved giving me a hard time about my accent and phrasing and, by the way, was a notorious cheat at Monopoly! I thoroughly enjoyed my stay with them and spent another night with their older son, Andrew, in Norwich on my way up to Scotland. I remember my pillow falling off the bed, hitting the space heater, and a hole melting in it, but I did not tell them for some reason. Andrew, If by cosmic circumstances you happen to read this, sorry! I owe you a pillow! I met a fellow that evening who claimed to have written a fair amount of Aqualung (b.s.) but owned a very cool Vox guitar with built-in effects.

I visited Leeds, Nottingham Castle, Kent (I had to), Yorkshire, where I saw a complete double rainbow standing on the edge of a castle in a fine sprinkle of rain with the sun shining through. Btw did you know that rainbows are actually complete circles, but the only reason we see

107

only an arch is that we are too close to the ground, and the bottom half is obstructed by the horizon? Just thought I'd throw that in there.

Anyway, it was magical. I spent one night in Wolverhampton at a hostel where the host was one of those people who mumble and never look you in the eye. He was, however, bold enough to wake us in the morning by playing the bagpipes badly, up the stairs. Badly, you ask? How does one know? Trust me. I headed for Scotland and had to buy a wool sweater in June! I spent a day seeing beautiful Edinburgh, Scotland, and, without notice, called one of the numbers in my book, "Buck Buchanan," in nearby Glasgow. Mrs. Buchanan answered and it took a minute until she realized who I was. She was an old WWll friend of my father's. She put her husband on the line, and they insisted that I go to the coffee shop at some hotel, and they would send their daughters to fetch me. I discovered that the coffee shop was close and under construction, so I assumed and waited in the coffee parlor for an hour or so before being found by two absolutely lovely Buchanan daughters, aged 16 and 19. They took me back to their parents house, where I met some of the nicest people I encountered that whole trip. They would have nothing other than for me to stay the night on a comfy fold-out in front of a blazing fire with a pile of comforters after a delicious meal of black pudding, fresh bread, and some pretty amazing Scottish ale. This was also the first time that I heard anything about having a Scottish ancestry. " Buck" Buchanan asked me "Ya know wheeerre yeeere fraam doont ya." I knew we were part German, and I believed English. "Nooo! Yeeere a Scot lad!" he exclaimed and pulled out a book of tartans and showed me ours. Years later, as I shared in a previous story, I was told that we were part of the McGregor clan, as in Rob Roy McGregor. Whether or not I'm actually distantly related to the main character in one of my favorite movies of all time, I choose to believe it!

Anyway, they convinced me to change my loose plans and see more of Scotland. I am so glad that they did! Scotland was second only to Switzerland to being the most beautiful country I saw, and I saw so little. I rode the train as far north as they went at the time to Aberdeen where I was treated to lunch and a beer by an old, old sailor who regaled me with WWll stories. It was the first and make only time I'd been referred to as a "Yank." When I'd had enough, I excused myself and caught the train south again. Missing pieces and an unsure order allow me to lump, condense, skip ahead. I saw Shakespeare's home town, Stratford Upon Avon, and visited Stonehenge before it was made impossible to walk among the stones. I, violating the rules, scooped a handful of pebbles from the site and maybe still have them in a box somewhere. Things like that are why you can no longer get close. My bad.

It was getting close to the end of my two weeks in Britain and I had realized that I had left my only nice pair of slacks at the Wood's house in Lincoln. I called and told them that I had left a pair of pants in the closet and asked if I could jump on a train from London and retrieve them. The gladly let me spend another night. Apparently, in England, the "closet" means the "bathroom," and "pants" means "underpants"! They looked all over that bathroom for a pair of Fruit of the Looms, wondering what was so special about them that I would spend four hours of train travel to secure them!

Anyway, from here, the story picks up from my trip to Dover and over to France in a previously shared adventure.

4. Jamie's Dip

Photo by Bruce McRoberts

I think we have all been in a situation where our words stopped working correctly. My friend Jamie Haslett, may he rest in peace, was a smart, funny, talented, sometimes arrogant, self-effacing, excessive, gifted graphic artist and terrific violinist. He was one of those people who smiled almost all of the time and would make jokes constantly but was dead serious when it came to his art and music. I consider myself lucky to have known him for the short amount of time that I was able to and honored to have shared many stages with him as the musical duo Going For Baroque and with a band that tried on several names, Nowhat, Poltergeist, and some I can't recall. Anyway, one day, we all decided to take a break from band rehearsal and run over to Swensens for

110

some ice cream. We approached the counter, and Jamie looked up at a very pretty young lady, probably 16, behind the counter, and his mouth stopped working correctly. What he meant to say was, "I'd like a DIP of Rocky Road, please!" What came out of his mouth were the words, "I'd like a dick...uh...uh...." He froze. The young lady smiled and replied, "I'm sorry, we don't serve those here!"

He died. Not then and there, but in a tragic and senseless auto accident a few months later. The world, minus his brilliance, is a dimmer place. His very best friend, Bruce McRoberts, named his son Jamie Drew after him.

One night, as I was walking down Greenville Avenue, where Jamie and I played frequently, I saw a fellow musician named Larry, whom I had heard had died and whom I had grieved for, approaching me, looking as astonished as I was. "I heard you were dead!"

He exclaimed. "I heard YOU were dead!" I exclaimed back. We both stood there grasping the other by the shoulders, looking as if we had seen ghosts. I imagine that someone had referred to Going For Baroque when passing on the sad news about Jamie, and Larry had pictured the wrong member. It was a weird situation that I think Jamie would have smiled at and made a goofy joke about.

New Orleans

Photo by Richard Watts

One of my favorite cities is New Orleans. Every time I have visited there I have come back with an adventure. Or two. Or five. My first visit there was with the salon staff from Hair Odyssey, the salon that I would eventually buy. Richard Watts was the owner at the time and took us all to a hair show in the Big Easy. Any time you visit New Orleans, expect to be approached by some street scam artist or another. It's just part of the ambience. Kids saying, "I bet you a dollar. I can tell you where you got your shoes and even what street in what city!" If you bite and say, "O.K., tell me," he'll reply, "On your feet, on Bourbon Street in New Orleans!" You got sucked in, and now you owe him a buck, which I hope you'll pay and walk away minus one dollar wiser.

Anyway, we were walking down Decatur near Jackson Square when a pretty blonde girl walked up and said, "You're the best-looking guy I've seen all day!" offering me a smiley face button and launching into a spiel about feeding the hungry kids or something. I replied with a generic foreign accent. "Sahrry, naw Engleesh!" She asked, "Are you Swedish?" I answered, "Yah, yah, Swedish!" She started talking to me in Swedish. SHE was Swedish! Busted, I gave her a dollar, took my smiley face button, and walked away minus one dollar wiser.

Later that day, we were walking down Bourbon Street, and I saw her again. I approached and asked, "Am I still the best-looking guy you've seen all day?" She paused, looked around, and inquired, "Give me twenty bucks?" Still thinking of the "feed the kids/smiley button" scam, I quickly said "No.."....then realized what she was proposing. Again, I replied, "No." and walked away an even twenty dollars wiser.

On that same trip, we walked into Jackson Square a beautiful park, and immediately, I was approached by a old guy who handed me a handful of birdseed. I was suddenly a very popular man with the hungry pigeons. "Say, brother, this birdseed costs two dollars a box. Can ya help me out?" He asked. Two timeless pictures later, I helped him out and walked away minus two dollars richer.

Another trip, a few years later, I was walking down Bourbon Street again and was approached by a sketchy guy. Assuming because of my long hair and Rock and Roll regalia that I was a partier, he said, "Hey man, I got whatchu need! I got weed, I got coke, I got ecstasy..." and showed me a cellophane bag containing some pills with the letter "E" on them. "See? E for ecstasy!" I replied, "No, E is for Excedrin, and even if I was interested, which I'm not, I sure as hell wouldn't buy it from you!"

Another time, after doing Bourbon Street and ready to call it a night, I was headed back to Lafitte Guest House, a nice bed and breakfast I often stayed at, when another seedy fellow appeared and said, "Man, you don't wanna go down there! That's the gay parta town!"I answered, "You know, I'm a lot less threatened by that than I am by you!" and continued on. I shared that story with my wife's uncle Duane, a very funny old guy who had lived in the French Quarter for 40 years and who passed shortly before Hurricane Katrina changed the face of New Orleans forever. He replied, "Gay part of town? Honey, you don't want to drop your keys in ANY part of this town!" New Orleans will always be a special place place for me. I've visited there probably more times than any other city that I've not lived in. That status could change.

Wedding Snafus

I have attended, done hair for, musically accompanied, or been vaguely connected with more wedding mess-ups than I can remember. At the end of the day, the brides and grooms all ended up married. Some of them still are. Some of them, I performed in some capacity at two of more weddings for the same people. I have wondered if it was my participation that jinxed some of them!

I was the best man for Vaughn Stockton, one of my childhood best friend's wedding. He married Michelle Bayles, and in spite of her breaking up with fifteen-year-old me to be with him, we have all remained great friends! Being a broke hippie/ camp counselor/ college student/ whatever, I didn't own a suit. Vaughn borrowed one from a soul bruthah he worked with, and somewhere along the line, I burned a small hole in it. I sort of remember breaking into his neighbor's house and borrowing a tie (which I returned, and it was someone who would be ok with it). I also forgot their wedding rings and had to race across town to retrieve them in time for the wedding. Yes, my absent-mindedness is not a new attribute. Oh yeah, and I had a black eye to boot. Not that I probably didn't deserve one from all the breaking and entering and running late and such, but I think it was actually from an airborne air hockey puck. At another wedding that I had just attended, Sally, the bride, kept getting down on her knees and back up and back down and so forth. It was my first Catholic wedding, and I assumed it was just a lot of kneeling or whatever. However, the groom wasn't doing it as much. Someone eventually brought out a folding metal chair from the backstage...or back alter, and she said, "I do!" Sitting down. She was fainting! As it turned out, the maid of honor had thrown the bachelorette party the night before, and the poor bride was extremely hung over. Good way to start things out! Another wedding, Patricia's and Tom's, I was playing guitar and had to change to an open tuning between songs and was trying to do so veeeeery quietly when "SPAAAANG!!!" I broke a string. Oops. Then, to upstage my distraction, apparently, someone had not locked the legs

115

on Patricia's side of the short kneeling platform, and it collapsed, nearly causing her to fall over sideways. Not my fault, that one.

Another wedding, same chapel at Old City Park in Dallas. I was to play "Greensleeves" when I saw the bride arriving in her horse drawn carriage and continue until she entered the back of the chapel. I began playing....and continued to play....and continued to play. Someone had intercepted the bride, my cousin Laurie, out of my line of sight to tell that her mother hadn't arrived yet. I continued to play until I thought my fingers were bleeding when someone got word to me, and we all enjoyed a few moments of silence.

And another! Ralph Fahrbach, my friend and bass player, and his fiancée were having a romantic dinner at The Grape the night before their wedding. Bruce, Jerry, Mike, and I, the other members of Jack B. Quick, came in wearing bandanas and kidnapped him. (Tona was in on it). We took him out and thoughtlessly got him snockered. I didn't realize how snockered until he leaned forward to me and said, slurring thickly, "You know?....... You......And me?.........And Kent?........ We're the Four Musketeers, man!" That's right. Both of us. He "decorated" the side of my pretty silver Saab on the way home. A stranger pulled up next to us and signaled Ralph to roll his window down. Then, he said with a thumbs up, "Hey! Nice paint job, dude!" The next day, Ralphie said, "I do." leaning against a pillar.

My long-time client/ friend Susan had a beautiful outdoor wedding and rode up in a horse-drawn carriage. They arranged to release hundreds of butterflies as they sealed their vows. What a super romantic idea! Unfortunately, most of them did not make it to the vows! I think some did indeed fly away and perform as planned. A bunch just fluttered to the ground. Those didn't count. They cost a lot, but at least the ground was pretty.

One more. One that I couldn't attend. My buddy Tim Stephens was supposedly taken out the night before and assured all night that the chairs for the wedding had all been taken care of (they hadn't), and as legend tells it, he was stranded in a bad part of town wearing a tutu. So the story goes. I wish I had been there for that one!

Although it could/should be said that you only get one chance, I did do the hair for one client for two different weddings. I'll call her Mallory for now until I get permission to tell her story. Mallory came in a couple of nights before her wedding for highlights. She was seated in my chair as we were about to begin when her cape came undone and it started to slip off down her front. I instinctively grabbed for the cape just as my friend Vaughn called my name from the front desk. I turned and looked at him but continued to grab. Suddenly, both of my hands were occupied. I jerked my hands back as both of our eyes shot wide open! "I am SO sorry!" I said. "She laughed and said "You're the LAST guy that will ever get away with that!"

Another time, another wedding. I was running out of ideas for bridesmaids' hairstyles. The bride wanted them all different, and I came up with a very pretty rope twisted-up style for my last bridesmaids hair. The only problem was that it was prettier than the brides hair style! At one point, I saw the bridesmaid surrounded by admirers of her hairstyle, and the bride was left standing alone, hands on her hips with a "What am I, chopped liver?" look on her face. Finally, one Saturday, I received a call from my friend from the bride and formal place across the street asking if I could help a woman who had come into her shop. She had had her hair done for a wedding at another salon and hated it. I told my friend that I really didn't have time to help her. " Well, could you just look at it and tell her it's o.k.?" my friend asked. " Ok! Send her over." I said. She arrived, and although a simple braid down the center would not have been my choice for her, it had been executed well enough, and she was not the star of that show anyway. the guest in my chair at the time said, "It's ok. I'm nothing in a hurry!" I undid her braid and did something a little prettier. Then, she had no money but agreed to bring me a check that weekend. After a couple of calls, her husband, not knowing of any of this, agreed to slide a check under the door, which he did. The punchline was, they originally called around five o'clock. She arrived about five-thirty. I finished about five forty-five, the wedding was at six o'clock across town, and what's more, she was the maid of honor, and SHE HAD THE BRIDE'S WEDDING DRESS! Anyway, as I said in Wedding snafus Pt 1, they all ended up married regardless of the complications. Yay.

Barby 2

Photo by Eugene Skinner

Like mother, like daughter. There is a genetic strain flowing through our mother's side of the family called Stinson Blood. It's a "take no crap from anybody" state of mind that surfaces occasionally. Our mom had it. Her mom had it, and her mother had it, and Barby inherited it. Balancing that feistiness is an equal dose of compassion and lovingness. No one fights harder or loves stronger than a Skinner woman, especially with Stinson blood in her veins. Barby is I survivor. She has been through some tough times and hard lessons but always survived and was stronger for them. One of the best things she did was was raise two beautiful and remarkable daughters, Rebecca and Bethany. They deserve their own stories, perhaps books. She has also been an outstanding aunt to my children. A birthday or holiday doesn't pass without her sending gifts or cards, even in the tightest of times. One of my other favorite things about her is her hearty laugh! She appreciates a bad joke or a good story!

Some of my favorite memories with my funny, feisty sister:

One time in Ohio, our sister Carolyn had left some blue crepe paper on the floor and Barbie sat on it and wet herself. The blue dye stained her cute little hiney blue!

When we lived in Massachusetts, she was probably three, and she had a cute little friend named Lynn Marie. These two little blonde bombshells would go to our neighbor's house and chant, "Fro sumpin' out the window!!" and the neighbor would toss the cookies or candies. This became a standard routine.

When our parents needed to go somewhere, Barby would plead, "Barby too! Barby, too!" When we lived on Nashwood Lane in Dallas, I heard her playing in her room with her Barbie and Ken dolls. She was maybe five. I got closer to her door and saw her shaking Barbie at Ken in rhythm to "Damn you damn! Damn, you damn! I hate men to pieces!!!"

One time, our parents went out and took Barby with them. I completely forgot where she was, and when she didn't come to dinner, we called her friends houses. No luck. No sign of Barby! Neighbors were knocking on doors. Everyone was in a panic. The police were called. They were about to start dragging the creek when my folks drove up with Barby! "Oh yeah!" I exclaimed, slapping my forehead. Doh! I was protective of my little sister. When she was a preteen and teenager, I literally had to chase boys away from our front door!

These are just a few of my favorite Barby stories. As kids, we fought a lot like brothers and sisters are prone to do. As adults, we don't talk enough and see each other even less, but there truly is much love between us! Oh yeah, when she was tiny if our parents were about to go somewhere, she would run up proclaiming, "Barby too!" Thus, the name Barby 2.

9. Die For You

In the beginning, there were the chords, and I saw that they were good. Did I mention that I am an insomniac? I awaken in the wee hours and have to do something to get my mind off of whatever is keeping me awake. I had a state-of-the-art transitional analog to digital synthesizer, and I would spend hours exploring. I stumbled on the core chords of this song. I made countless 4 track recordings, trying out vocal tracks and using mostly nonsense lyrics. They did begin with "See how they run... when the ending has come. Can't you see how I tried..for you? I'd die for you." I remember playing a rough take for some friends, Tim and Mary Stephens, who may not have been in their most lucid frame of mind... or maybe their most? Mary(r.i.p.) was in tears. That is the goal of every songwriter: to instill a significant emotional response in their listeners. O.K. Maybe not tears, but the potential was there. In the past, I had a tendency to dwell in the past. The grass was always greener on the back side. Stupid, I know. Anyway, I was stuck for too long in a "not right" relationship and had a tendency to miss the good parts of previous ones. I took that frame of mind and translated it into lyrics. I had one of many takes of "Die For You" on a mix tape that I played in my salon. Yeah, tapes. I remember one of my stylists' guests remarking, "What is this, a funeral parlor?" Still not, my hopes were fulfilled. Anyway, I pulled "Die For You" out of the bag at several open mics and the occasional Jack B. Quick gig and eventually recorded it with Marc Mydill, the result of those sessions you hear here. I think of it as my late 80s power ballad! Find it on SoundCloud if you like.

Dale Robert Barton Mark Meyler

Photo by Kent Skinner

Having been raised in a house with guns on the wall, being taught to be careful, and being a pretty good shot, it's odd to say that the only living creature that I ever shot was my absolute longest-term childhood friend, that I still talk to, although too infrequently, Dale Meyler. We met in fourth grade while members of the We Hate Girls Club. Understand that we never really hated girls, but it just wasn't cool yet. Give it a year. I think what we really hated was having to square dance on Fridays in gym class, where you had to actually touch girls, even the ugly ones! We all secretly had our crushes but dared not reveal them yet. It wasn't cool. Honestly, I had way too many! I was always a player in my fourth-grade mind.

Anyway, Dale and I connected on that gym floor. We hated this. We would deliberately choose the most neutral girl as our square dance partner, thus negating any "Kent likes _____" drama. Like anyone really cared. Remember, functioning as a 4th grader.

We soon discovered a mutual passion for monsters. Monster models, monster magazines, monster movies, monster...yes, cards. Anything monsters. Later, when grounded, my dad would take away my monsters! So, we would get together and play monsters. Our mutual friend Vaughn got dragged into this later. Dale's monster lust led him to collect short monster movies on 8mm film and eventually to collect movie posters and memorabilia, a passion that provided a livable income as an adult. We shot a fun, grainy sci-fi movie entitled "Beasts From Planet Xerox," I believe. I suspect the major corporation must have copied him. Hahahahaha...copied him? Ok. Sorry. It might have been "Zerox," but I have it on VHS somewhere.

Anyway, I shot him. We were at my family's land in Kaufman County, just popping around with pellet guns when mine jammed. I tried to force the safety, not knowing that I just had to re cock the gun. The gun spun around and fired, hitting Dale in the foot. A little blood, maybe tears, but definitely, guilt was shed. A quick trip into Kemp and he was good to go. So much for gun safety.

We got into one fight, as I recall, in 7th grade. I don't remember if he really liked her or not, but I told Roberta P that he did, thinking that they would be good together. He was pissed, and push came to shove, ending with my fist hung up on his braces. I still have the scar.

The Beatles landed while we were in fifth grade, and we got our first guitars. A brief career in a band we named "The Mysterians" ensued. We were an undiscovered sensation in my garage. Also, it was just Dale, me, and a kid named Larry playing the wastebaskets. Dale and I did play in a couple more bands over the years. In high school, I recall us driving around White Rock Lake for half a night looking for the Dreyfus Club, where we were supposed to be playing a church youth club party and arriving in time to play three or four badly rehearsed songs before it was over.

Our senior year in high school, Dale landed the lead role in our senior play, Tom Jones. He played a handsome, good-intentioned, socially awkward young gentleman. He was perfectly cast. I played an inept would-be highwayman as comedy relief from the comedy.

I may have mentioned in a previous story that Dale had a store in Austin where he sold movie memorabilia and comics. I painted a huge mural on the side of the house starring the Marx Brothers, The Shadow, Clark Gable, and a few other golden age stars. I lived in the back of the unheated store for a winter during a particularly low spell. During this time, Dale worked several jobs to get by. I know he did a night shift at Denny's washing dishes and was working on a book about blowing the lid off the money game. I think a good word describing Dale is "adamant." Whatever he was into at any given time, he was adamant. Be it his religious phase, his hobbies/ profession, parenthood, survival, whatever, he was adamant!

Dale was married to his high school sweetheart for a while and fathered two remarkable children, raising them through hard times and good times. Later, living in east Dallas in a very diverse neighborhood, his kids could be seen heading to 7-11 at night to get some "pwotein"! They grew up in a survivor mode and not only survived but triumphed. I know he's proud.

Once in that same neighborhood, Dale had befriended a woman in his building and apparently enraged her ex-husband to the point of waking him up with a baseball bat, permanently changing his hairline. Dale has led a colorful life.

I remember a phone conversation with him regarding his meeting a woman he described as a very artsy Jewish girl. I envisioned a petite Jewish artsy type along the lines of his ex. I don't recall how much time passed before I met Jill. Jill was not at all what I had imagined. I could not have imagined Jill. Jill was big, loud, gregarious and commanded the love and attention of all in her presence. She was smart, hilarious, an extremely talented artist and teacher and you could not help but fall head over heels with her within the first five minutes of knowing her! I may own own of the largest collections of her art in existence, including some amazing masks, paintings, wood sculpture, and a guitar that she painted for me. Glenna and I also had her do our wedding portrait. Bravely, Jill lost a tough battle with cancer a few years ago. Dale and the world lost a brilliant, loving, and funny artist and friend. This plane is truly a dimmer place for her absence. The next one is surely filled with its inhabitants wearing Raybans. I know I'll think of many more stories and will be reminded of obvious omissions by our mutual friends but I will close this with my stating, as I have to him, that I envy him the simplicity and focus of his life. The big house the fancy cars were not his priorities. He has lived his life his way with the people that he loved and is loved by and done the things he wanted or had to do. His health has not been good, and I don't see him often, but he will always be one of my favorite people in the world.

JP's Party

Before there was a Paul Mitchell school, before there was a Paul Mitchell Advanced Academy, before there were Paul Mitchell National Educators, there were Paul Mitchell Associates. I was one of them. Actually, I became one shortly after Paul died. I had always wanted one of the shiny banners with my name on it that said PAUL MITCHELL ASSOCIATE KENT SKINNER. Unfortunately, they ceased awarding those to new Associates right before I was invited to audition. I got a black bag for my product knowledge kit. Oh well. Anyway, I soon became one of the busiest Associates and got an award or two. As you may have read in earlier stories, I got to travel a lot. I loved it. There was another group within the PM Associate family called Task Force. I eventually was accepted onto this "elite" team. Lots of people wanted on the team not realizing how much work it was. It was an honor to be on the team, but Task Force meant forced to do tasks! We did so willingly.

One time, a bunch of us flew out to L. A to attend a workshop with John and Suzanne Chadwick on show organization and backstage skills. It was helpful and fun, but this story is really about a different reward. John Paul found out that we had come out on our own dime and decided to invite us all over to his place in Malibu for dinner. He hired a bus and drove us out to his hilltop ocean view palace, where we hung out on his patio and enjoyed Krystal champagne and, of course, Patron. We also enjoyed some of the best fajitas ever cooked personally by Wolfgang Puck! We got a tour of the house and saw his original Rembrandt. Wow. One of my friends had told me to ask John Paul about his stereo system. He replied smiling, "I really cant tell you a lot about it! I hire people to take care of those things for me! I can tell you that the speakers are made of Kevlar and go for about ten grand apiece!" He showed it to us. I know good sound when I hear it, but honestly can't discern $20,000 sound from $2,000 sound!

Outside, one of my friends offered him a cigar, which he politely declined, offering one of his own Cubans instead. Later, a fellow associate that I barely knew leaned across the patio table and, in a strong southern accent, said, "Hey! Try this!" and handed me a flask. "I asked her what it was, and she replied, "It's moonshine! I gave JP a sip, and he said, "You have to send me some of this!" It was serious stuff. The next time I saw her at a training, she had brought me a full bottle of it. She warned me to go easy on it because it was 190 proof, and you could go blind if you weren't careful! I did. I did be careful not go blind. It was definitely a night to remember! Someone told me that JP's neighbor Cher came by although I never saw her. Anyway, I'll always remember the night I sat on JP's patio eating Wolfgang Puck's fajitas and drinking Patron (and moonshine)!

Butterflies

No, not the stomach kind. Actual butterflies. I have no logical reason to believe this, but I want to. In times of worry or stress, the appearance of a butterfly can alleviate some of my dread or drama. Call it a good luck sign, an omen, or just naive hippie b.s., whatever. These stories are absolutely true.

Butterfly story #1 took place at the old Paul Mitchell distributor C.B. Sullivan /Paul Mitchell Dallas. They had a big education room for classes and shows. It had very a high ceiling, and one day, looking up, I saw a large Monarch butterfly flying in the rafters. One of the girls exclaimed, "Poor thing! Can't we catch him somehow and let him out?" With no reason to think it would work, I walked over to just below where he was flying and raised my hand up with my index finger extended. Immediately, the butterfly descended and landed on my finger! Everyone was astonished! Me too! I calmly walked out of the room, down the hallway, and up to the front entrance. I walked outside and held up my hand. The butterfly turned a half circle facing me and took off! I was as amazed as everyone else, but of course, I acted like, like that kind of thing happened every day! Actually, I guess a lot of things like that do happen every day. A lot of times to me. Butterfly story #2- When my son Zane was very small, we went to the museums at Fair Park. One thing we wanted to see was the Butterfly Zoo, an outdoor butterfly exhibit. It was a screened-in area with lots of plants and more than a few butterflies. You could walk around inside and see the butterflies in their own environment. Zane has a slight phobia about bugs that may stem from a traumatic run-in with a bed of fire ants when he was very little, so when a butterfly landed on his chest, he panicked and started slapping at his chest, yelling, "No! Get it off!!" The poor butterfly spiraled to the ground, mortally wounded. The Butterfly Zoo staff member, with a forced calm, said, "That was a rare specimen of the Lepidoptera (something something) family!" We apologized and slunk away. My daughter Savannah just informed me that there was an episode of SpongeBob SquarePants where a butterfly had terrorized Bikini Bottom. That may have factored in.

Perhaps the "good luck sign" butterflies are actually Butterfly story #2's pals come in times of stress and worry to mock me! "That's that kid's dad! Get him!" I'll worry when they evolve opposable thumbs.

Rats!!

Art by Zane Skinner

Again, I begin not sure how far this will go or if it will be entertaining or not! I lived in my old house for about 20 years. It would be paid for by now, but we'd be in an old small house infested with memories and at times, termites and rodents. I discovered the termites one day, lying back in the tub enjoying a leisurely warm bath with my feet on the far wall. Suddenly, the tile shifted, and my feet were a couple of inches farther than they had been seconds before. It seems that the builders had installed the green board (basically sheetrock with a waterproof plastic coating) backwards, so when the grout started to deteriorate, so did the wall. Wet sheetrock and wood are like strawberry shortcake to termites. Even after treating for termites and redoing the tile myself, there were repeat visitations. Nothing like starting the day finding a tub full of swarming, winged, unwelcome housemates.

I don't guess the termites were near as big a nightmare as my fabulously furry freeloading friends were. It started with a little scratching noise in the wall. I lived by a nature preserve and above a creek, and I naively thought, "Well, ok. No big deal. Probably a cute little mousie." Yeah, well...one night not long after that, I couldn't sleep, so I got up to do some laundry.

Suddenly, a rat jumped out from behind the dryer! I literally jumped out of my slippers and screamed like a girl! He looked at me like, "What?! I thought we were roomies!" I ran to the all-night Walmart and got sticky traps, which my dog Bananahead got into. Great! The instructions said to use warm, soapy water in case of such an incident. Worked like a charm. Later that night, I heard a ruckus in the kitchen, and the dogs were going crazy. I opened the laundry room door, and there he was, stuck to the sticky trap with a length of chain that I'd never seen before. Maybe he had planned to use it on me. Then I asked myself, "Now what!!!" What do you do with a live pissed-off rat? Being the soft-hearted animal lover that I am, I decided to scoop him up with a shovel and dump him in a bucket. I filled another bucket with warm, soapy water and carried them both down the street to the nature preserve. When I got deep enough in, I dumped him and his sticky trap into the bucket of water. Worked like a charm again, and I tossed the warm, soapy water, the sticky trap, and him as far as I could throw them. I went home and back to bed, satisfied with my humane solution. Well, either he loved his bubble bath and came back for more, or he had friends because that didn't end anything! A few nights later, Glenna and I were watching tv when suddenly she shrieked and jumped up on the chair. Down the hall, jumping like a rabbit, came a big f...ing rat! It ran past her and behind my antique pump organ. No jokes, you weirdos! That's a musical instrument. He had made his home there and had chewed through the bellows, rendering it a large antique door stop. I invested in a "humane" trap. A steel mesh box that closes suddenly, trapping said rodent if you can lure him inside. Contrary to popular belief and countless cartoons, cheese isn't a rat's favorite food.

They do, however, like peanut butter. I finally caught him and decided to dump him out in the country. When I let him out, he ran straight for my truck and disappeared. I don't know if he hitched a ride back or not, but I caught him or his pal the next day in the humane trap. I was headed our of town for a work trip and was going to dump him on the way, but completely forgot until I got to the airport. I'm sure he found friends there.

I began to lose my humane qualities when the attic started leaking rat urine. This was war!! You know, you hear about rat poison that makes them thirsty, and they supposedly go away seeking water and die somewhere else? False. Somewhere else means your attic and in your walls. There's no description worthy of that smell. I cut and patched and used so much Lysol that I wish I was a stockholder. I had the whole attic insulation vacuumed out and replaced, but as fond as I had once been of that house, it was forever tainted. We luckily sold it in 36 hours after it went on the market for more than our asking price and built-in Wylie next to a green belt and a creek, but fortunately, we've had few issues with critters. Knock on wood.

Convolution

It was one of those dreams like where you are in a class about to take a test you haven't studied for, only in the one I had last night. I was suddenly performing one of my songs in public only to realize that my band was not all there. While it could be argued that that was always the case, in this case, it was literally true! I was already singing while climbing up the rocky edge of a water-filled crevasse when I noticed that there was no guitar. I wondered if there was one nearby I could snag and continue. There wasn't. I just kept singing and climbing and finished the entire song sans my guitar parts. It felt triumphant. The song Convolution actually exists and can be heard on SoundCloud. It started out to be about relationships but ended up being about everything. Some of you have heard me talk about the rhythms and patterns we create with the people and world around us. You can create a Moire pattern by holding two combs flush together and sliding them longways. Two individual sets of teeth create an illusion of a set of larger teeth. The same thing happens driving by a fence on the highway and also watching the blinkers of your car in conjunction with the car in front of you etc, etc. anyway, this song is about those relationships and being part of something much bigger than you may be able to see all at once. Have a listen if you like. I never liked my lead vocal track. I think a woman's voice might have been better, but I love everything else about the song. It took weeks to record. I kept coming back to my music partner, Marc Mydill's home studio after driving around singing with the preliminary tracks and saying, "We gotta add this part! We gotta add this part!" At some point, you have to let go and let it be what it is, both in life and in the recording studio.

Convolution

Everything changes. Listen to me.
The heart rearranges to what has to be.
Perpetual strangeness is how it all seems,
And love can be dangerous, led by dreams.
It all has a reason that's hard to conceive.
Conflicting cohesion, try to believe.
And everything boils down to part of a whole,
With parts interchanging, they join our souls.

Everything leads into something that touches and changes and takes you to somewhere else, guiding you, pushing and pulling and lifting and coaxing, refracting, reflecting in countless directions, affecting another set, spreading out, and setting up rhythms that build into patterns so infinite. Try to imagine a piece of the puzzle complete in itself yet still incomprehensible.

A rhythmic confusion too vast to explain,
Bizarre convolution, the Cosmic Refrain!
A symphony played out for those who can hear,
who dance to the music and love without fear!!

Tickets To Ride

I'm sure that we all have had our share of traffic tickets. In fact, I have one waiting for me to plead "not guilty" to as we speak or, rather, as I write and maybe as you read. My very first traffic ticket was when I was in 8th grade for the horrendous act of riding double on a bicycle with my good friend Kyle Evans. We had to perform, I think, 48 hours of public service to amend our wrongs. I'm sure this foray into the world of crime led us down our individual paths of evil and debauchery.

For years, as I traveled for Paul Mitchell, I listened to books on tape and, later, CDs to help the miles fly by. I listen to lots of things, including motivational, historical, mysteries, detective fiction, comedy, biographies, and so on. I have quite a library if you'd like to borrow!

Anyway, on one trip back from Houston, I approached the southern mixmaster in South Dallas. While the miles flew by, I also flew by a police car! Crap! I got pulled over. The cop asked why I was going 87 mph in a 65. I replied, "I know it's no excuse, but I am listening to a Tom Clancy novel on tape and..." He interrupted, asking, "Which one is it?" I showed him the box. "Aww! That's a good one! Where are you?" he asked. I answered, "Right where the helicopter is hovering over the train, and they're extracting the good guys..." He continued, "Well, I have already started writing the ticket, so I have to issue it, but when did you last take defensive driving?" I replied, "Maybe a year and a half." He said, "Well, if they won't let you take it again, please plead, "Not guilty." You might have to do a little detective work, but unless you reach out and punch me or something, I probably won't remember this particular incident." I did as advised. I figured that he must be out of the Southside station, and I called him when my court date drew close. "Nope. I don't remember you at all!" he said. He didn't show up to court, and I walked away like a free man. Another work trip took me to Paris...Paris, Texas, that is. It was about 6:30 and just barely starting to get dark. I passed a speed limit sign that said 65/60 meaning 65mph during the day and 60mph at night. My headlights weren't even on yet because it was still light enough outside to read fine print on a map, not to mention a bold-lettered street sign! Flashing red and blue lights. I pulled over, confused. "You were going 67 in a 60 mph zone." the cop said. Explaining that it wasn't night yet didn't help. Neither did my having long hair. "What's in the box?" he asked looking through the window of my Montero. "Heads," I answered. "I mean.. dollheads..mannequin heads!" "Why do you have a box of mannequin heads?" He asked, bewildered and not comfortable with the whole thing. I explained that I was going to teach a long hair styling class at a spa in town for Paul Mitchell. "Who?" "Paul Mitchell...you know, the shampoo?..." Nope. "Never heard of it." So, being a long-haired hippie hairdresser from out of town with a box of heads and driving 7 mph over the speed limit "at night," there was no way I was skating away from this ticket. I let the weeks go by, and it was a day or two after I was supposed to contact the court. I called the judge in Paris...Texas and told her my story. She asked, "What spa?" I told her, and she replied, "That's where I get my hair done!" and gave me 60 days probation. I carefully avoided driving at dusk 7 mph over the speed limit anywhere near Paris... Texas. for the next 60. days.

GTFOOMS!!

Art Kent Skinner

As I've mentioned before, one of my favorite cities to visit is New Orleans. One of my favorite school groups to do trainings for were the Vanguard Paul Mitchell schools. On one of these trainings, my co-trainer was Dave Holland. It was a pleasure to work with Dave because in addition to being a great teacher and cutter and a deep thinker, he has a great sense of humor, nearly as warped as my own.

On a previous trip to New Orleans with my wife Glenna, we were walking down Bourbon Street and stopped at a doorway to listen to a band playing The Eagles' "Hotel California" and doing such an astounding job of it that I had to go in and see if they were lip syncing or playing with a prerecorded track. The double guitar lead is not terribly complicated but is not easy at all to play. It was completely live and spot on. The band was called Rockbox. We had to stay and listen to these guys and, in fact, return every night of our trip.

Back to the main story. Dave and I went down to Bourbon Street the Sunday night that we arrived and headed for the Famous Door club in hopes of catching Rockbox. Unfortunately in the music biz, various things can break up a band. I have no idea if it was personal differences, ambitions, friction, or what, but I found that they had split into at least a couple of splinter bands. The band at the Famous Door called themselves Rockshow. They were adequate talent-wise, but the sound was really bad. The funny thing was that there may have been 10 people in the club but the band acted like they were in a packed concert hall. "GOOD EVENING NEW ORLEANS! ARE YOU READY TO ROCK?!! SOMEBODY MAKE SOME NOISE!" So, it became a running joke for Dave and me. At odd times during our training, one of us would suddenly yell, "SOMEBODY MAKE SOME NOISE!!" And somebody would. At one point in the show, a couple of drunk girls got on stage saying that it was one of their birthday. The singer, a short, wide mini Axl Rose wannabe, tried to get them to do shots. Birthday girl wisely declined and was met with verbal abuse. "YOU'RE F----ING WORTHLESS! GET THE F--- OFF OF MY STAGE!!! That, too, became a running joke. Too bad about Rockbox! Sometimes, the chemistry is such that it could take you far. Again, I haven't a clue why they broke up, but I sorry I won't get to enjoy that particular combination again. Sometime later, I heard that Dave was going to do a training in Germany. I had a multi-linguistic friend translate, "Somebody make some noise!" "You're f---in worthless!" And "Get the f--- off of my stage" into German and sent it to Dave, telling him, "Here are some helpful phrases that will come in handy." and said that they meant, "You have beautiful hair!" "Nice weather we're having!" and "Can you recommend a good restaurant?" Dave and I both retired from Paul Mitchell Advanced Academy. The memories remain, and the jokes continue. Santa: "Get the fog off my sleigh!" And "Get the duck off my stage!" are a couple of forgettable ones.

One other memory that I have of that trip was the Education Leader at the time for those three schools apparently told the teachers to do separate full page haircut diagrams of each step in nine haircuts. We had to inspect their diagrams and coach them for certifications. There were DOZENS of three-ring binders brimming with paper! A full set of diagrams can easily fit in a single paper folder! I think she wiped out a couple of forests with that misunderstanding!

Vaughn

Selfie by Vaughn Stockton

I have referred to my long, long-time friend and brother-in-arms/ partner in crime, Vaughn Stockton, several times in these stories. I have many friendships, but few that can rival the time, adventures, and experiences that we've seen. We have remained friends for over fifty years through marriages, shared housing, practical jokes, thrown objects, rock festivals, hitch hiking, mind expansion, hirings and firings, girlfriends, and other natural disasters.

We met in fifth grade. The teacher, Mrs Petty, who should have retired sooner, introduced the new kid to the class. "This is Vaughn Stockton." I'd never heard the name Vaughn before, and he had an odd expression, and my first thought was that maybe he was a foreign kid. "Sit there behind Skinner!" the teacher said. She never called me anything but "Skinner." Everybody else had a first name. I was sitting up front probably because of some distraction I'd caused. I was also wearing a black turtleneck and a scowl. Vaughn later said his first impression of me was that maybe I was a troublemaker. I don't remember for sure if it was part of our assignment, but Vaughn leaned up and asked me, "Hey, what's purple and has Beatles on it?...... Grape Britain!!!" Thus began a lifelong friendship. It was cemented a week or two later when he was visiting our mutual friend Dale Meyler, who lived on his street. Dale is the one close friend that I still stay in contact with who predates Vaughn. He deserves his own story and plays a pivotal part in this one. Dale said, "Let's go over to my friend Kent's house. He always has pretzels and orange drink!"

Reason enough to start a friendship. We all shared a passion for monsters, The Beatles, movies, and girls. Vaughn was always a little cooler and more popular than us. His parents moved a lot, but the bonds of friendship held strong.

As young teens, we fell in with Mike Bayles. He was over the top. He had a hysterical laugh and had no fear or boundaries. We would sneak out at night, and he would manage to "procure" beer from unlocked garages. We were mostly guilty of harmless hooliganism. Actually, Dale had gone out with Mike's sister Michelle, a pretty, spunky blonde girl. That didn't work out and I asked Dale if he minded me asking her out. He was cool with that. We went out for a short while until Vaughn entered the picture. It began the night before my 15th birthday. Dales birthday is the day before mine, and at his party, Dale suggested that we all sneak out and come over later. Mike and Vaughn were spending the night at my house, and it was easy to get out and return to Dale's. Not much went on. It was mostly about the thrill of roaming the tough streets of fashionable far North Dallas. Suddenly headlights! It was the police. Instead of staying the course and maybe answering questions and probably getting sent home, we ran. Mike and Dale got away. Dale's sister Vickie and I were caught. Her friend also escaped but had to return since she lived in Highland park. Dale came back because they had his sister, and Vaughn returned because he was staying over my house. We were all brought home. Dale's mom was outraged. Mine were disappointed and grounded me for three months. Vaughn got off light, having a cool mom. Anyway, I was allowed to have my birthday party the next night, but as you can imagine, the turnout was light. I remember playing spin the bottle.

There were sparks between Michelle and Vaughn that night, and they are still married today! Of course, my teenage heart was temporarily dented, but who and where we are is a result of every happenstance and decision that has occurred in our lives. I wouldn't change a thing.

Oh, there's plenty more to tell, but it will keep for now.

Kevin The Cop

One of my long-time friends began as a client. Kevin "Cagey" Bailey was fresh out of the Dallas police academy when I first cut his hair. He's a wild man, good ol' boy, good-hearted guy. He's shared some of his war stories with me, and he's had some good ones. He retired not too long ago after a series of practical jokes on a supervisor (not proven who was responsible) was blamed on him.

He disappeared from my chair for a while. One night, I looked towards the front of the salon and saw some long haired guy in my station. I walked up and asked, "Can I help you with something?" He turned and smiled. "Well, hello, Kent Skinner!" It was Kevin, the cop! I asked him, "What's with the hair? Are you working undercover or something?" He wasn't. It seems that he was just seeing how long he could get away with it. He was gelling and spraying it down and tucking the ponytail into his collar. He also had a small diamond earring that he had to remove for inspections. He sometimes forgot. "Bailey??!!" One night, around 11:00, I got a phone call from him. "I need you!" He exclaimed. "What?" I responded. "I need you to shave my head!" he said. "Why?" I asked. "Me and Vicki were in the hot tub drinkin' some wine and I leaned back on a candle and caught my hair on fire!" he said. I said, "Come on over!" He did. He managed to make via the back roads from Allen to Wylie without incident. Yes, there was no way for him to go to work the next morning, looking like he did. Fortunately, his skin wasn't burned as he had dunked his head under the water as soon as he realized he was aflame. The only clippers I had with me were some small neck trimmers, and they clogged up pretty quick, so I resorted to scissor over comb. Considering that it was midnight and we were outside on my patio with a just a 40-watt bulb for a work light, I did a damned good job. When he tried to pay me, I refused. It's always a great idea to have a cop friend owe you one! The next morning, I found a hundred-dollar bill on my kitchen island. I called him. He said, "Don't worry about it. You guys are buying diapers these days."

My wife Glenna does an annual girl-cousin getaway, and a couple of years ago, she was in the elevator at her hotel when she heard a voice behind her say, "Well, hello, Glenna!"

She turned and saw a very long-haired and bearded biker-looking kind of guy smiling at her. "Who is this?!!" She thought. "Kevin Bailey!" he said. Small world. Anyway, Kevin "Cagey" Bailey is the kind of friend that may move in and out of your life easily, is always good for his word, and will always do anything he can for you. The "Serve and Protect" mindset doesn't go away.

Update: we lost Kevin after an emotionally devastating divorce.

143

Lisa and Gabby Hayes

We had two women named Lisa working at Hair Odyssey/
Rembrandt. Both were blondes, but Lisa P was blonder in every sense
of the word. I found her in a high school cosmetology class that I was a
guest artist at. She was eager and had long, pretty hair, so I hired her as
a stylist and used her as a long-hair model. She worked at the salon for a
couple of years. A notable habit of hers that eventually drove me nuts was
that she would NEVER SHUT UP!!

One day, I came in, and her male guest was sitting in her styling
chair shirtless and grinning ear to ear. She had her hand on his chest and
was holding his chest hair between her fingers. "What are you doing?" I
asked. "He asked me to trim his chest hair!" she replied. I explained that
we didn't offer that service but let her finish up. Another time, when we
were preparing backstage for a hair show, she asked if anyone had a mirror
so she could check her makeup (one of her favorite pastimes). Someone
handed her a two-sided mirror, and she looked into the magnifying side.
She exclaimed, "Ommigawd! My face looks so huge!" I said Uh. Lisa?
Would you mind taking your head into the next room? It's creating a
vacuum in here, and my blow dryer won't work!" She replied wide-eyed,
"I'm sorry!" and left the room."

Doug Wick was a happy-faced, long-haired stylist that worked in
the station next to me. He was also a drummer. One day, I overheard
him telling his guest that when he was a kid, his dad took him to see
Buddy Rich, a famous jazz drummer, and that he got to sit on his drum
stool and that Buddy had given him a pair of drumsticks. "And so I grew
up to be a drummer!" he said. I joined in. "When I was five, my parents
took us to New York and Maria. Callas (a famous opera singer) came to
our table and kissed me on the forehead, and I grew up to be a singer!"
Just then, I saw Lisa walk in. I continued, "and when Lisa was a little
girl, GABBY Hayes....." O.k., maybe that was only funny to me. You see,
Gabby Hayes was a western movie actor that... Never mind. Sometimes,
I just crack MYSELF UP.

My Summer of 69.

My buddy Vaughn Stockton and I were still working at the Target snack bar, and we and some of our other budding hippie friends (picture us in heavy, starched white short-sleeved shirts and paper hats) were talking and dreaming about running away and going to Woodstock. It wasn't realistic. Who would serve the "tender, juicy Target hot dogs" and make 9-cent Target popcorn announcements? Well, someone surely would have. Anyway, it was all academic because Woodstock came to us! Some of you might remember, but most of you have probably never even heard of the Texas International Pop Festival. It took place at the Texas Speedway in Lewisville in August of 1969, the same month that Woodstock changed everything.

Being 15 and not able to drive yet, my mother drove us out to Lewisville, about 45 minutes from where we lived in "fashionable far North Dallas, a tidy upper-middle-class neighborhood. My mom probably had no idea what she was allowing us to experience. Vaughn's dad was supposed to pick us up later that night. More about that later. The entire raceway area was packed with the hip and wannabe hip. I think we straddled that line. I certainly was wanting to be. Vaughn was always cooler than me. Anyway, the roster included big names like Janis Joplin, Ten Years After (a band that nearly cost me a hundred bucks decades later.....different story), a fledgling band called Grand Funk Railroad, blues legends Freddie King and BB King, soul act Sam and Dave (Soul Man, Boogaloo Down Broadway) Santana, Spirit, Johnny Winter, Sly and the Family Stone, Chicago, and newbies on the scene, a little band from England called...Led Zeppelin. Side note: I bought Led Zeppelin's first album based on the reviews in Rolling Stone, listened once, and put it aside thinking, "This guy sings like a girl!" I guess I was used to manly baritone voices like Jim Morrison, John Kay of Steppenwolf, Justin Hayward of the Moody Blues, etc. Well, I was wrong. Honestly, Led Zeppelin is one of the only acts that I still have vivid memories of from that day. "Dazed And Confused" and "You Shook Me" became emblazoned in my brain. I remember singing them later at the top of my lungs, crossing the cotton fields that are now Lincoln Center at 635 and the North Dallas Tollroad on my way to Target to sell my soul at the snack bar.

Anyway, other highlights of the day include collecting underground newspapers, some of which I think I still have somewhere, and seeing.... not smoking....thank you, Bill Clinton....marijuana for the first time. I remember two very cool-looking girls rolling tobacco out of a cigarette and replacing it with a green leafy substance. I did not inhale....o.k. they didn't even offer.

We didn't see Janis or a couple of the other big icons, only being there for one day. Later that night, we waited for Vaughn's dad to show up and drive us home. And waited... and waited. Eventually, I flagged a police car down and had him call my mother. I guess my dad was out of the country for work. While we waited, we laid back on the hill below the shoulder of I35 above a line of trees. We were air guitar soloing and making Jimmy Page guitar solo sounds as best we could with our mouths when a naked hippie stood up behind the line of trees and said,

"Hey man, there's people trying to sleep down here!" Not cool! Not cool! Embarrassed, we quietly awaited my mother's arrival. Years later, she told me that she had been impressed by my problem-solving ability, having flagged down the cop and having him call her. I always wondered what adventures might have ensued had I not.

Near Death Experiences

Somehow, I've managed to make it this far. I suppose everyone has a few of these situations that might have gone bad. The fact that I'm writing and you are reading this is evidence of luck, happenstance, or divine intervention. You pick.

My first car accident was shortly after getting my driver's license. I was traveling north on the service road to Central Expressway between Walnut hill and Royal Lane in my father's Pontiac Executive. I looked to my left to see if anyone was coming down the exit ramp. No one was. However, the guy in front of me stopped completely to check. Bam! It was more than a fender bender but not enough to total the car. A piece of metal trim pierced the trunk of the car ahead like a spear. I found a phone and called my dad, afraid of the conversation to come. Of course, he was more concerned for me. I'm glad that I didn't have to make the call that the dealership repairman ahead of me did. He was taking the car in to have a "small rattle" checked out. "Um...sir?.....you know that small rattle?..."

One time, while driving the Camp Kiwanis bus back from a field trip to the Ft Worth Zoo, traffic had slowed to a crawl ahead. That's when the brakes went out. Fueled by panic and adrenaline, I quickly down shifted and used the parking brake. We were almost stopped when we gently bumped the truck ahead of us. No one was hurt, and there was no appreciable damage to either vehicle. I let out my breath when some smart Alec kid said sarcastically, "Way to GO, Kent!"

My last scary car accident was around 1980, when I moved back to Dallas. It was the summer when Dallas had suffered through a heat wave with 69 days over 100 degrees 42 of them consecutive. No rain means lots of oil accumulation on the highways. It had already been a great day, beginning with my retrieving my grandfather's ring from the toilet trap, buying my first of many acoustic twelve-string guitars for a pittance, and putting a new tape deck in my Opel Manta. It was also the first day of rain in three months. I was driving my friend Vaughn Stockton to Valley View mall, heading east on 635 between Midway Rd and Welch Rd. Traffic was moving very slow because there were already accidents ahead because of the slip n slide nature of the wet, oil-slick highway. All that accumulated oil had risen to the surface. We were in the middle lane, moving slowly, when I felt an impact at my left rear fender. We were whipped around sideways, and looking to my left, I saw the grill of an 18-wheeler! We slid down the highway for maybe 150 feet before he noticed us and hit his brakes. I was in automatic get the hell outa the way mode and got over to the inside shoulder. Again, no injuries or broken glass, but side left side of my little Manta was caved in. I remember the truck driver saying, "I wuz just drivin' along, didn't hear or feel nothin' when I looked down, and there's this little white car drivin' sideways in front of me!" We were lucky that the road was slick enough that we slid vs being crumpled, but then again, if the roads hadn't been so bad we wouldn't have been in that situation to begin with.

Anyway, everything you've been through has lead you to where you are today. There's been a lot of joy and life since then. I'll do my best to be able to say that again in 71 more years!

Pottery Plus

Again, I begin unsure if the unfolding recollections will be as entertaining to the uninvolved as they may be to those present during their genesis. Wow! Great opening sentence, Kent! Thanks, self! After working at Target, my friend Vaughn and I went across the parking lot and applied for jobs at Pottery Plus, an offshoot of Pier One that specialized in dinnerware and gourmet foods. The store hadn't opened yet, so we were hired to help build it out, set it up, and eventually to work in the warehouse. At this point In my life, I discovered the joy of hot glue. I think it may have been a fairly new invention, or we would certainly have had it in my house. Anyway, we used a lot of it, including this mishap. Our bosses, Bob S and Jerry N (I'm not sure which one thought of it), had us get up on a ladder one morning and glue several very nice plates to the metal siding above the Pottery Plus sign outside. Key word: morning. It looked great. Oh, did I mention the words "metal," "hot glue," and outside? As nice as it looked, it sounded even better when the plates answered the call of gravity and escaped the grasp of the glue. Good call, Bob and/or Jerry.

Another quick memory: covering with a price tag the word "Meat" on cans of "Reindeer Meatballs." Hey! We were 19! Neither of the bosses liked hippies, so imagine me with my shoulder-length hair stuffed in a cheap short-haired wig that fooled no one working in the warehouse where no customers would ever see me. Cute. Occasionally, a boss would tell me to take off the wig and follow a suspected shoplifter. There was one guy that was so good that we never caught him. One lady that we did catch managed to sneak enough merchandise out of her coat and hide it while being held in the office to make her arrest a misdemeanor vs a felony.

There was a sweet naive young girl working there named Mary Evelyn from Tennessee. She mentioned Tennessee enough that it became her nickname. There was another stock guy whose name was also Jerry.

Well, call him Jerry 2. Being the wise guys that we were, we had to subject to our cruel humor. One day, we let her "catch" us practicing our karate moves on the cardboard boxes out back. We convinced her that we were Masters of Tofu. She apparently hadn't read the labels in the food section. Another time, Jerry and Jerry 2 told this poor girl that my sister was giving a ballet recital at the Dallas Music Hall and that she was world famous. "Go ask him about her!" they said. She came up to me and said eagerly, "I heard your sister was a famous ballerina!" I replied, "That's very funny." and continued my work. She went back to the two Jerrys, confused, and told them of my reply. They burst into laughter and said, "His sister doesn't have any legs!!"

She returned immediately to me in tears, apologizing! "I'm so sorry! I didn't know!" I felt horrible! I explained that it was just a terrible joke and apologized back. I don't think she ever really trusted us much after that.

Anyway, manager Jerry eventually fired or laid both Vaughn and me off, hippies that we were. I did, however, take great pleasure in seeing him shot multiple times. (He was also attempting an acting career and got blown away by RoboCop in the second movie.)

AA Practical Jokes And The Tree Free Experience.

I have spent the last several years proudly training and teaching and continually earning my spot on the Paul Mitchell Advanced Academy Cutting Team. People have come and gone for various reasons. It is not easy to earn or even maintain your spot on the team. Among these creative and bright people, there are inevitably going to be some practical jokers. At one of my early trainings, then Team Leader Andrew Carruthers was stressing the important fact that when attempting certification there are no "passes" or "fails." You either complete your certification or you are given the coaching needed to help you complete in the future. He held up a guide and said, " Nowhere in this guide will you find the word "fail"! In fact, I'll give anyone $100 if they can show me the "word "fail." The next day, someone held up their guide and pointed, saying, "Mine says right here "If you don't complete your certification, it means that you have failed." Someone else held theirs up and said, "Mine does too!" Andrew turned a little gray as he started doing math and probably wondering, "Can I expense this?" It turned out that future and current Team Leader, Mike Helm, had taken the files and, changed the wording, and printed, punched, and bound some "special" copies!

At another early training, an anonymous person made legal-sized "WELCOME!" collages with some really raunchy pictures and slipped them under the doors of select members. The main problem was that some members had changed rooms and some random hotel guests may have received an unexpected surprise! I, in fact, have no idea who was responsible, and thus, they will maintain anonymity. Doubtless, they are long gone anyway.

At a training in San Antonio, a well-known Paul Mitchell artistic director got sealed in his hotel room with a sheet of plastic taped to the frame of his door. Inside the plastic was Easter basket grass and other paper-based filler. When he emerged, he didn't really know how to respond other than to do a superman bust through. No big, haha there.

One of my favorite ones I wasn't present at but have to recount for posterity. Brennan Claybaugh, the top dog at PMAE, rented a car to drive to the training. He parked under a tree, and when he came out that afternoon the car was completely covered in bird poop. They drove through a car wash several times before it all came off. The next day, Brennan made a point to not park under the tree! However, Andrew got hold of the keys and moved it back under the tree! Once it was returned to its previous smelly white state, he moved it back to it's tree-free parking place. When Brennan came out later, he was reportedly speechless. If I know him at all, that didn't last long. One training in Las Vegas occurred on my birthday. At one point, Mike Helm started to speak, and it seemed that he was having a hard time getting to his point. After a couple of minutes, he looked to his left down a hall an began to laugh. We all looked right towards the hall and saw an intense glow getting closer and closer. It was a birthday cake for me!.......with the whole surface covered with lit candles! The combined flames easily reached a height of 2-3 feet! Mike was apoplectic. I was astonished, flattered, and insulted (not really) at the number of candles. I may be the oldest person on the team and prone to "When I was a boy..." stories, but there had to be 3 or 4 times as many candles as required. It was great!

There haven't been as many legends or practical jokes in recent years. I'm sure they are coming.

This wasn't a practical joke, but I think warrants retelling. At one of countless Advanced Academy trainings in Costa Mesa, my cutting teammate Doug Christensen and I had gone to dinner in his rental SUV, and when we returned, he parked on the far side of the hotel. The next morning, before my coffee had fully kicked in, I looked down that direction and saw a black SUV. I dragged my bags to the rear of said SUV and, seeing that there was someone in the drivers seat, knocked on the rear window. Nothing. I knocked again. Still nothing. Once more and nothing. I stepped around to the side and realized that it wasn't Doug! The older lady in the drivers seat looked like she was about to have a stroke! I genuflected and backed off apologizing. Doug had gone out again after we came home and had surrendered his spot to a similar-looking vehicle. Once again, Kent Skinner scares the crap out of another poor old lady! Speaking of which.......

Kent: The Dark Side!

This might surprise you. Probably not. Like many of us, I can be and have been at times an a__hole. A girl once told me, "If you weren't such a nice guy, you'd be a real a___hole!" Or.. maybe it was the other way around. I won't say that I'm proud of my actions, but I confess to a little guilty pleasure at the time for having committed them. Years ago, I was written a bad check by a good friend who later made good for it. However, it caused a couple of my own checks to bounce. One went through on the second submission, but the other, written to the dry cleaner two doors down from my salon, went straight to a collector. The fee was $40 on a $19 dollar check! Had the owner of the dry cleaner accidentally bounced one on me, I would simply have walked next door and said, "Hi! It seems that you have accidentally written me an NSF check!" and would have accepted the $19 and his apology and all would be well in the world between two neighbors. This didn't happen.

I drove down to the collection office. At that time in my life, I drove a pretty silver Saab with an excellent sound system. I also wore my hair to the middle of my back, and in my black leather jacket and Oakley sunglasses, I just might have projected a less-than-conservative or passive image. I pulled up to the front door at an angle and parked with my front wheels on the sidewalk. With the door still open and Rammstein blasting from the speakers, I entered the office.

A woman came to the bulletproof collection window and asked, wide-eyed, "Can I help you?"

"I want my check!" I replied. She repeated, "I'm sorry. How can I help you?"

"I WANT MY CHECK!"

"What's your name?"

"Skinner."

"Beg your pardon?"

"SKINNER!!" She scurried off and returned, saying in a shaky voice, "Tha...that will be $59." I pulled out exactly $59 in change and, wadded up bills and tossed them through the recessed tray below the bulletproof window. Money scattered everywhere. She gathered bills and change and finally gave me my check. I left feeling simultaneously triumphant and guilty for being an a__hole to an old lady who was just doing her job. She did, however, work for a collection company, so I am sure that I wasn't the first. Rationalize...rationalize.

Sometime later, I tried it again. Different agency. Different result. Also, the bounced check was my fault, so this time, Kharma stepped in. I walked in angry and demanded my check. I was asked to take a seat. I refused. I was told again to take a seat, and I refused. I leaned on the counter, and it broke off! It hit the ground and I stepped back as surprised as everyone else! A very big man came to the window (no shaky little old lady this time) and demanded that I sit down. I, in return, demanded my check. He said that first I had to pay and, that the check would be mailed to me, and that it wasn't even at that facility to give to me. I continued to express my anger, and he turned to the woman and said, "Call 911." She did. So much for intimidation. I then remembered that I had a firearm (legal) in the car from a trip to the farm and also a previously opened bottle of single malt scotch. No, I wasn't drinking. I decided that I really didn't want to deal with the police right then. I paid and left with my tail between my legs. Kharma can be a bitch!

Meet Me At Kenray

Art by Mark Thompson

The nice thing about getting into fights as a kid was that usually, somebody broke it up before any permanent damage was done. I never picked a fight, but I found myself in a few of them. I never backed down from one although I did avoid a fight if I could. Because someone usually intervened, I rarely lost one, either. Here's a rundown of the few that matter. Cast of characters: Mike R (already sounds like a tough guy, r.i.p.), Rusty K (also r.i.p.), Ricky S (we eventually made peace in the clinic co-dodging class while faking illness), Elizabeth T, Duane C., and me.

In 4th grade, I remember Mike extorting our lunch money from my friends and me. I refused, tussled, got separated, and ended the problem. I eventually bought some tires from him a decade later. Maybe that one was not that memorable.

In gym class, there was this triumvirate of evil consisting of Ricky S, Rusty K, and Duane C. I don't know, looking back from an adult perspective, what their motivations were, but essentially, they were bullies. This had gone on long enough, and I consulted my dad, who advised that I make sure that there was an equalizer of some kind nearby at any given time. I took that a little too literally. One cool thing about my dad was that he showed me how to do stuff, and I had complete access to tools and, equipment, and supplies in our well-stocked garage. I took an aluminum pipe and cut it off to about five inches. I took an acetylene torch and melted enough lead to fill it but didn't pour the molten lava until I inserted a length of bicycle chain into the tube. This fits nicely into the rings of my notebook.

The next time, I found myself in the middle of "You wanna see a fight between me and Ricky?" I whipped out my weapon and laid into them. One of them managed to pull the chain free of my hand but not until I did some damage. We all went to the principals office, and my dad had to explain his advice for me to the principal. "I didn't mean "Carry a weapon!"

Anyway, nobody went to jail or the hospital or got suspended. There was a car dealership called Ken Ray Ford near Marsh Jr High where people would meet to settle their differences. "Meet me at KenRay!" was a not uncommon challenge heard at recess or in class. To save face, one would accept this, and hopefully, justice would be delivered. I don't remember what started it. Certainly not me, but I had a date with destiny, or rather Duane C., at KenRay. It was over very quickly. Rather than traditional fisticuffs, Duane boxed (slammed open-handed simultaneously) my ears. Both ear drums ruptured. Fight over.

After a conversation between my father and his parents, expensive doctor visits, and sleepless pharmaceutical-influenced nights, Duane unwillingly became my guardian angel. "Don't mess with Skinner! He'll

158

get you in all kinds of trouble! The only other fight from that time that springs to mind wasn't really a fight. There was a girl that hung with the "tough guys" named Elizabeth. One day, my friend Kyle Evans and I were at Park Forest shopping center, and we asked her friend some nonsense question like "Are you green or blue?" as we had asked several people just to get a reaction. Just being goofy kids. She straddled my front bike wheel and punched me in the face."What'd you call me?" She asked and punched me again. I didn't know how to react? I had been taught from an early age not to hit girls. One had never hit me before, either! We rode away, confused and embarrassed. My dad later asked, " Why didn't you hit her?" Aside from yanking a thief from my van in the '70s (not really a fight), I have only been in a couple of grown-up fights. They were over very quickly and were both between me and my long-time friend RW. One was outside a hair class in the parking lot, and I have no memory of what it was about. It was really just a shoving match. The other was when he was going though a recurring rough patch with a girlfriend, and I was mostly listening over margaritas and Tex Mex. I said something like, "I can't feel what you're feeling, but I can see that you're going through a lot." or something. Rich misunderstood me, exploded, dumped the table over, and stormed out. The owner came running out yelling, "This is my place! This is my life!" I gave her more than our bill would have been and went after RW. I found him in the alley behind the restaurant. I tried to calm him down and explain what I said when he turned on me. He grabbed my shirt and shoved me against the wall. I reacted by throwing my arms up between his and breaking his grip. I came back down with joined fists, and I broke his glasses and his lip. I was driving that night (probably not a great idea), so I loaded him into my truck and took him home. We didn't talk for a few months, but one day, he showed up at my door and apologized. His brothers had convinced him that it was a good idea. "Kent's your brother, man!" They were right. Brothers sometimes fight, and they get over it.

I have known people that enjoy picking fights knowing that the other person is likely to back down. This is usually evidence of some self-esteem problems and a need to prove themselves....to themselves. I've known a couple guys that could certainly do some damage in a fight but choose to use humor and their brains to avoid fighting. One old client of mine couldn't help but notice a very pretty girl at a club. He didn't try anything at all, but her boyfriend had to get macho and ask, "What're you looking at?" My friend replied with a smile, "Well, right now, I'm looking at the luckiest guy in the club!" Situation disarmed. Another time when challenged (it seemed to happen a lot), he said, "Now I don't know whether you can kick my ass or not but either way, both of us would leave hurt or f----d up. So, how about I buy you a drink, and we see who can tell the best Aggie joke, and we'll both go home happy?" Brilliance!

Contrary to the image this story may convey, I am not a fighter by nature. I have spent a few years taking Tae Kwon Do and can usually handle myself pretty well in a controlled ring. That's much different than a street fight. I hope I never have to test it in a life-threatening situation!

Jury Duty

I have only been chosen twice for jury duty. Initially, I wasn't thrilled to have my days messed up, but in retrospect, I wouldn't have missed it for the world. Well, maybe the world. Anyway, I'm glad I did it.

The first time around was the tougher one. We were told that it was a carjacking case. I sat through the selection process with either a bunch of clueless prospects or clever duty dodgers. The lawyers went down the line asking, "If the defendant WAS found guilty, could you assess the death penalty?" One good ole boy replied, "Well, I'd have to hear his side of the story." The attorney tried to clarify: "Now, this is assuming that you HAVE heard his side and have already found him guilty." "Well, I can't say without knowing his side." "Assuming that you DID hear his side and you DID believe him guilty...." "Well, sometimes they make toy guns that look like real guns and...." Forehead slapping ensues. Another couple of prospects were very adamant about their willingness to fry somebody. During the whole process, the defendant, a big Mike Tyson-looking kind of guy, slouched in his chair, not taking anything very seriously, and was trying to flirt with the court reporter, who looked like she was going to poop her pants. Eventually selected, we were asked to wait in the hall for a couple of hours. Finally, a spokesperson came out and thanked us for our time. I guess a couple of the more radical pro-death people must have scared the defendant because he opted to do seventeen years without parole vs going to trial. The spokesperson informed us that rather that just a carjacking case, it was the South Dallas Rapist, as the media referred to him.

The second tour of jury duty was easier but stranger. Both the prosecution and defense teams were of a like mind that the defendant was not just guilty of robbery, assault, and drug possession but was verifiably nuts. They both just needed us to listen to him and to agree that he needed mental health care vs hard time. Somehow, I ended up being jury foreman. I don't remember how. Anyway, there is an actor named Brad

Dourif. If they made a movie about this guy, Brad would be the perfect actor to play this guy. He looked just like him and Brad has played more than a couple of nut cases. See "One Flew Over The Cuckoos Nest," "X Files," and "Dune." You'll recognize him. The prosecutor was trying to get him to agree to going to the hospital rather than jail. He refused either option. "Naw....I'm going to stay with my pastor! I don't need to go nowhere. Jesus has already forgiven me, so I'm going to stay with my pastor!" Not sure how the pastor felt about this. After a couple of rounds of this, it was easy to say, "Yep! He's crazy!" Anyway, proud to do my duty. Will do so again if called.

3s&7s and Coolhand

I don't think one should chose one's own nickname. I have a softball jersey from when our school had a softball team with the name "Coolhand 37" on the back. Someone asked me the other day if she should call me Luke. It has nothing to do with Coolhand Luke. It's a combination of a nickname and my "lucky numbers." I really don't know what to make of this, if anything. I just think it's interesting.

Throughout my life, there has been a repetition of 3s & 7s at important milestones. First, I was born at 3:07. I weighed 7 lbs and 3 oz.s. My birthday, 3/17/53 added together equals 73. My best friend in fourth grade, Dale Meyler, and I had the same phone number, except that mine ended in 3 and his in 7. My children were born on the 3rd and 7th. Glenna's birthday is 7/13, mine 3/17. To top it off, if my legs get any sun (not so much these days), with a little imagination, my birthmark shows 317. So, I'm either a pawn in a cosmic joke, a bit player in a big coincidence, or the second coming here without an instruction manual. Whatever. The name "Coolhand" came from Denise Van Deusen. When I first moved to Dallas from Austin, fairly fresh from beauty school with a smattering of brief salon jobs behind me to work with my pal Vaughn Stockton with the goal of eventually opening a salon together, I started working at Regis in Richardson Square Mall. At the time, it was the #1 Regis salon. I struck a deal with the manager that I would do all of the popular Bo Derrick braids, and I would not have to do any of the BHLs (blue-haired ladies) roller sets. I admit, it was more from fear than anything. I had gotten through school having done one roller set plus the set at state board exam, which I lucked out of. (Another story). I was a fairly private person. Vaughn and I, being best pals, hung out together, and a couple people, including Denise, assumed that I thought I was too good for them or something. "Mr. No sets and cool braids." I would come in to work, and Denise would say with a slightly snide tone, "How's it goin'..........Coolhand?" She and they eventually realized that I was o.k., but the nickname stayed. To this day, pushing 50 years, Denise still calls me "Coolhand." I guess there are worse nicknames. I admit to liking it.

Bloody Fingers

Photo by Glenna Skinner

I still get out and play music when I can. I prefer to play to an audience that came to listen to music. Most of my repertoire consists of original music of my own or close musician friends or radically reworked pieces from famous sources. I believe that if you cover someone else's music, you owe them the respect of nailing it as they wrote and performed it or that you put your own stamp on it, effectively making it your own. Anything in between usually comes off as a lesser attempt or, worse, an amateur imitation. The author should also be acknowledged.

I decided a few years back that I wouldn't do any more background music gigs. If the audience doesn't stop talking or at least clap, then how much better is my effort than a juke box?

I will occasionally try out new material at an open mic. Often, I am excited or obsessed with an idea or song that, once performed live, didn't quite represent the masterpiece in my head. The audience at an open mic is typically mostly fellow musicians doing the same thing, trying something out, working out some bugs in a piece, or people that just enjoy performing. The non musician listeners are open for anything and are almost always appreciative.

I have been very fortunate to have shared a stage, a gig, or opened for some of my heroes and influences and more than a few local successes. The weirdest combination was opening for Robert Fripp of King Crimson and the League of Crafty Guitarists. We had to set up on the floor in front of the stage and could not run lines into the house system besides our vocal mikes. The entire stage was taken up my Mr. Fripp's and his bands gear. I am a huge fan of his music, but I didn't see his and mine being a great mix. We did our best and got a decent response. Surprisingly, a couple years later, as I was squeezing through a row of seats at a Laurie Anderson concert, a guy asked me, "Didn't you open for Robert Fripp?" "Why, yes, I did!" I replied with some astonishment. "You guys were great!" Wow. (Because we weren't.) "Thanks!"

I've lost track of how many times I've opened at Poor David's Pub for the legendary songsmith Shawn Phillips. (A much better combination) The first time I was booked as a solo act and was anxiously preparing for this groundbreaking gig, buying his more recent albums so as to not be uneducated if the opportunity presented itself to discuss music. I had no idea what to expect. Shawn's music is clever, socially commentary, political, cosmic, and uncategorizable. The best tag might be "Folk Rock." Would he be nice? Arrogant? Humble? Rock star attitude? Who knew? As an amusing side note, in the '70s, girls would scream and "Ooh! Aah!" when he let his substantial ponytail down. I tried copying that move in a few hair shows in the 80s and 90s. Nobody screamed or "Ooh! Aah!! Ed. Oh well. Anyway, about ten days before the big gig, I reached into my Paul Mitchell travel bag and came into contact with an open razor and cut the, you know, what out of my left-hand middle finger. Basically, I took the tip almost off. For the next few days, I tried everything that people suggested. I used Aloe Vera, vitamin E, positive visualization, prayer, and everything! It was coming along pretty good when one afternoon, I was in the theater parking lot at Brand and Beltline, and a girl that I dated briefly pulled up next to me and asked, "What's up!" I stuck my finger out to show her, and...she stuck her head out and BIT MY FINGER! I've never been a very good dancer, but if it weren't for the less-than-elegant verbiage spewing from my pie hole at that moment, I might have made it to the next round on Dancing With The Stars. Two days before the big show, one of my clients, Beth Mydill, suggested that I call her husband, Marc, a terrific guitarist. I had a couple of his CDs and knew it was a great idea. We got together, clicked, and, with the help of several layers of liquid bandage, managed to pull off a good show! During our sound check, an older (than me, yes, they exist) guy in a fireman's shirt walked in the back door and, with a Texas twang, said, "Hi guys! What's happenin'!" I said, "Just doing a sound check." He smiled, extended his hand, and said, "Shawn Phillips!" "Well, I'll be damned! Kent Skinner!" I said and began an ongoing tradition. He is a very person who does what he does like no one else and, after the last couple of gigs, has had some great comments and suggestions for me.

A few years ago, five or six of my high school classmates, none of whom I was close friends with, showed up to hear me. It was both flattering and intimidating. I knew that at least three of them were good to really good guitarists and they sat at the front table maybe ten feet from me. About three songs into my set, I grabbed my twelve-string acoustic and found it severely out of tune. It may have fallen off of its stand and been put back up or as someone suggested later, someone may have pulled a crappy joke. I prefer to believe the former. Tuning a six-string guitar on stage is distracting enough. Tuning a twelve-string is twice as annoying. I should have just handed it off to one of the guys and said, "Hey, do me a favor and go tune this!" I finished my set on the six. I got a couple of compliments from the rat pack afterwards and one or two stayed for Shawn's show. It's weird to have jr. high social order vibes trickle out of your psyche 40 years later.

Target Stories

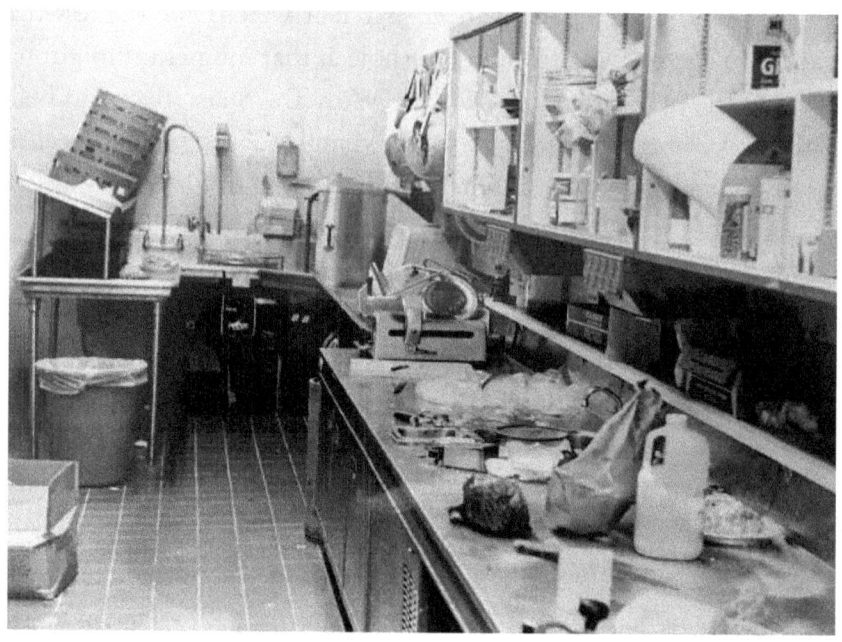

One of my earliest jobs, my second one, actually was at the first Target store in Dallas. I left my cushy $1.40 an hour bus boy position at Fred's Barbecue to accept the substantial raise to $1.60 an hour and the rise in social status associated with working behind the nut stand at Target. Just down the counter, a few feet was the candy department. Lori was a cute, flirtatious brunette who had us all eating out of the palm of her hand. "Don't let Candy Girl play with your nuts!" Said my boss, Jim Berg. He had a strange nasal Midwestern tone to his voice, and it always seemed that he felt he was destined for bigger things. The Nut Stand soon went away, and we were reassigned to the Snack Bar and the restaurant. Jim's one-liners live on today in the reminiscences of my friends and me. Once, when I asked what we were planning to do with the days-old mystery meat that I was putting through the grinder (chicken, beef, whatever). He replied, "We'll call it "Sarcasm On Toast" and serve it on white rye and a raisin." Whatever that meant. Actually, it was used for stuffed peppers. I never tried it. "I'm not paying you to play grab ass with the girls!" was another favorite he used on my pal Vaughn Stockton.

As a kid, my voice changed early. Picture Froggy on the Little Rascals. Maybe not that bad. I had a deep voice that didn't belong to a skinny blonde kid. Picture Barry White.....again, maybe not. Anyway, I was given the privilege of making the "Attention Target shoppers.." announcements. One day, when Jim supposedly gone for the day, I wrote a joke announcement taking the words of the 9-cent popcorn special and the hot dog special and mixing them up. My "friends" talked me into making it. "I'll give you 5 bucks!" "I'll give you a matchbox!" Not that I'd admit to accepting bribes or other extra-legal activity, I made the announcement. "Attention Target Popcorn! For the next nine cents, you can get a foot-high bag of tender juicy Target Shoppers for only fifteen...." or something like that. It was hilarious....until Jim Berg walked up and said, "Skinner, come with me!" He was in the store shopping, not that it would havemade any difference, there being LOTS of other managers in the store. We went back to the management (it felt like the principal's) office. After some minor begging, I was told that if I got a haircut that, maybe I wouldn't get fired. I agreed, got a haircut, and got fired anyway. I didn't tell my dad. I hung out at the Skillerns Drugs soda fountain, reading comic books for a few afternoons. The guy behind the counter asked if I needed a job. I took it, and then told my dad that I had decided to take a different job. It turned out that he already knew the whole story. What were the chances? He had met the Target store manager at a dinner party and heard it all and was just waiting to see what I would say to him. Anyway, to make an already long story not as long, I'll just say thatI was not destined to be a soda jerk at Skillern's for long. I found out that the "Assistant Manager" who offered me the job was just another flunky like me. I was made legit after a few days when the actual manager showed up. We never mopped or anything. The most we did was to heavily spray Lysol around the floors and corners, which also masked the suspicious smoke that the bogus Assistant Manager added to the already irresistable bouquet of the kitchen. I quit after two weeks.

I asked in a previous story if you had ever found someone so attractive that you couldn't even talk to them. I had a crush on a girl in high school....actually a lot of girls. I kind of liked this senior girl that I didn't really have that problem with, nor was I likely to get anywhere with. We just talked in the library. "SHHHHH!" So, she graduated. The next year, her younger sister showed up. I did have that problem with her. The best I could do was "Hi!" passing in the hall. I did get my nerve up and approached her in the library and gave her a picture that I'd drawn of her. As I recall, it wasn't too bad an effort. "I remember her looking a little stunned but saying, "Thanks." I walked away embarrassed and thinking, "Stupid! Stupid!" The term "stalker" hadn't been coined yet, but I felt like one.

You ask.. "Wait! Isn't this supposed to be more Target stories?" It all comes together in a minute.

Another time, my younger sister Barby had a friend spend the night. In the morning, I answered the door in the jet plane pajamas that my grandmother made for me that had a gaping fly that had to be held closed. The sister that was picking Barby's friend up was my crush.

"Be cool." (Too late) I told myself. "Stupid!!, Stupid!!" the voice in my head chanted. Whatever.

So, a few months after my unceremonious exit from the Target restaurant, I was in the store shopping, and guess who was working behind the snack bar. Yep. I went back to the restaurant and approached Mr Berg. There was a novelty toy called "Bag O' Laughs," a plastic box in a cloth bag that, when pressed, would laugh uncontrollably. I had one in my jacket pocket. "Mr Berg? I was hoping I could talk to you about maybe getting my...("Har! Har! Har! Har! Har Har)...... job back.?" I had accidentally hit the button. I fumbled the battery out and shut it up. Jim didn't seem to have noticed. He might have wondered about the panic on my face. We sat down, and he finally said. "You're on a months probation. In a Month, I'll either fire you or give you a raise. If you're only worth a nickel raise, I'll fire you!" I never worked with crush girl. She got fired within a week, and there I was with my crappy job back! I got the raise. 10 cents, I think. I worked there for another year or so, rotating between shoes, jewelry, and back at the restaurant before moving across the parking lot to Pottery Plus....another story. Years later, I thought I recognized a woman in the salon. She was that original older sister. I told her about giving her younger sister that picture. She said, "She had that on her wall for years!"

Oscar The Magic Owl

You never know what kind of impact a few minutes spent with someone may have. One of my brief but interesting jobs while I as in college was for Britannica doing magic shows in daycare centers promoting a cheesy reading program that involved a plastic owl named "Oscar the magic owl" that had contacts on his feet and would light up when placed on the metallic tape by the right answer in a book. Oscar was not to be relied upon because whether the answer was right or not, he did whatever he felt like. I had nothing to do with the sales or quality control. My job was to go into pre-arranged daycare centers, be "Uncle Kent," perform a less than amazing thirty-minute magic show, pass out Oscar the magic owl rings and letters asking the parents to send them back so that a "teacher" (salesman) could contact them. When I was asked to be one of their "teachers," I declined. I probably worked for them for a month.

Two years later, on a campus bus, I noticed a kid peeking over the back of a set a few rows ahead of me. I didn't think anything of it. I smiled and waved. Before he and his mother got off of the bus, she came back to me and said, "Excuse me, I know this is a weird question, but... are you "Uncle Kent"?" I was pretty astonished. Her kid recognized me from a less-than-awesome magic show two years before! Maybe Oscar really was magic!....... Naw.

Thumbs Out

I'm not sure why my dad thought that this was a good idea, but at fifteen, when I couldn't drive, and even at seventeen, when I should have been driving, I did a lot of hitch hiking. He didn't know that I was doing it until he pulled up beside me on Forest Lane (another whole source of stories) and said, "Get in!" After discussing it with my mother he told me that it would be o.k. but to use good decision making. It was a way to get around without accepting the responsibilities involved with two tons of steel, glass, and explosive liquids. Again, too many stories! My bff Vaughn- I can't believe I just used the abbreviation, 'BFF,' suggested a couple of our hitchhiking adventures. I'll start with the most amusing one, short and not-so-sweet. Thumbs out, we were heading north on Marsh Lane around Royal Lane and walking backward. Years before, the civil engineer or whoever plans this stuff had no idea that a fifteen-year-old would be traversing the very path that a fire hydrant interrupted. In the words of Jim Nabors, "Surprise, surprise!." I seem to recall both of my feet leaving the ground.

Another trip, an older black gentleman picked us up, and I sat up front. He started saying things like, "I'll treat you lack mah own keeids," and reaching over and touching my watch, "My, but that shore is a purty wristwatch!" and just generally making us nervous. He also predicted our future careers. He pointed at Vaughn and then me, saying, "You gonna be a doctor.........and you gonna be a judge!" We had him drop us off a block over from our destination.

Hitching down Forest lane to Vaughn's house one time, a somewhat older hippie type and his dog picked me up. He asked where I was headed, and I told him the major crossroads. He said that I have to tell him where to go because he wasn't from around here. I asked him, "Where are you from?" He said, "Topanga Valley, you know?.....where Crosby, Stills and, Nash.....and Neil Young are from?" When I got to Vaughns, I told him the story of my trip. He said, "Wait a minute," and pulled out one of Neil Young's albums, which had a picture of him and his dog together. "Is this the guy?" Vaughn asked. It did look like him and his dog. I thought, "maybe so!" So there is a slight chance that I may have bummed a ride with Neil Young!

This one isn't particularly funny. As I mentioned in the previous "Thumbs Out" story, I did a lot of hitch hiking back in the 60's and 70's. They were different times, mostly safer, but not always. My father's approval of that mode of transportation was perhaps naively based on his own experience and from living in less scary times. Most of my rides were pleasant, or non memorable riding with normal, nice helpful people. There were, however, terrible things that happened to some of my friends and acquaintances, including robbery, rape and murder but as a young man, I believed that I was immortal and that those things would not happen to me. I was lucky that the things that I experienced were at worst uncomfortable.

One good experience involved Vaughn Stockton and me hitching to Austin to see his friends in the bands Crackerjack and Blackbird playing at an outdoor concert. I remember some wasted old black guy getting thrown off of the stage after commandeering a microphone and announcing "Well, I went an did it! I got LOADED and STONED TOO!" Blackbird and Crackerjack were two terrific bands including a couple of people that later made it big including Stevie Ray and Jimmy Vaughan, Tommy Shannon and Chris Layton of Johnny Winters band and later SRV's Double Trouble and Kim Davis of Point Blank. The trip down was mostly uneventful. The concert was amazing. The trip back was a grueling all nighter with scarce traffic. The best part was having that adventure with my bud, Vaughn.

I played in a band in Dallas on weekends for a while when I was in college at U.T., and I would hitch up and back with my guitar, amp head, and my dog Alabaster. She was well-known around campus and probably had more friends than I did. I got rides with people that knew her and not me. "You must be o.k. if you're with her!" someone one said to me! One time, I got a ride with a creepy, puffy guy who drove with his little fingers extended from the steering wheel who asked me if I wanted to look at pictures. I asked, suspicious, "Uh..what kind of pictures?" "You know, pictures of women...and men...." Me: "Naaaaaw! I don't think so!" We rode in silence for a couple of minutes before I said, "Yeah, this is a good place to let me out up here!"

Another time, I was picked up at the same spot by another weirdo who started telling stories leading up to some kind of proposition, but I nipped it early by telling him about that previous ride. He got the message and, after a minute, "remembered something that I left back at work" and dropped me off. Whew. The next ride on that same trip was a redneck truck driver that pulled over, relieved himself on the shoulder of the highway while Alabaster and I caught up. First, he said, "Cain't haul at dawg!" but changed his mind and let us aboard. Just to set the record straight, so to speak, I told him about those two rides. He said something like, " He probably just wanted to....." I thought, "Oooh, Nooo!" He changed the subject. He asked what I did for a living. I told him that I was a student and worked for YMCA Urban Services. "Yew work with a bunch a n_____s?" He talked about wishing he could drive through South Dallas and shoot as many of "them people" as he could. He also pointed out a restaurant in Temple with the "best-looking hookers this side of the Rio Grande. And CLEAN! And you better be clean too, or they're liable ta inspect ya and disinfect ya!" I rode in silence, just wanting to get home to bed. I did. He actually drove his semi within 2 blocks of my house. Close enough. I exited the truck feeling morally soiled. Goodbye redneck mother.

During a particularly rough patch when my van was broken down in Dallas, my left arm was paralyzed, I was living in the back of Dale Meyler's store, an old house with no heat, struggling through school and trying to maintain a relationship in Dallas...whole different story...I would hitch down to San Antonio from Austin just to take a hot shower! One ride, I was picked up by Cheech and Chong's real-world counterparts in a blue Volkswagen bug with a four-foot bong. Although I pulled what decades later might be called a Bill Clinton and "didn't inhale" (I was going to see my mother after all), I got moderately incoherent and couldn't hold on to a train of thought while trying to converse with my confused Ma!

On one of my return trips from San Antonio, another Volkwagen pulled over, and the driver, a Mexican guy, asked, " Where you goin, man?" I told him, "Austin," and he said, " Get in!" I did. After a couple of miles, he said, "I'm taking this broad to Michigan...to see her old man!" It was winter. They had no coats or luggage that I could see. Until then, I thought the passenger was a big Mexican guy! No, just a big woman! We drove a while before he had to pull over to "water the plants," as he put it. While he was outside, she turned around and said, "When you get to Austin, call the police! He's taking me to see my old boyfriend who he thinks I'm still in love with!" Before I could remove myself from this Mexican soap opera, the driver was back, and we carried on. I figured I would do as she asked as soon as I was able to. Remember, VW Bugs were two-door vehicles, and it wasn't likely that I would be able to jump out of that little bitty window. Eventually, in San Marcos, he pulled back over and said they were heading back. He was bluffing but succeeded in scaring her....and me! I should have called the cops anyway. I suspect that I could be dropped off blindfolded anywhere on I-35, and after walking five minutes either north or south, I could tell you where I was and how far it was to Dallas, Austin, or San Antonio.

Things change and the world is a more dangerous place. I pass up hitchhikers with a small pang of guilt. Also, I will not be as accepting of my son riding with strangers as my dad was with me!

Even More Salon Silliness

My good buddy Vaughn Stockton reminded me of a couple good quick ones. One of my favorite Steve Martin movies "All Of Me," co-starring Lily Tomlin, had just come out, and I asked a guest, an older woman that I had only had in my chair a couple of times, "Have you seen "All Of Me" yet?" She replied, "No, and I think it's best that we keep it that way!"

Things actually heard in a salon that can be misinterpreted:

#1 "Unless you can think of something fun to do with it, just get it out of my face!"

#2 "How long do you like your bangs?"

#3 "Did you layer in the back?" "No, I just met her!"

#4 "Lie back. I'm going to give you a deep penetrating protein treatment!"

Unlike my neighbor in the packaging and shipping store next door who was constantly running people out of his one parking space just to be a prick, I had "Welcome!" stenciled on our parking places, believing that the occasional parker might say "Hey, there is a salon here!" One day, Vaughn and I were at the desk and a guy in a Land Rover parked right in front of my front door. He climbed out glaring as if to challenge us, saying, "Go ahead, you silly hairstylists! Make my day! Say something about me parking here!" He went next door to Albertsons. Vaughn said, "What an a__hole!" and grabbed paper, scissors, and tape and, made new letters, and changed the rear Land Rover label to read "Land Boner". The guy eventually came out, glared, and drove away. I'm sure at least a few people driving behind him enjoyed it!

Then there was the woman who called and complained to me that the shampoo girl had used something on her to make her hair stop growing. Not a good business plan for a hair salon! She said she was going to call the police and tell them that we were selling drugs out of there. (Not sure I would take whatever she was on.) I suggested she do just that and to be sure and mention that part about making her hair stop growing. Finally, one day, I came in from lunch, and I sat behind the desk. A man approached and said, "I'd like you to read this," and handed me a photocopied manuscript. I tried to read and understand it, but it was gibberish, pseudo-religious gobbledygook. It made no sense whatsoever. He had returned to Mario's station, where Mario was attempting to do a young woman's hair while he read the same rubbish from his manuscript about loud. She had dark circles under her eyes and long sleeves in the summertime. The man claimed that she was one of his wives and that he rescued them from the gutter and offered them salvation. If she said anything or touched her hair, he would launch into her. "GOD BROUGHT YOU HERE AND GOD BROUGHT YOU TO THIS MAN AND YOU ARE INSULTING GOD, THIS MAN, AND ME!" She cowered and apologized. Yes, his check bounced. According to a small article in the Dallas Morning News a couple of weeks later, he was running for president, and the accumulated hotel bills and restaurant and business hot checks were God's contributions to his campaign fund. Yes, it takes all kinds.

Clients From Hell

Most of my clients/guests were or are amazing. Every once in a while, a crazy one or two might pop up! One Monday morning around, I was awakened by a phone call from a total stranger. "Hello?" She said in a panicky voice, "This is Linda C_____, and I tried to frost my hair. It's all different colors! Can you fix it?" She had apparently bought a home frosting kit but didn't understand that the plastic cap included is used to keep the color off of THE REST OF YOUR HAIR, and she just put bleach all over and panicked when it started turning all the different shades possible between dark brown and blonde. For those of you that are not privy to the workings of hair color, brown has to go through red, red, orange, orange, orange, yellow, yellow, and pale yellow before it gets to pale blonde. She stopped halfway and was stuck with every possible variation. I told her that I was not working that day, but I could at least look at it on Tuesday. "I CAN'T GO TO WORK LIKE THIS!" she exclaimed. I suggested that she call the salon when it opened that there was a good colorist that worked Mondays. She did. A couple of hours later, I got a call from that stylist." Heh heh heh heh!" she said. "Guess what YOU'RE doing tomorrow?"

She did come in and it took about 5 hours in between clients and doing one little bit at a time. I remember having to charge her around $350 for the correction. I did her hair for a couple of years, and she always whined and complained about my prices and was never happy with my work. Then, one day, SHE DID IT AGAIN! She tried to highlight her hair at home and made just as bad of a mess as the first time! I suggested that I would be glad to refer her to another stylist that she might be happy with. I have only "fired" a couple of clients in my career. Later she wrote me what I assume was a scalding letter. I only read a couple of lines before trashing it. One day, I got a call from Millee, our terrific front desk coordinator, saying that one of my clients had met the guitar player from Huey Lewis and The News in Atlanta, and they had swapped gold chains or something, and he was in town and needed a cut. I thought, "Great! Things like this can happen." I came in and cut his hair while his girlfriend got a manicure and her sister got a braid. He had all of the patter and seemed legit. After he left, he called and was concerned about the cheap sunglasses that he had left behind. Hmm. Ok. Whatever. I looked closely at a Huey Lewis video on MTV, and there was a guy that looked kinda like him, mullet and all but was not the guitar player. Then his check bounced! It turned out that he had stayed at my client's house, rummaged through the trash and, got his American Express number, and ripped him off for a few thousand dollars. Just a con man with a pretty believable scam.

A43zb

Here are a couple more Hair Odyssey/ Rembrandt stories. It's an old joke now but nonetheless a good one worth unearthing. I had a guest in my chair that was a good sport and a lover of practical jokes. I had her call the salon and ask for the owner. Good old Richard answered the phone. She put on her best telephone operator voice and said, "Yes, this is Mrs Filbert from the phone company, and we just need to verify that you received your a43zb regulation plastic bags." "Now, wait. What?" Rich asked. She responded, "Your a43zb regulation plastic bags." He replied, "I have absolutely no idea what you are talking about!" She said, "Your a43zb regulation plastic bags!" "Lady! I don't know anything about regulation plastic bags! What are you talking about?!!!" She replied, "We're about to blow the dust out of your phone lines, and if you don't cover your phones up with a43zb regulation plastic bags, you'll have dust everywhere!" "I DON'T HAVE ANY REGULATION PLASTIC BAGS!!!" "Well, do you have any plastic bags about the size of the phones with elastic around them?" "Well, yeah! I have lots of those," he replied, thinking of the plastic processing caps we use in the salon. "Well, if I were you, I'd hurry and cover those phones up before you get dust everywhere!" A few minutes later, I saw Richard covering up the phones between each station with processing caps and grumbling, "This sounds like a bunch of s___ to me!" Sorry, Rich, it was too good a story to not tell it!

Wow. Too many to tell. A couple more that spring to mind: I had only been at Belt Line Hair Design (good name! It narrows the location down to somewhere on the perimeter of Dallas), which later became Hair Odyssey and even later Rembrandt The Salon when I bought and remodeled it....don't you love run-on sentences?....for a couple of weeks when I was sitting behind the front desk waiting for a walk-in guest and tipping back on my stool when the legs went out beneath me! I went down. That being bad enough being the new kid on the block, but I hit the retail shelf behind me on the way down. Actually, all four shelves were connected by a metal band in front, so imagine a large Venetian blind with rows of shampoo, conditioner, styling, and finishing products from multiple lines on each slat collapsing in unison and dumping their contents directly on my head! Continue to imagine me on my ass, red-faced with ruptured cans of hairspray hissing around me like a pit of aromatic snakes! Not a good impression.

Memory #2: Richard Watts, the owner of the salon and I were standing at the desk one day when a man walked by the front of the salon and grabbed his ear and snarled! I asked Richard, "What was that all about?" He replied, " I cut his earlobe off!" I responded, "What?" "I accidentally cut his earlobe off!" Astonished, I continued, "And he didn't sue you?" He responded, "No, but every time he walks by here, he looks in here and makes that face!" So, a couple of years later, I came in from lunch as Richard was telling a client, "No, don't worry! No charge!" After she left smiling, I asked, "You're giving away free perms?" He replied, "I did it again." I asked. "What?" He pointed at the ledge of the window between stations at what looked like a small piece of bacon fat. I paused and then asked, "Is that....?" He answered with a nod. Fortunately, she was visiting from out of the country and also did not press legal action.

More Salon Silliness

Have you ever thought of what you should have said five minutes after it would have been funny? Yeah, me too. Every once in a while, it just pops out immediately. Here are a couple that still crack me up. One day at Hair Odyssey, the eventual Rembrandt The Salon, one of our stylists named Annette Burns was sharing the fact that some days she went by her first name, "Kristin" and sometimes by her middle name, "Annette I piped up with, to the tune of the Almond Joy commercial, "Sometimes you feel like Annette.......Sometimes you don't!" O.k., Maybe you had to be there. Another time, I was just finishing a delicious muffin from my friend's baking company, "Muffin Doin'!" (I thought of the name, thank you very much) when my client "Edith" walked in. I held up my hand and did the "Sorry, my mouth's full!" Sign language. She smiled and said, "Oh, that's o.k.!" Finish your cake!" I swallowed and replied, "This is great! I get to have my cake and Edith, too!" Ba dum sss!

Another that I immediately wished could have been rewound and erased. There was a new stylist in the salon, and as is often the case, not that it mattered. There was some speculation about his orientation. While standing around the front desk, someone passed around a roll of lifesavers. However, New Guy was bypassed. He asked, "Don't I get one?" Someone replied, " We haven't gotten down to the d___ flavored one." Silence. Shocked looks. New Guy, red-faced, held up two fingers and said, "Woah! Two points!" Joke is well taken. Whew!

Car Stories With Bruce

My long-time friend, Bruce McRoberts, and I have seen our share of adventures. Many of them took place in a time where the times themselves offer possibly plausible excuses. I first met him at a party. I, by request, had brought my guitar in only to have it hijacked by a guy. "Hey, that was great! Do you mind if I play a song?" Six songs later.......some guy with long, straight brown hair, an intensely serious look on his face, a CAPE, and a star painted on his forehead was sitting at the piano bashing out power chords to some unknown, all-over-the-place piece of music. I wasn't too impressed. It wasn't until a few months later when I was living in The Big House, an early 1900s two stories on a hill above Northwest Hwy between Midway and Inwood, with a bunch of people that, for the most part, I barely knew. A couple of guys were invited over by one of my housemates, Sandi. One, I believe, was violinist Jamie Haslett, the star of a previous story pertaining to a dip of Rocky Road. The other was Bruce playing mandolin. We jammed a little bit and I came to realize that Bruce was a prolific songwriter. We did connect this time. Many bands, band members, houses, and girlfriends came and went. We are still good friends today. One of many road stories took place in his old Toyota Corolla. As many as four, maybe five of us, possibly including Bruce, myself, probably Jamie, and maybe Tim Stephens. Too many brain cells ago. Anyway, we were in no shape to drive but decided to do the drive-thru window at Jack in the Box. After staring at the menu for what seemed like a very, very long time, we realized that we had put the order taker off several times. " I said, may I take your order, please?" "Just another minute!" Hysterical laughter ensued. Minutes passed. "May I take your order, please?" More laughter with tears and gasping. Bruce finally took control of the situation and just drove away without any food being ordered. He had to stop in the middle of Royal Lane to let the laughter subside before he could continue to drive. We were very lucky that night.

Another time, he and I were headed to my house which faced a small park the size of a small city block. It was the next place I lived after the Big House was torn down. It was the first time he'd been over, so as we approached the middle of the park, I said, "Turn here!" He did in the middle of the park. We bounced over the curb, and he cut across the grass to my house. "He gleefully exclaimed, "I've always wanted to do that!" Another little one that springs to mind: He and I were driving to Austin, and I was suffering from a mild digestive issue. I tried to sneak one out silently and succeeded but was busted when the air in the small enclosed space suddenly went foul. "Oh MAN! Really?" I replied, "I'm sorry! I guess that was what you call silent but deadly!" He said, "I don't care what you call it! If it came out of your ___, I don't want to breathe it!" Good point. Well put.

On another trip, this time, I was moving from Austin to Dallas. We had secured my belongings in the back of his pickup truck with a 9'x12' oval braided rug covering them and ropes lacing across everything. I remember drinking a Mickey's malt liquor from a wide-mouth green bottle. Every once in a while, I'd look back and see that everything looked intact. Then, one of those times, I noticed that the rug was gone. We pulled over, and in fact, it was. Everything else was there, and the ropes zig-zagging from every direction were still taut. Just the rug was missing! It must have been a magic carpet because it didn't seem possible that it could have come out with the ropes holding it down. Oh well. Maybe it was the Mickeys.

Have you ever found yourself in the middle of a story and you realized that it wasn't as entertaining to your audience as it was to you? You are tempted to add some spice..."And...and the... Aliens! We were abducted by aliens.... and..." I hope that doesn't happen here. There are many, many more stories to come involving all of these guys and The Big House. I hope they are as fun for you as it is for me to recall them.

My Sissy

photo by Kent Skinner

I don't know how old we were when I stopped calling her Sissy. Carolyn was always the one in charge. She took me to the movies, taught me songs, blackmailed me, all the things that a big sis should do. I suppose I regret starving her chicks by eating their chickie mash. I was very young and hungry.

Carolyn had very long dark hair. When she got it cut above her shoulders, our small town paper thought it was newsworthy and ran a story with before and after pictures with me holding a ruler to her hair. Earth-shattering stuff! I credit her with instilling a sense of melody and harmony in me. Every night, we washed the dishes and sang to pass the time and make it somewhat My. To this day, I can remember most of the songs from Camelot, Oklahoma, The King and I, Brigadoon, and Irma La Duce.

Carolyn was Daddy's girl. She was and is a good girl with a lot of spunk and maybe missing a filter here or there which was the cause of a few reality shifts in later years. I lost daily contact when she went off to U.T. Austin. She got her degree in teaching and worked for years, teaching mostly in private schools and later as a librarian and substitute teacher. She has many, many funny and heartwarming stories of being one of the few white faces in a school in South Dallas and not being afraid to get down and talk smack to little smarty pantses. She taught as long as she could and was wise enough to retire when it became too hard.

She is also the only one of our immediate family after our father to serve in the military. She retired as a Major in the U.S. Air Force after serving in Thailand. I know our father is proud.

She had a few boyfriends in high school, the best of which stuck around since 1962, and has been married to her for over thirty years! A brave and patient man! During the same time she stopped teaching full time, our mom's health began to decline. Carolyn took the lead in caring for her, a job that she had time for and did well. We all greatly appreciate it.

She is one of the few people to ever beat me at Scrabble. I've often said that although we have different tastes, our brains work on similar frequencies. She has a huge heart and an odd sense of humor, which I greatly relate to. I love her very much! I love you, Sissy!

Son Of The Return Of Kent Skinner's Stories

Son Of The Return Of

Kent Skinner's Stories

Art by Kent Skinner

Christmas Trees

Photo by Kent Skinner

When I was a kid, our family tradition was to decorate our Christmas tree on my father's birthday, December 15th. I know that's a little late in the game for most families, but it was what it was, and I wondered why all of my friends' families jumped the gun by decorating the weekend after thanksgiving. I clung to this tradition for years, even after my father's death as a way of honoring him. It wasn't until recent years, when I had a family of my own that I realized and accepted that there were other family traditions and desires that I had to acknowledge and let go. I also realized that decorating the tree had become a somber and reverential ritual instead of a joyous celebration for me. However.....I have a couple of good Christmas tree stories to share!

The first one involves the artificial tree that we had in the wood-paneled basement den in our tiny house in Fairborn, Ohio. My sister Carolyn and I remember this story differently. I will share my remembrance. I was 4 or 5 years old but I remember it not being a very convincing tree. It was kinda sparse and skinny. My dad being in the air force (why we were in Fairborn to begin with) and my mom got to travel a lot and had collected Christmas tree decorations literally from all over the world. Some of them were very fragile and delicate. We also had a cat. Not just a cat but a brawny character named Pedro. His brother Pancho got smacked by a car less than 2 weeks after we got them.

Carolyn thought that it would be a good idea to put the little catnip mouse that we had gotten Pedro on the tree. Surely, he wouldn't try to get to it before Christmas!

Considering velocity + trajectory+ Christmas tree, it was surprising how few fragile and irreplaceable ornaments were lost. My father was not happy. She had been told that this was not a good idea. His reaction was the desire to give Carolyn a lecture and spanking, but our mother intervened, and Carolyn got off with a lecture.....until she did it again! Here is where Carolyn and my versions diverge. She does not recall replacing the catnip mouse and repeating the previous scenario, more ornaments going south, and her getting the spanking. The next story took place about three decades later. I was recently single and was reestablishing my reality. As per my family tradition, I put my tree up on 12/15. I bought a nice blue spruce and decorated it with stars, planets, and various celestial ornaments. I used the packet of tree food provided. As the food dried up, I improvised with watered-down maple syrup. Hey! It was tree blood, right? It worked. After Christmas, I kept it going. There was minimal loss of needles or greenness. February came along, and I decorated my healthy (looking) tree with hearts. March came by, and I celebrated my birthday, March 17 with shamrocks. Easter arrived on time and in time to witness bunnies and Easter egg decorations! I had plans for a red, white, and blue theme for July 4th, but my friends, worried about my safety and sanity, staged an intervention. Down came the tree! I woulda coulda made it until Halloween or Thanksgiving! Oh well!

The last episode took place around 15 years ago when my sweet daughter, Savannah, was not even a toddler! Her very first word was "Da..da...da..da...Daddeee!!! upon my return from a 5-day trip for Paul Mitchell. Her first sentence happened a few weeks later while we were Christmas tree shopping. Glenna, Savvy, and I had been to probably 4 or 5 Christmas tree lots, seeking that one special tree that says, "I'm yours!" None of them were saying that. Finally, at a lot in Rowlett, we were looking a particular tree and pondering ownership when a tiny voice firmly commanded, "PICK IT!"

Stunned, we said, "We'll take this one!"

"Yes, Ma'am!!"

Joe eddy

If someone were to ask me to name someone who was the epitome of "Cool," I would have to say Joeddy Hines. We first met when we were attending Vogue Beauty Academy. He was one of those guys who always had a funny remark and a smile unless he was immersed in one of the things he excelled in, such as playing the guitar and, for years, cutting hair. Then, you would see his focus and brilliance show through. He is the guy who introduced me to the genius of Paul Mitchell, which, of course, impacted my whole career.

Photo by Allyson Frost

The Joe I met in school was a was a tall, lanky, slightly goofy guy and was definitely attractive to the ladies. He was a great storyteller and I have shared many, though I won't share all. He was one of those smart, funny people whose very presence makes any occasion memorable, whether he's on stage, behind the chair, telling stories or just hanging out. Our friendship was one of those that could be neglected for months or even years but could be plugged back into and instantly be running at full speed. I wish I had plugged in more often. I assumed it would always be available.

Probably the cement of our bond occurred during the times he, Kip Caven, Lee Steel, a friend or two and I would take too long a lunch break and enjoy some awesome carne guisada and a beer at a nearby Mexican restaurant before returning to hair school and its harsh reality! Soon after graduating from school we went to work for a guy named Glen, who was opening a salon near the UT campus in a former Church's fried chicken drive-through. That's a story by itself.

His stories need his expressions and gesture to make them magic. I wish words could convey them. One story Joe told a few times was of a Latina woman coming in and asking how much a haircut was. I don't recall what we charged, but it was more than she had. As she started to leave, Joe said "How much you got?" She replied, "Five dollars." He gestured and said, "Sit down." She said, "I wan a change, but not too short!" There was a huge pair of cheap but sharp probably Indian steel shears there and Joe pulled her hair up into a ponytail and. Two quick hacks, she left happy with her "chag but not too chort." Hey, five bucks is five bucks! Another favorite of story of his took place after a late-night gig with one of several great bands he played in long before Buick MacKane, Alejandro, Hellapeno, Los Tailpipes, etc all. Two big girls apparently invited a couple of the guys in the band home and cooked them breakfast. Bacon, eggs, and toast make for quick sobering up. Sincere thanks were given, and the boys were on their way!

The Rockin' Devils were a terrific streamlined Rock/Rockabilly/New Wave unit that got a story in Rolling Stone after a flood filled their studio and Scotch rescued the tapes of their new album. Joes guitar sounded like a military assault. This story isn't directly about Joe, but I enjoyed Joes's telling of it. They shared a gig with some "big national act" that no one remembers today. The Devil's lead singer, Larry, got fed up with the other band's singer and his "star" attitude and proceeded to pick him up on stage and drop him on his head. I recall him telling about meeting Allyson. The way I remember it, he was at a party and saw her dancing. (maybe on a chair?) he pointed at her and said, "I'm going to marry that girl." He did. I attended their wedding ceremony, which took place in their back yard. It was a beautiful ceremony, joining two beautiful people. I remember stopping at the liquor store and impulsively buying an unfamiliar bottle of east European liquor. The label said something about exotic herbs and spices, and the bottle looked like it was carved from stone. It tasted like the liquid from old lawn clippings smells. It was awful. So awful that after gagging down a sip, you had to pass it on and say, "Here, try this!" I heard that they finished the bottle, and there may have been hallucinations involved. I never saw another bottle of it again. Joe left us last night, less than a week from his and Allyson's 33rd anniversary. These disjointed and mostly true stories are just small tips of the huge iceberg of a life of cool. I, along with scores of other people whose lives he touched and made better, will miss him terribly.

Car Talk

Art Kent Skinner

There are many milestones that we use to measure our lives. Most of us use several different overlapping units of measure, such as houses, schools, relationships, hairstyles, favorite songs, presidents, etc. One of many that I use is cars. I don't know if this will be as interesting to anyone else as it is to me, as we all have a long line of cars with their own stories in our lives. Some were/are more iconic than others. We'll see how this story plays out. While writing and rereading, I am finding that it is crossing into other stories and connecting some pieces of my life.

My first car was a deep metallic green 52 Chevy with 50,000 original miles on it! It had three on the tree and a start button. It was my grandmother's car. She was like the proverbial "little old lady from Pasadena" who never drove over 40 mph, maintained the car religiously, and, to the best of my knowledge, only received one traffic ticket and had one accident. "Well, I think this is ridiculous! I stopped at the stop sign like I was supposed to!" She did, however, fail to yield right of way to the person on her right. Bang. No serious damage.

My sister Carolyn had "The Green Hornet" before it was mine to drive. She had a minor run-in with a VW Bug in a parking lot. The Bug suffered way more than the Hornet. It was built like a tank. It did look like a large bug in the insect and the VW "Bug" sense. It looked like a huge, pregnant VW Bug. I took the back seat out and put in green shag carpet imagining it to be my love machine. No such luck. Underneath the shabby after-market seat covers was a nearly mint-condition front bench seat. I also installed a cassette deck given to me by a neighbor who was in the toy and novelty business. It was unique in that car decks were at least a couple of years away from being common, and odd that it was not stereo but mono. He also gave me a rear window suction cup mounted sign that had three messages it could show: "TOO CLOSE!," "DIM LIGHTS!" And "SOS," A little crafty exacto knife work, and "SOS!" became "SOB!" One night after driving my friend Vaughn Stockton home I was driving east on Forest Lane when someone pulled up too close behind me. Awesome! I get to use my new toy! I switched on "TOO CLOSE!" He stayed right on my butt and switched his brights on. "Grrr! I'll show him!" I thought and flipped on "DIM LIGHTS!" Nothing changed. "Oh yeah?" On went the "SOB!" light"! Suddenly, he swung around to the left and caught up with me. I looked over expecting some form of road rage (I don't think there was a name for it yet), and saw Vaughn in his Nova with the windows down, laughing his ass off! There may have been honking involved too. Anyway, the Green Hornet served me well for a couple of years before my father inexplicably decided we should sell it. I did sell it for $500 to a friend who to this day, laments not maintaining it well enough and saw it's last days. I'd love to have it back, restore it and add it to my currently non existent garage full of Kent Skinner's Iconic Car Collection.

I next drove my parent's Pontiacs, a dark blue Bonneville, and a white Executive, which I crashed into a stopped car while looking at an exit ramp on 75. See "Near Death Experiences"

When my mother moved away to San Antonio, she bought me a white Toyota Corona Deluxe. It had a half roof of white and flashy light blue faux leather vinyl. Watch out, ladies! It was iconic in that I experienced one of the coming of age milestones that should only happen in the the reclining front seat of a compact car. No names. A gentleman never brags. Another memory was picking up a displaced (doubtless, stolen) tombstone that a friend had found in a field next to where he worked. I don't know why I wanted it. I later returned it to the aforementioned field. I also needed to be in class at UT Austin for a major project presentation by noon. I drove most of the way doing 100 miles an hour and just made it on time. Travel time: about two hours and forty five minutes. No tickets and luckily no accidents. I imagined getting pulled over and the tombstone having MY name on it. (Twilight Zone music)

My next vehicle was one of the most iconic. I paid $500 for the old 65 Dodge van I drove while working at YMCA Camp Kiwanis. If that camp's name resonates for any reason, check out the Camp Kiwanis Alumni Facebook page. It had double swing-out doors on three sides, no insulation, and rust holes in the floor that you could see the road through. The heater didn't work, the air conditioner didn't exist at all, It had no back seats, and the classic slant 6 engine was mounted inside the cabin between the two front seats. This was the vehicle that the YMCA deemed safe to transport children on field trips, etc! Maybe that was why they sold it. Anyway, I put shag carpet in the back and imagined, although never accomplished, the fancy mural that I would paint on the sides. To its dying day, you could still read YMCA on the side. It did get me out of a parking ticket once. Not concerned with its current paint job, I did once bust through a tow yard gate that someone was holding closed. Sometimes, there are benefits to not g.a.f.

I drove it for a couple of months until it broke down while I was moving back to Austin for school near the town of West Texas, which is really more central Texas, but whatever. I hobbled it to a church parking lot, where it rested for a few weeks. I hitchhiked to Austin with what valuables I could carry and returned for what remained unfiltered later. The V.A. coughed up some delayed payments and I was able to get the engine rebuilt a couple of months later. I probably put another 100,000 miles on her. Interesting fact: the width of the cabin right behind the seats was exactly the width of two huge Altec Lansing A7 Voice Of The Theater speaker cabinets that were efficient enough to be driven by the Craig slide mount 8 track deck I had on my dash. This impressed many a hitchhiker. This was when hitchhiking was somewhat safer. You could sometimes get gas money from a rider. I made a couple of trips to and from Dallas with no money of my own. Also, putting it in neutral and coasting down hills conserved gas.

She eventually developed transmission problems, and I attempted to fix them myself, resulting in her losing all but second gear and reverse. This caused some very long and noisy trips to and from Dallas. After living at the 21st Street Co-op for a year or so, she died. I hauled her to the lot behind my next house on 6th Street and later gave her to some acquaintances who were building a house in the country. They gutted her and backed her up sideways to a hillside, buried her for insulation, and supposedly lived in her until they could finish their house. I don't know what, if anything, became of her after that!

Upon returning to Dallas, my mother gave me her old Opel Manta. Its strongest memory was the day I was pushed sideways down 635 by an 18-wheeler whose driver had no idea that I was there. "I didn't hear or see nothin'! I just looked down, and there's this little white car drivin' sideways in front of me!" Insurance paid $800 for it, and I drove it like it was until I got my next love, a Datsun 280Z 2+2, one of the rare ones with a back seat!

My mom had started to feel old a few year after my dad died. My sister Carolyn pointed out to her that she was beginning to act like her mother. She snapped out of it, dyed her hair red and paid $10,000 cash for a little bronze 280Z with standard transmission. It was a great little car and was my inspiration to someday have one of my own. This was the first car that I ever bought on my own through a bank. I drove it for several years before succumbing to pressure from my soon to be ex and trading it in on that suburban iconic vehicle, the Dodge Caravan, the first minivan. This is one of my lifelong regrets!

After our split up and losing the minivan (no love lost there) I briefly drove my sister's white 73 Pinto station wagon. Like the first Dodge van that I loved, it had no heater and was so loud that I had to wear headphones to listen to music. This didn't last too long. I treated myself to a pretty little silver Saab that my lawyer friend Sam Emerick sold me. One shouldn't buy a nice car if one can't afford to maintain it! I went on a couple of first and last dates with women who weren't impressed with my pretty little Saab that had to be pushed out of parking places after it lost reverse? What is it with me and transmissions? I spent about 3 grand on her in the last year I owned her. I sold her for half of that.

My next vehicle was a Ford Bronco 2. After the exploding Pintos, rolling Explorers, and driving the awful but free Pinto station wagon, I had sworn to never own a Ford, but I considered this one to be just a transitional vehicle. My friend Susan Jordan's dad, Al Jordan, (r.i.p.) bought and sold cars on the side and was kind enough to sell me this one for what he had paid at the auction. It got me by. I'll admit to liking it.

The next vehicle was another minivan. I had gone to look at a Mitsubishi Montero, which was my dream car at the time, but I gave in to practical and financial reality and bought the vehicle next to it, an Oldsmobile Silhouette van, the one with the long and extremely slanted windshield. It looked like some kind of moon vehicle. It was actually pretty comfortable on my long Paul Mitchell Educator road trips. The only story worth telling was about the time I heard on the news that a killer storm with potential baseball-sized hail was coming. I pulled the van as far as I could under the eaves of my roof and covered it with a king-sized mattress pad, closing the doors on the edges to hold it in place. Well, the pad acted as a giant wick, and the front hood vents were right under the edge of the roof, and thirstily accepted the full runoff from said roof. I had zero hail damage but about eight inches of water to drain and dry. I sold it to Richard Watts, who eventually drove it to its doom. I then finally got my Montero. It was one of my better choices.

It was another deep green machine. It had all the whistles and bells available, rode high, and felt solid. I spent a few nights in it at the Kerrville Folk Festival and on Mount Nebo. I won't say that they were comfortable nights but I did stay dry in a pummeling thunderstorm on the top of

Mount Nebo. I had very few mechanical problems except the first time it rained. The windshield leaked, and the stereo and whole dash shorted out. It was a "program vehicle" with about 7000 miles on it when I bought it. They neglected to mention that it had been in a wreck and that the windshield had  been replaced with a non-Mitsubishi windshield. They wanted me to pay for the repairs, but I pointed out that the dash and stereo were between the front and back bumpers and, therefore, should be covered by the "bumper to bumper" warranty. I also mentioned that my job as a national educator and salon owner put me in front of a LOT of people that cared about what I had to say and that I could be their best PR guy. Things got fixed. I put almost another 100,000 miles on it before the electric windows and rear door stopped functioning. I traded the Montero in on a Nissan Murano when they first came out. It was, at the time, a unique-looking vehicle. It had all of the comforts of a nice car, the same engine as the Z cars, a super smooth automatic transmission, and plenty of room for amplifiers and guitars. The Murano was originally intended to be released as an Infiniti but was kept back in the Nissan line for some reason.

We went car hunting and considered another sports car. I told the salesman that if they made a 2+2 like my old 280Z, he'd have a deal. He told me, "Well, we kinda do!" and let me drive a nice red Infiniti G35 with black leather, basically the same engine as the Z and the Murano, and it had back seats. We also traded Glenna's Jeep in on a PT Cruiser, seeing as how we needed another family car with the arrival of our daughter Savannah. After the brakes went out, you can probably imagine who got to drive the G35 and who got the PT Cruiser.

The only story worth telling about the Cruiser was about getting t-boned by a stupid bleached blond wearing flip flops and gym shorts in

38-degree drizzle who, while trying to run from the scene of the minor fenderbender she had just been in, ran a red light and plowed into the right side of the Cruiser, knocking me about twenty feet into a Krystal burger parking lot. Oh yeah, it was also "Rock Star Day at work and I was decked out in goggles, a full length black trench coat with chains and snaps and straps and knee length boots. I'm sure I was a sight standing in the rain talking to the cops and swapping insurance cards. The car should have been totaled but it wasn't. It needed a few weeks of physical therapy, as did I.

Next trade was for an Infiniti FX. It was basically the Murano's sci fi influenced big brother. It was also a great car and one of 4 Infinitis I leased or bought. Glenna got the baby blue G37 convertible with the very cool Transformer robot hardtop and I traded the FX in for a black G37 sedan. I never fell in love with it.

In an effort to cut back on expenses and to get out from under a thousand bucks a month in car payments, we bought a used Toyota FJ Cruiser.

I auditioned several and found one in almost mint condition. When the salesman, trying to convince me to buy another truck, an older 4Runner with body damage and cigarette smell, said about the FJ, "This is really a young mans truck!" my mind was made up. The FJ it was. The general manager of the dealership, who is the father of one of my favorite ex-students, said "You're family!" and kindly took my offer of $15,000 cash. It is still one of my favorite rides ever. Around the same time, Glenna's mother, realizing that it was time to stop driving, generously gave us her old but well-kept Chevy Impala, eliminating our other car payment. It's not sexy or luxurious, but it's free! Glenna named it "Vlad."...the impala. Bdum..sss! Vlad got traded in for a Hyundai Santa Fe, and the kids each have a red Nissan Rogue. Hopefully they won't come with the adventures my rides did.

Daddy's Last Day

I've written about my dad a couple of times. I don't think I've tackled his last day. It was November ninth, 1971. I was in my first of several years of college and just a few months back from my European adventures. It was mid-morning when I answered the phone. It was my dad's secretary. She told me that my father had had another heart attack and was on the way to the hospital. This was attack number 3, I believe, and since he had survived the previous two, I was concerned, of course, but it didn't occur to me that he might not make it through this one.

I called my mother at the neighbor's house, where she was playing Bridge. She headed for the hospital. My buddy Vaughn Stockton was at my house because we were supposed to be leaving for class at Eastfield Junior College. An hour or so later, my dad's best friend Charlie Kent, who I was named after, showed up and was doing something I don't remember when I asked him how my father was. He looked slightly surprised and said, hesitatingly, "Kent....your daddy's dead." It seemed unreal. The flack metal in his chest since WW2 finally got him. For some reason, Vaughn thought that I might want to be alone and took off. I went upstairs and laid down. I searched my mind for the moments that I had last seen and spoken to him. I had missed him leaving that morning. I was still in shock and couldn't believe that I would never see him again. A couple of hours passed and my mother returned home. One of the first things she did was she got a metal box from their bedroom, removed a sheath of papers, and laid most of them on top of the logs in our fireplace. He had asked my mom to destroy certain documents in case of his passing. I don't know what most of them were, but having been involved in some "secret mission" stuff in the Air Force, I think some of the documents might have pertained to that. I did however recognize some of the papers. One time, while inspecting my school notebook in 8th or 9th grade, he had found a bunch of drawings that my friend Kyle Evans and I had done depicting our favorite superhero characters in "compromising situations"! Consider, if you will, alternate reasons that Superman, Doctor Strange, and Wonder Woman might go by those names. Imagine the consequences of the love lives of The Human Torch and The Incredible Hulk! Anyway, my dad had saved these masterpieces with, I assume, the intention of sharing them with me, maybe over a beer sometime down the line. I wish that we'd had that opportunity! I watched them burn with the other mystery documents. If you have ever lit a fire in a fireplace you know it is not necessarily an easy "one match" task. I remember her lighting the edge of those papers and them catching easily. So did the logs. That's strange enough.

As the day progressed, the house filled with people. My mom floated through a sea of condolences on Valium. I know it is awkward to find words of sympathy for some people, but my mom recalled one of her "friends" confiding to her that "of course, some of her other friends would not be comfortable with her being around their husbands." Huh?

At the end of the day, my mother and sister went to bed. I walked through the house, turning out lights, and upon flipping the den lights off, I noticed the last flame in the fireplace flickering out. That fire had burned all day, and to the best of my recollection, it had not been fed. I don't know if it meant something or not but it felt like a moment meant just for me. More snafus. My father selflessly donated his eyes. They forgot to take them. The obituary said that he was a pilot in WW1. He was born in 1919, a year after WW1 ended. According to the Dallas Morning News, I have a sister named Mrs Seymour Johnson Base. Funny! My sister Carolyn was stationed at an Air Force base by the same name. The vultures circle. Someone actually called and offered to sell us laminated copies of the obituary. My mother laughed at them and slammed the phone down. You could do that, then.

A year later, my Mother and sister Barbara moved to San Antonio, where my dad is buried.

I was living in a garage apartment behind my Aunt Jean's house and in my second year at Eastfield. One night, I was up late reading. I'll say that I was studying and that there were no comic books involved, but I won't swear to it. I heard a noise over on the desk. I didn't figure out what had made it but I noticed that the clock read 12:00. I shrugged it off and went back to uh..studying. A few minutes later, I looked at the clock again, and it still read 12:00. I looked closer and realized that the noise I had heard was the minute hand falling off of the clock and resting in the plastic front. The next day, I happened to call my mother in San Antonio. We chatted for a couple of minutes before she asked me if I knew what day it was. I didn't. She reminded me that it was exactly a year after my father passed. Several times over the years, I would just happen to call her on that day. I probably had a subconscious calendar reminder working for me.

I sometimes have dreams where my father is offering me advice. When I could remember and decipher it, it has often been good.

More Salon Stories

Not an earth shaking coincidence but maybe evidence of a cosmic prankster. One morning, I looked at my books and noticed that my morning consisted of Dawn Franke, Vickie Danke, Gary Shanke (probably misspelled but all rhyming), Marla Finco, and Jim Stanco (close but no cigar). Good enough for a quick, mildly amusing blurb, but here's where it all goes dark and queasy!

Mr Shanke was a good guy, if a little exuberant. He worked for a meat factory and commonly came in on his lunch hour smelling strongly of raw sausage. He told a story of a meat processing plant that he may or may ot have worked for.

Here's where the faint at heart might want to scroll on to a post of someone's cat or what they ate for dinner.

According to Gary, the meat plant would collect the blood from the slaughterhouse and it would be dried and stored for selling for other uses. I can only imagine what. Anyway, the powdered blood would get sucked up into the air ducts in the ceiling and would collect moisture, thus reconstituting back into blood. One day, the workers heard a horrific grinding and squealing sound. It was the steel girders bending from the weight of the reconstituted blood! Suddenly, the ceiling collapsed, drenching the factory floor and the unlucky workers in tons of blood and maggots!! O.k. Breathe! I warned you!

I don't think it was the factory that Gary worked at at the time. I can't help though, thinking about this story whenever I see their delicious products on the shelf at the grocery store. Vegetarianism anyone?

Lil Abner Adventure

One of the stories from my early childhood that comes up at family gatherings is about he time I took myself to the movies. I was 5 years old. The deal was, if I finished my lunch in time I could go with my sister Carolyn to see "Lil Abner" at the nearby theater. It was maybe a mile away and an easy hike. Well, time was up and I had not finished my lunch. Carolyn left and I was not happy. I wasn't going to let that stop me. I had no idea what "Lil Abner" was about. Most of you reading this probably never saw or heard of the long-running (1939-1977) comic strip.

Anyway, I took off to the theater. Being 5 years old I had no source of income, so I boldly went up to a stranger's house and rang the doorbell. An old man answered. "Yes?" I told him that my sister had left me and gone to the movies without me and I asked him if is could have some money to join her. He seemed amused and asked how much I needed. I guessed, "A dollar?" He looked surprised. "A dollar? For a little boy like you to go to the movies?" I was a little embarrassed. I didn't know what it cost! He complied, and I thanked him and ran to the theater. I gave the girl in the ticket booth my money and to my surprise, she gave me change back! Wow! I then went to the concession counter and got a Coca-Cola and some candy. I handed the guy my change and he handed me some back! Wow! What a concept! This time, however, I didn't receive as much back as I had at the ticket window. Hmmm. I didn't understand how this all worked. I asked, "Can I have some more?" "More what?" He asked.

"More money?" I still remember the confused, maybe annoyed, look on his face.

I found a seat at the back of the theater and watched the second half of "Lil Abner." I liked it enough to sit through it from start to finish again! My sister never saw me. I finally moseyed on home to find my parents in a panic. They had called all of my friends parents and asked all of our neighbors if they had seen me to no avail and were about to call the police when I wandered in. I told them my story, completely unaware of any wrongdoing. My being a basically good, slightly shy kid, it stunned my parents that I would trek out on my own and ask a total stranger for movie money! They did not punish me for my little outing. I think that maybe they thought it was a good sign of independent thinking and problem-solving. I did get a lecture on talking to strangers. They had me show them where the old man that financed my adventure lived, paid him back his dollar, and had me thank him again. I remember the amused look on his face as he said, " I thought that a dollar was a lot of money for a little fella like him to go to the movies!" It turned out it cost 35 cents. Even with candy and a Coca-Cola, I still went home with change in my pocket and a story to tell 59 years later.

Rocket science and sushi

One of my favorite foods is sushi. Good sushi, that is. There's an old joke that applies to pizza and Mexican food. "Pizza (or Mexican food) is like sex. When it's good, it's great! When it's bad..... it's still pretty good!" This doesn't work with sushi. When it's bad, it's bait. One of our favorite sushi restaurants is Sushi Sake in Richardson, Texas. The food is always fresh, well prepared, and well served. Our favorite item is salmon roe with a raw quail egg on top. Try it. Trust me. Just do it. A small dollop of wasabi, a quick dip in the soy sauce, a toast with your dining partner, and past your anxious lips. Let the quail egg roll down your lucky tongue. Close your eyes and enjoy the veritable cornicopia of palatable and olfactory delights. Gently burst each tiny sphere of wonderfulness and let them slide down your gullet towards the embrace of your waiting tummy!..... Did I just invent food porn?

For a while, we had a favorite waitress named Mary. On top of not speaking English well, she was pretty much a dingbat. She had lots of personality and decent enough waiting skills. As I speak for her, please excuse my stereotypical spelling of her thick accent. I do so simply to demonstrate the difficulty in understanding her. One of the first nights she waited on us, she said to me, "You ah rook a rike.....you know.... man?... man?.... t.v....man.....you know, t.v...man? You know... man... Dog? T.v.?" Then it came clear. As most of you know, I wore my hair long for most of my adult life. She was saying that I looked like Dog The Bounty Hunter! I was hoping she was referring to some handsome TV. Star but no, Dog The Freaking Bounty Hunter! Oh well. You know we all look alike.

Mary disappeared from that restaurant one day. I don't know where she went. I'd like to think that she left to pursue her Phd in rocket science.

The Jokers

My dad was many things. He was a very intelligent man. He was a war hero, an engineer, a lover of music, and the best dad he knew how to be. He also loved a good joke. He was a member of a loose-knit group of practical jokers headed by his long-time friend and attorney, Bob Lockhart. There were no by-laws or even a name for the club. One only had to survive one of their pranks with class and desire to join in the fun.

One of the pranks was on a would-be entrepreneur who was always trying to jump on the "next big thing!" At the time, there were a lot of armadillo novelty items. Armadillo purses, keychains, etc. They printed up a flyer touting the inevitable success of the armadillo industry and anonymously sold him a bunch of rabbit cages labeled "Armadillo Breeding Hutches." When he found out the truth, he didn't appreciate the humor and was instantly eliminated from the possibility of membership.

Another fellow worked for the U.S. Patent Office. I believe it was Bob who found a nondescript machine part, polished it up, and sent it to the patent office guy with no explanation, name, or return address. Every couple of months, he would call, disguise his voice with, as I recall, a German accent, and inquire about the status of his "framistat." Without responding to the request for more information or even a name, he would work himself up into a rage over the lack of progress being made and hang up. I don't know how long this joke went on or its eventual conclusion.

One that my father was involved directly had the host of a party walk in on Bob and my mother apparently kissing in a back room. The embarrassed host excused himself and, in an act of righteousness, went to find my father to inform him. While he was absent, Bob and my dad quickly switched places via the back window, and the host barged back in only to find my mother in the arms of my father kissing passionately and both of them and Bob incredulously and vehemently denying any of the aforementioned shenanigans!

This one is a little complicated. I don't remember any of the actual names save for my dad's and Bob's. "Jim" was showing Bob a supple deer skin that he had picked up at a garage sale or something. Bob suggested that they play a prank on "Frank," who was an avid outdoorsman and hunter who had recently returned from a deer hunting trip empty-handed. They decided to tell "Frank" that "Jim" had been driving up on Balcones Drive, that a deer had wandered into his path, and that the deer was frozen in his headlights and wouldn't move. "Jim" supposedly reached into the back seat, grabbed his son's 22-caliber rifle, and dropped the deer with a single shot. "Jim" was excited and thought this was a great idea! They set up a little dinner party with "Jim," "Frank," and their spouses. There was one more person there that neither "Jim" nor "Frank" knew. As I recall, it was my father. It may not have been, but for the sake of the story, it will be. When they are introduced to my father, he says, " Hmmm! "Jim Smith... Jim Smith. Why does that name sound familiar?... Oh well, no big deal." As the night progressed, he pondered a couple more times, "Why does your name ring a bell with me? Oh, it's probably nothing!" Eventually, they got around to showing "Frank" the deerskin and spun their yarn. "Frank" wouldn't buy it. "No, really!" said "Jim." "One shot! Right between the eyes!."

Then my dad slaps his head and says, "That's it! That's why I knew your name! Oh...I'm so sorry! I work for the Texas Wildlife and Game Commission, and we heard about a deer being shot up on Balcones and. I'm here in Austin to investigate! And to make things worse, this is a doe skin! Even if it was deer season, this would be a problem!" "Jim" started back pedaling. "No! Wait! This is all a joke! I got this at the flea market and....." My dad said, "That's a good story. Stick to it. We don't have to spoil this pleasant evening with all this. We can meet Monday and discuss it." Panicking, "Jim" insisted, "No, really, it's all a joke!" My dad followed through. "Seriously, let's not talk about it tonight. I shouldn't have mentioned it." "Jim" stewed all weekend. They all met for lunch on Monday, and the wicked truth was revealed. They all remained friends.

One more concerning this group. The time: during WW2 when rubber was being rationed. The owner of a mechanic shop near downtown

Austin wanted to count himself among the jokers. One Monday morning, he noticed that the traffic near his shop was ridiculously dense. He couldn't even get near his business and had to park and shuffle though a small mob to get to his door. He asked, "What's going on? Why are you all here?" Someone showed him a page from the Sunday paper. There was a big ad with the words "TIRES! TIRES! TIRES! ALL SIZES! LOW PRICES!" He had to humbly apologize and explain that he knew nothing about the ad and, in fact, had no tires! Luckily, he was not lynched. After some pondering, he decided that he had figured out who was behind the prank and attempted retaliation. He went to every locksmith in town and bought hundreds of random keys, which he loaded on dozens and dozens of key chains, each with a tag that read "If found, return to ---- -----St. For $5. reward." He then drove through the poorer part of town, scattering them on the streets. Supposedly, for years, the resident at ---- ----- St. had people knocking on the door expecting $5. The sad/ funny part of it is that that poor fellow residing at ---- ----- St. had nothing to do with any of this and, for years, had to turn away countless disappointed reward seekers!

As some of you know or don't know, my father was mostly bald. His hairline resembled Patrick Stewart's and he kept the wreath of remaining hair cut short. One day, he came home with a salt and pepper men's wig. I can't imagine that he intended to seriously change his image but he wore it to a neighbor's dinner party. He rang the doorbell, and when the host opened the door, my dad barged in, asking, "Where's the food?" Minus his glasses and wearing the wig, the host had no idea who my dad was. Dad made a beeline for the table and started loading up a plate. "Excuse me! I don't think we've met!" said the host. "Nope!" Barked my dad. "I'm Mike Pace." said the host, offering his hand. "Good for you!" snapped my dad. Mr Pace was about to lose his temper when someone intervened and told him, "Stop! That's Gene Skinner!" Altercation averted.

My mother also had a wicked sense of humor. There are pictures of my mother dressed in a ridiculous bold striped outfit with a turban and sunglasses on, posing as if she were a fashion model. My sister Barbara just reminded me that she was wearing a corset over the striped pajamas! One of the officer's wives at the Air Force base fancied herself to be just such a glamorous type and was, of course, in the local fashion show. It was being put on in a house with doors leading from room to room, and the attendees were scattered throughout the house. The models would walk from room to room and show their outfits. Mrs Glamour Model was walking through the house and couldn't figure out why people were laughing uproariously every time she exited a room. My mother was following her unseen and mocking her every exaggerated move. With the turban and sunglasses, no one could tell who she was!

It may or may not have been the same woman, but there was a loud, flirty woman getting on my mom's nerves at an outdoor party. My mother and friends were sitting on the grass, and the obnoxious woman was standing in front of them, occasionally standing tip-toed with the back of her shoe flopping down. My mother "accidentally" poured her drink into the woman's shoe. "I'm so sorry! Did that get in your shoe?!!" she exclaimed. I would love to know the rest of that story.

I know that there are many more that I never heard and, doubtless, some more that I'll remember. Stay tuned for more episodes of "Those Wacky Skinner's!."

Zere

One of my old clients was a gentleman by the name of Zere. Zere is from Ethiopia and then once they had achieved independence, Eritrea. Anyway, he was referred by a long-time client named Mike. On his first visit, Zere was quiet and very polite. The next time he was in, I thought I'd drag him out of his shell by asking him to tell me a joke, preferably one from Ethiopia. He obliged. "O.K. There's this guy? And he's riding the bicycle? And suddenly, he falls off of the bicycle, and his pants are on backward? He says, "OH NO! I AM STANDING BACKWARDS!!!"

He erupted in shrill, hysterical laughter! I couldn't help but crack up myself! This quiet, polite man was in stitches, and the salon was filled with his laughter! Everyone was looking up at my station and wondering what it was all about. There's no way to explain.

He tried again. This one was a little better, and I got a little history lesson. "O.K. So, my country is in a civil war, and our leader was once a poor man, but now he is very wealthy. So, his wife is out shopping, and the shopkeeper is on the ladder, getting things down for her. Suddenly he........How do you say?... Blows out the back?.... He frat? Yes, he frat! The wife says, "I beg your pardon!" And the shopkeeper says, "Your husband has already shut my mouth.

You would have him shut my ass too?" More laughter, more looks.

I won't swear it was him that told me this one but it fits. "In my country we are in a state of martial law. So there's these two policemen and they are walking down the street. Suddenly one of them pulls out his gun and shoots this other man. The other policeman asks "Why did you shoot this man? He was doing nothing!" The first policeman says "Yes, but I know this man. He lives very far from here and by the time he got home it would be after curfew!" More laughs.

The strangest story he shared was something that he experienced while out jogging. This took place in suburban Richardson Tex, a ways from the countryside. He said he was jogging along when a coyote ran up and snatched some woman's little poodle or chihuahua or some little dog and ran away with it. Needles to say, the woman was hysterical. Zere was also in hysterics... the other kind. There are some serious cultural differences between us and Africa for this to be funny but again his laughter brought out the giggles in me in spite of myself. I must give him credit for introducing me to some of my favorite cuisine, Ethiopian food. He told me of a neat restaurant called Queen Of Sheba on Lemmon Avenue near McKinney and I had to try it out. It became one of my favorite places and I eventually proposed to my wife Glenna there. Zere suggested the I try "fitfit," a rare and spicy beef dish. When I ordered it the very gracious server asked if I'd ever had it before. "No" I replied "but it was suggested to me." She had a concerned look on her face and said "I don't think it's a good idea!" I had their vegetable platter instead and it has become my standard dish along with "silsi" puréed roasted tomato, garlic and jalapeños. Mmmmm. Anyway, thanks, Zere!

Allison Wonderland

After I returned from my backpacking trip to Europe my friend Dale Meyler suggested that I go check out a place called Allison Wonderland on Knox Street in Dallas. It was an old movie theater that the owner, Jim Allison, had turned into a cool weekly multi-media show with live music, serial movies, weird flicks, and the most amazing light show. Dale had been doing lo-tech multi-media shows in his garage for years, and he wanted me to try and figure out how Jim was doing his light show. I was flummoxed. All I had to do was ask. I introduced myself to Jim and played some original guitar pieces and songs while we talked for a while. I ended up playing there almost every week for a while. After that initial chat, Jim asked me, "OK. So you're name isn't really Cat Skinner, is it?" Laughter. He had misheard. "No, it's Kent Skinner!" I corrected him. He gave me a tour backstage and demonstrated the instrument he had built and named the Crystalume. He would manipulate a collection of lenses and crystals and various pieces of cut glass and lucite, working in and out of multiple focal points of light from a 1000-watt projector. By playing the beam of light with his fingers and varying the rhythm, intensity, and size of the imagery, he created what he called "Vusic" or visual music. This was leagues beyond the cool but splashy psychedelic light shows that one associates with the 60s. This was a polished, practiced visual interpretation of music. This was art. Jim would drop little nuggets of information occasionally but he let me discover on my own. I had to build my own setup. I experimented and went through a couple of Lumes before building one that was portable and powerful and is sadly gathering dust in my garage as I write. I convinced the art department at U.T. Austin to give me six hours of credit toward my Art Degree. I named my show "Talking Lights" and later, "Choreoptics" and always acknowledged Jim as the source of my inspiration. But this story is not mine but his.

Jim is a visionary. In the early 70's he anticipated a day when you would be able to buy your favorite album of music and take it home and watch it! I remember him owning an early videotape cassette recorder and, in later years, playing with lasers. He should have become more famous and known for being the pioneer that he was.

The theater, Allison Wonderland, did not endure. There was conflict between partners and it eventually folded. Jim moved away for a while and, as a parting gift, gave a bottle of Aramis cologne and a fantastic set of pen points and Rapidograph pens, which I used for years. I wore the Aramis, too.

After a stay in Natural Dam, Arkansas, Jim lived with his lady friend and manager, Mary K Wilson, in a house near Inwood and Mockingbird Lanes in Dallas. Although they were probably about 15 years older than me, it was cool to go hang out and listen to his stories. Jim is one of those people who has this incredible charisma that people are drawn to. Within five minutes, no matter where you are, there will be a crowd of enthralled listeners. Occasionally, at this house, there were altered consciousness states to be entertained by although I don't remember personally participating...specifically. One story involved a guy named Flip. Flip was probably an ex-jock turned hippie and was one of the early "Oh woooow." kind of guys. He was young and had a bad sense of timing. One time when Jim and friends were tripping, Flip burst in exclaiming "Oh my god there is a horrible accident with blood and gas and cops and fire engines and.......!!" Jim interrupted in a calm voice, "Flip......we're tripping." Apologies. A week later, same circumstances, Flip started talking about an episode of The Outer Limits or some such show where someone had inserted earwigs into someone's ear and it was crwling around and eating his way out and..... Jim interrupted again, "Flip,...we're tripping" "Oh! Sorry man!" etc. Another week went by and

Flip popped in to find Jim alone sitting in a living room chair with his eyes closed. Jim opened his eyes and turned to Flip. Flip asked "Tripping?" Jim nodded. Flip left. I understand that Flip, like some of us, grew up and still remains friends with Jim and Mary-K (as she spells it today).

There were also rumors of their cat "Slo," short for "Speed's little one," relaxing in a giant glass brandy snifter while smoke was blown through the center hole of an LP placed over the top. Liquid cat. He could slosh him around like a giant furry shot of cognac.

I lost track for a few years and, by chance, ran into Mary-K in Austin. She put me back in touch. Jim was living in Houston with his new lady, Judy Zekowski. We had independently discovered and were using some of the same music for our shows. I refer to it as graphic music, music that begs to be augmented visually. Jean Michel Jarre and Mike Oldfield for example.

I visited a few times, sometimes to help Jim out of a manic funk. It could be brutal. His moods would swing extremely wide. He could be the happiest and most enthralling person on one end.

Again, I lost touch for a few years. I don't recall how, but we reconnected again in the late eighties or early nineties and collaborated on a show with Judy's son, Greg Zekowski, who had taken up the Crystalume himself at the White Rock art facility, The Bath House. Three Crystalumes! It was kind of a mess, but it was cool to perform as a peer with my once mentor!

Greg's sister, Jeanne Champion, has her own Crystalume and still performs today! I need to drag out my Lume and clean her up. I may have been intimidated by the amazing visuals possible with digital technology today, but thinking more about it, I can make impressive music in the studio with only my computer, but it will never replace the satisfaction and the purity of sitting and playing my guitar.

Jim is living somewhere in a small town near Houston. We have reconnected and will hopefully do some more work again soon!

Update: I did reconnect, and I rebuilt my Crystalume. We had many wonderful conversations, one of which informed me that I had been included in the Lightshow Hall of Fame. I'll bet you didn't know there was one. Neither did I. One day, his stepdaughter Jeanne called and let me know that Jim's house had been hit in a bad storm and Jim had been pinned in the wreckage for a couple of days. He was passed food and water by rescuers and came out mostly o.k. But his roof needed replacing. Jeanne and I (she mostly) raised enough to repair his house and Jeanne's husband Chris went down and got his house livable again. Sadly, his beloved panel truck that had carted him and his Crystalume around for decades was flattened. A couple of years later, I saw that Jeanne had posted on Facebook that he had passed. It's now up to us to keep his legacy alive.

Old one, my version:

I was in the back of "Big Bad Billy's Bar and Billiards" in Biloxi playing a little blackjack with the boys, listening to Bobby Bland's Blues trio on a boom box and imbibing a Bacardi Breezer when in barged this big black bear named Bruno, from Birmingham. Bruno bellied up to the bar and beckoned the bartender. "Barkeep! Bring me a beer! A Budweiser in a Bottle! A big one!" To which Bob, the barkeep, barked back, "Buddy, at Big Bad Billies, we don't bring bottles of beer to big brown bears. Especially big brown bears wearing beige berets. So, beat it!" Well, Bruno barked back, "Listen, Buster! You'd better bring me a big bottle of Budweiser, or you see that buxom blonde bimbo in blue at the end of the bar?" "Who, Brenda?" asked Bob. Bruno: "If you don't bring me a Budweiser, a big one in a bottle, I'll bite her on the buns! Bad!!" Then Bob the barkeep belched and boldly bellowed, "Buddy! Like I said before, we don't bring bottles of beer to big brown bears! Especially big brown bears in Bermuda boxers! So, beat it before I bring out the bat and break some bones!" So Bruno from Birmingham bounded down to the bend in the bar and bit Brenda, the buxom blonde bimbo, on the buns! Bad! And bounded back. "You ready to bring me that beer? The Budweiser in a bottle? A big one?" Bob replied, " Buddy, just like I said back in the beginning, here at Big Bad Billy's, we don't bring bottles of beer to big brown bears. Especially big brown bears on drugs!" Bruno blinked. "Back up! Back up! Drugs? Drugs? Who said anything about drugs?" Bob, the barkeep, replied, "The buxom blonde bimbo at the bend of the bar that you bit so badly on the buns?" "Who, Brenda?" said Bruno, barely breathing.

Bob: "Don't you realize that was a barbiturate?" Badump ssss.

Again, only true in my head...

In addition to my years as a marine biologist/ surgeon/ superhero/ rock star/ hairstylist, teacher, etc. I also spent some time as an anthropologist. Here's one of many tales.

Working for Texas A.&M. (Aliens & Mopeds, not the other one), I was given a grant to study a particular tribe in the Amazon. I was asking for more money, the subject matter being even more fascinating than I originally thought, and I was asked to present my findings to the committee.

"We have already granted you more than enough!" they said. "Just what is it about this particular tribe that you think warrants us giving you more?" "Well, they have a fascinating natural herbal medicine system!" I replied. The chairman said, "They ALL have some kind of herbal medicine system. What is so special about theirs? I answered "Well, for example, they take the leaves of this one palm plant and roll them up and use them for suppositories!" The Chairman replied, "Well, while I'll admit that this is rather unusual, it hardly justifies the amount of money you are asking for." I countered, "You don't seem to understand! With fronds like that, who needs enemas?" Again, not entirely true...

You may be surprised to know in another life I was a marine biologist. Yes, there was always something fishy about me! Anyway, I received a large grant to study a subspecies of porpoises that apparently had zero mortality rate. They had been living so long that there was no procreation either. No need! I brought a few of them back to The United States for study but to my great dismay, they began to fall ill, and I nearly lost a couple of them! I was in a panic! I didn't know what to do! They were too weak to make the return trip home. Then, by a weird fluke, I discovered that it had something to do with a symbiotic relationship they shared with a rare breed of seagull. Not just any old seagull. Again, I had to go to the coast of Africa to try and retrieve some of these birds in the hope of saving our amazing sea brethren.

Luck was with me at first, and I located and corralled some of these birds who, missing their fishy friends, came willingly. Our return trip to the airport was stalled. In order to get to the plane, we had to travel through some dense jungle, and at one point, our path was blocked by a huge, majestic lion asleep across the trail! There was no way around on either side so I realized that the only way was over him! We cut down some bamboo, and with the caged birds strapped to my back, I pole-vaulted over our fierce, slumbering obstacle. Immediately, I was surrounded by the Jungle Police! "You're under arrest!" they exclaimed! I asked, "What for? What are the charges?"

He replied, "For transporting gulls over the stately lion for immortal porpoises!"

This story came to me in a dream.

Few people know that before he was famous, the late Johnny Cash tried a chip full of salsa served backstage in Possumneck, Mississippi, that changed his life. It was spicy and tangy and smoky and so good that he just couldn't get it off of his mind. Unfortunately, there was no jar, no label. Now, there have been rumors that Johnny had kind of an addictive personality. He would sometimes disappear for days on end. People attributed it to drugs or alcohol. The truth is that he would roam the country searching for the special hot sauce of his dreams. He heard rumors and whispers of the deadly condiment and followed them to countless dead ends. He stopped at every Tex-Mex restaurant, truck stop, and Mexican grocery in the South without finding what he sought.

One day, he heard tell of an old woman, a witch down in the Mayan peninsula in Mexico whom, it was said, made the best salsa in the world! He canceled his next five gigs and headed south. He rode donkeys, Jeeps, and horse-drawn wagons. He traversed deserts, mountains, and jungles before finally reaching the fabled village where the old bruja lived. He found and entered the old woman's hut. As luck would have it, she was one of his first big fans, having caught one of his shows at that Holiday Inn in Possumneck, Mississippi, while attending a Salsa Aficionado convention where one of her jars of salsa mysteriously disappeared and somehow made its way to a bowl backstage. She consented to sharing her secret recipe with him only after he agreed to write a song for her. She shared the special Tomatillos grown in Mayan soil. She gave him the seeds from a rare Mexican pepper and showed him the special pan with a rounded bottom, similar to those used in the Far East that she would use to saute' "las limas" or "the limes," the source of the salsa's tanginess. He asked her if he could just use his regular flat-bottomed pan, but she insisted that he must use the round-bottomed pan. From this came the inspiration for the lyrics: "Because you're Mayan, I'll wok the lime!"

I'll bet you thought this was leading up to a Ring Of Fire joke.

Pianos And Guitars: Their Stories and The Ones That Got Away

I took piano lessons for five years, from age 6 to 11. You'd think I could sit down at a party and impress someone. Not really. Yes, 5 years, no to impressing anyone. You see, my first teacher had me learning The Marines Hymn. My dad, being in the Air Force, moved every two years or so, and with every move, I got a new teacher who would ask me what I wanted to learn. I'd reply, "The Marines Hymn!" I can still play the heck out of it, but if asked to play at a party, I decline. Not exactly a crowd pleaser.....unless you are a Marine. If you are, well, Semper Fi, buddy! Not gonna play it. I don't wanna insult anybody and get my ass kicked. My last year in piano was a tough one. I had already picked up the guitar thanks to The Beatles and was not practicing piano regularly.

If I missed my daily 30 minutes of scales and exercises I might have to sit at the piano in the garage for hours "practicing." That pretty much burned me out on piano. My 5th grade piano recital was 8 or 10 kids at pianos simultaneously playing "God Of Our Fathers." I knew most or at least part of it and smilingly fake pounded away at the ivories with no one the wiser. One day my dad told me that if I didn't practice, they would take away my piano lessons. Free at last! I only did it because I thought they wanted me to! In retrospect, I'm glad for the musical foundations I gained. I actually can play parts in songs when recording but not necessarily in one take. I hauled that old player piano from house to home for years. It sat in the garage too long and the tubes that provide suction for the player function deteriorated. I finally found it a loving home with an appreciative young couple in Garland who restored it and play it regularly.

That brings me to my first guitar, a Silvertone acoustic. I was 10, and The Beatles had just conquered America. I think Kyle Evans or Dale Meyler showed me an E minor and maybe an A minor. I figured out a few more on my own and we started a combo, The Mysterians! No relation to the later somewhat famous Question Mark and The Mysterians. A few people rotated in and out, and we never played anywhere but our garages. I needed an electric guitar!

I had resorted to putting little pieces of aluminum foil on my strings to make them buzz. By 7th grade, I had learned a few more chords. My parent's favorite song was "Laura's Theme" from Dr Zhivago, also known as "Somewhere My Love." My dad bought a cheap Japanese electric guitar and amp from Olsen's Electronics, a predecessor to the Radio Shack market. I was only allowed to play it while figuring out and practicing "Laura's Theme." I could call them mine once I had mastered and performed said piece for my parents. I did. I played that guitar for another 5 years though I heavily modified it.

I stripped,stained and refinished it a cool blue color. I tried several different pickguards. I cut one from a piece of mirror (unsuccessful), one from a 33 1/3 record album, and finally, a sheet of copper that held up well. I eliminated the volume and tone controls and wired each pickup to its own switch and jack, thus creating what may have been the first stereo guitar. At least that I had seen. I know Vox did some in the '60s.

It didn't occur to me to have one stereo jack and cord. I have one cord going to a washroom pedal and the other to an echo unit. I got tangled up a couple of times, pulling my amp over on top of me. I bought a do-it-yourself organ kit and wired each fret to the positive contacts that would have gone to the keys and grounded the strings so that when they made contact, supposedly, the appropriate note would play. It was a cool concept but was very noisy and scratchy and undesired notes would emerge. I basically ruined an already crappy guitar. I sold it in a garage sale.

My next guitar was an acoustic by Prairie. It was an at at-a-glance knockoff of a Gibson Hummingbird, only at a glance. It was serviceable and I carried it with me all through Europe after high school. On the flight to London via New York, I foolishly checked it, and it got a hole punched in it. I never saw it between flights, so I couldn't prove whose fault it was (besides mine). I eventually traded it for a Maestro by Guild, a nicer, inexpensive guitar. One more tidbit concerning the Prairie: I found it again in a resale shop on Exposition and bought it for $20 if I remember correctly. The neck had been broken off and badly repaired. I rebroke it and did a slightly better job repairing it. I signed it and had a couple of somewhat famous friends autograph it, too. Sarah Hickman and I think Josh Alan signed it. I gave it to Susan Jordan to give to her little boy, Jeremy. I don't know if he learned to play or not.

The Maestro briefly served me well until I traded it in on a Hofner Beatle violin-shaped bass, one that I should have kept. It cost me $90 and the Maestro. It's worth a couple thousand now.

I dabbled at playing bass for a short while. I tried playing with a slide, thinking that would be my gimmick. It got traded for a sweet early 60s Gibson 330. I ran into Bugs Henderson at Arnold and Morgan Music on day when I brought it in for some adjustment. He looked at it and said, "I won't swear it, but I think this used to be mine!."

Ovation was a new player on the scene, and I was intrigued by their round back, space-age material, and the general aesthetics and I traded the 330 in on one of the original models. It was another "Wish I hadn't!" moment, but it played fine and made me happy. I played the camp song on it daily at Camp Kiwanis (another story or three) and wrote some pieces that I still play today. It almost met its end early on when I stopped quickly in my 71? Toyota Corona Deluxe, realizing that I had left it on the roof of the car. Its case was built like an armored coffin, and the guitar was fine. I stopped trading guitars about this time, so the Ovation stayed with me for a long time. In the late 70s, I left it at Bruce McRoberts' house, and Danny M, a friend of his roommate, Jay Hillendahl, leaned it up against the piano after playing it. Ovations are round-backed, and even though they had a thin rubber pad to help avoid such slippage, it didn't help here. It fell, and the neck snapped off. I had a local luthier do a decent repair job that Danny paid for, and it lived a while longer. Some time in the early 80s, my friend Dale Meyler asked me if he could borrow it. I told him that I'd rather not loan it because of the previous accident. Not long after, he happened to be at my apartment and said, "If you don't mind, I'll just grab the Ovation." I hesitated because I had already said "no," but for whatever reason, I said "ok." A few days later he called and apologized because there had been an accident. I found a really good luthier who did an amazing repair job and Dale paid for it. He laminated the front and the back of the headstock with cherrywood and possibly birch and did a mother of pearl inlay of my initials in place of the Ovation logo. It lasted another 6 or 7 years until I personally kicked it over in the dark while jumping up and looking out the window for reasons I will not go into here and having leaned it up against a wall WHICH I KNEW PERFECTLY WELL NOT TO DO! There was a strange sound sounding something like "TWAAAK!." Third time was the charm. She lies peacefully in her case in my music room closet.

Rewind a few years to 76. I was looking for a hollow-bodied electric that I could also play acoustically. Some kind of jazz guitar like a Gibson ES 150. What I found was a 64 Gibson 335 12 string for $500 at McCords in downtown Dallas. I remember seeing one of Willie Nelson's black and white 5x7 promo pictures on the wall.  He had short hair and a spiffy cowboy outfit. Shoulda snagged it! Anyway, it was the first of many 12-string guitars in my life! A few years later I loaned it to Alex Chilton to play at Raul's in Austin and on another night to Elvis Costello. She still plays and sounds like God.

My next guitar was a Yamaha 12-string. I had fallen in love with my Austin housemate's Yamaha 12, and it was a very strange day when I got mine. I had moved back to Dallas and was renting a room in an old, long-since-torn-down house near downtown. The plumbing was ancient and you had to avoid flushing the toilet if you were about to take a shower if you wanted something other than scalding water. So, I had used the facilities and waited to flush until I exited the shower. Immediately after flushing, I grabbed my towel and heard a clink. My grandfather's diamond ring was missing. I had left it on the towel! It took 2 weeks of not using that toilet until I could get hold of the tools I needed to pull the toilet up. I finally did, and the ring was lying in the trap! I was so happy! I decided to go buy the guitar that I'd seen in a nearby pawnshop. It was a great day until I was broadsided and pushed down the highway by a semi that afternoon! Details can be found in a previous story, "Near Death Experiences." Years later, I had my artist friend Jill Parr paint it. She did an amazing job on it. Unfortunately, the paint and sealers killed the tone of the guitar so it mostly hangs among my favorites as a work of art. Update: the decades have allowed the varnish to cure and she sounds wonderful again!

I think the next member of the family was a beautiful dark mahogany Takamine 12 that I found in a pawnshop in Waco. It was missing a tuner,

so I got it for a song. I have plenty of parts lying around, so it was an easy fix. However, I got a speeding ticket on the way back to Dallas so what savings I had accrued were negated.

I was doing a lot of traveling for Paul Mitchell at the time and saw a Les Paul style guitar by Electra/Univox in a pawnshop in Abilene. It had built-in effects (mostly useless but unique). I didn't buy it immediately, but it stuck in my mind, and it was still there my next trip to West Texas. 80 bucks well spent. It's actually not just a novelty but a nice playing instrument.

Next came a Giannini six-string acoustic.I had seen it in a pawnshop....seeing a pattern here? It is a strangely shaped guitar with a good neck and interesting tone. My girlfriend at the time bought it for my birthday. It doesn't get played as much as some of my nicer guitars, but it is eye-catching. Wow. I think I just hurt its feelings! It is a little high-strung.

There's an old joke where a guy goes into a music store and asks, "Can I get a set of strings for my Ovation?" The salesman replies, "Sure. That sounds like a fair trade to me!" I still own a beautiful Ovation 12-string. It is not the best playing or sounding guitar in the fold, but is definitely one of the prettiest. I used it on my Lord Of The Rings medley. https://soundcloud.com/kent-skinner/07lord-of-the-rings-medley

I owned a green shallow-bodied Ovation that I picked up in, yes, a pawnshop. It was my travel guitar for a while. I broke the vow to myself to not trade or sell my guitars again, but it was seldom played, and one of my students needed a guitar, so I let it go, and a Steinberger headless electric 6 string took its place. It's smaller, travels well, and plays, and sounds great. I found an Epiphone acoustic/electric at a neighbor's garage sale. He never played it much and wanted $20 for it. I only had $17 in my pocket, and he took it. I didn't need it, but I couldn't pass it up for $17! My daughter Savannah plays it occasionally.

Seagull is a Canadian guitar company that makes some simple, not outrageously expensive, quality guitars. I played one, a twelve-string, in a pawnshop (No!) that was hanging next to a Martin12 string. It played and sounded better than the Martin. I had a figure in my head that I thought was fair and asked what the best price he could give me was. He suggested, "Oh, I'd take $160." That was much less than I had expected. I, straight-faced, asked if it came with a case, and he said he'd find something to put it in. He gave me a really cool brocade heavy fabric gig bag that I have received many compliments on. It has since had its neck broken and repaired by Mark Bander, a skilled guitarist and guitar repairman that I've known since junior high band days.

Another gem in my crown of axes is another pawnshop find. It's a Fender Stratocaster 12 string. Same story as the Seagull. It had been there for a couple of weeks, and when I asked for the best deal they'd make me, it was well under the $500 I was willing to pay. It chimes, it roars! It sounds like a schizophrenic Mark Knopfler! It needed to be mine!

Call me self-indulgent, but I became infatuated with a Taylor T5 which is an acoustic with electric guitar pickups and a multitude of switchable settings to meet almost any live need. However, they are very expensive, and I waited. Then I read about an Ibanez Montage, which had similar features plus built-in reverb, chorus, and distortion effects! And it

could be had for almost two grand cheaper. It's pretty but not near the quality of the T5. However, it's very playable and versatile! With the right settings, it sounds incredible. I used it on our Christmas CD "Walking In A Skinner Wonderland" which can be had for the asking.

I really wanted a really nice acoustic 12-string. I auditioned Taylors and Martins walked away from but dwelled on a black Taylor at Guitar Center. It wasn't what I had been hunting as it was a 6 string, but it had a cool Johnny Cash vibe to it. I called my regular salesman and said I'd be there the next day. As I was on my way to pick it up, sales guy called me and apologized, saying that when he got to work, it was on the way out the door! I was heartbroken! I actually felt very sad that it had gotten away. A week later, I saw a Breedlove 6 string in, yes, another pawnshop for a ridiculously low price and I snagged it. Breedlove was started by a head luthier at Taylor and was supported in his endeavors by the owner of Taylor. It was fate! It was Destiny! It's very pretty and sounds fantastic.

I still wanted a very nice 12, so I ordered the Breedlove's Big Brother. I know my other guitars are jealous of the attention these two get another

prize. I saw and played a supposed Gibson Les Paul 12-string at the Dallas Guitar Festival in 2015. Love at first play, even though the vendor admitted that it was a counterfeit. I paid a fraction of what the real deal would cost. The mother-of-pearl inlays are gorgeous, and the electronics are decent. I had Mark Bander do some repair and setup on it, and it is one of my favorites. I have also found a Gibson SG knockoff for $30, a Teisco (Japanese 60's department store electric guitar) at Salvation

Army, and had Mark Bander fix them up. Both are quite playable. I stumbled on a pretty black LTD 12 string at the same pawn shop where I bought the Strat 12. It played nicely, and I finalized a deal. I knew that they didn't make a case for this model, so when I asked if they had one, I expected that he might offer a gig bag for it. To my surprise, when he returned from the back of the store, he was carrying a huge coffin-shaped case. It was probably meant for a bass guitar and likely targeting metal players but it fit the 12 perfectly. It was also lined in crushed red velvet! One night, when I couldn't sleep (like most nights) and probably still enjoying the benefits of the martini I'd had before bedtime, I was scrolling on FB Marketplace. A guy had posted a couple of guitars for sale. I think he was asking $180 o.b.o. for a Telecaster style 12-string electric. I offered $100 for it and completely forgot about it. A couple of days later, I got a message from him saying, "I can do that." He had bought it intending to convert it to a left-handed guitar but never got around to it. The Tele design doesn't really lend itself to that kind of sacrilege anyway. It sounds great and is the only Telecaster I've owned. I also saw an old Silvertone acoustic for sale on Marketplace, marked down to $65. I couldn't tell for sure, but it looked a lot like my very first guitar (see picture at the beginning of this story with 12-year-old me kneeling with my young bandmates Kyle Evans and Daryl Peaton, both no longer with us. I met up with the seller and was still unsure whether it was a match with mine. I asked what's the least he'd take and he said $50. He didn't have a change, and I didn't have a ten, so he gladly accepted $40. Once I got home, I dug up that picture, and lo and behold, it was exactly like my first guitar. I strung her up and played the heck out of her! It was like running into my childhood best friend again! I have a few favorites. O.K.! They are all my favorites!

My Dad's Stories:

Art Kent Skinner

I won't swear to the authenticity of the details I provide to these three short stories, but I will share them as best as I can, recalling them coming from my father's lips.

The first recalls a friend of my father who rewired the coil of his car (there used to be coils, part of the electrical system) so that it had a switch which would reroute the current to the body of the car so that anyone in leather shoes or barefoot touching the car would provide a ground and complete the circuit providing a potent but non lethal shock. One day, my dad's friend saw another friends car ahead with a policeman standing with his hand on the roof of the car and speaking the the driver. Supposedly, my dad's friend inched up slowly and, touched numbers with his unsuspecting friend's car and flipped the switch, sending the stunned officer a few inches into the air. He rolled back and watched the fun. True or not, it provides good imagery to those who can imagine!

The second story also involves electricity. My dad discovered that the frame surrounding the window of the pharmacy, which had a neon sign, would provide a shock to anyone who touched the metal frame of his bike if he leaned it against it. One time before he could intervene, a dog wandered up, cocked his leg, and baptized the wheel of his bike. According to my dad, "It literally shocked the piss outa him!" I'll bet that he took to squatting after that, and if he ever fathered puppies, they came out chihuahuas.

The third involved an automobile, though not electricity. A friend of my dad, Possibly the same in story number 1, and either if not both, might have been his practical joker and attorney friend Bob Lockhart mentioned in a previous story, "The Jokers," rigged his car so that he could control the steering wheel with his knees. If he had an unaware passenger with him, he would pull the steering wheel off, saying, "I don't feel so good! You drive!"

As I said, I can't authenticicate any of these, but upon recalling them, I felt that they needed sharing rather than letting them slip away into the ether, as too many good ones do.

Stormbringer

I never use the term "back in the day" because I still consider this to be my day but this was back in an earlier day! I guess it was mid-eighties, and my friend, Richard Watts, asks me to tag along while he ran an errand out by Lake Lavon, where he kept his boat. He arrived at my house late in the morning while I was trying out some new music equipment. He asked, "What's up?" I replied, "New toys!" "Let's see!" "O.K.!" So, I turned on my new digital delay, Roland drum machine, and Juno 106 keyboard (which has since bitten the dust) and hit an a minor chord, tapped out a drum rhythm, and I grabbed my flute. I just sort of improvised for a couple of minutes and liked what was happening. It was kind of an ominous tune with a martial, driving beat and the trailing echoes of flute lines and trills, and it impressed us both. With that sound track in my head, we headed out to the lake. I don't remember what the task at hand was. I do remember that the rain was coming down in sheets, and I do remember Richard's fancy custom van running out of fuel in the middle of nowhere and watching him stomp off in the rain to the beat of the tune in my head to get gas. As I waited in the comfort of the van and with that tune driving and echoing in my brain, I was suddenly startled out of my reverie by a bolt of lightning striking a tree no more than 25 feet away from me! The images of lightning striking as portrayed in movies or, drawings, or still photography don't do it justice. Instead of a forked flash of light hitting and vanishing, it instantly appeared at the tree and hovered and writhed for a brief moment before shattering and fragmenting in the air. The fragments shimmered for a fraction of a second before wriggling off like a fantastic fireworks display! Rich returned about 45 minutes later, sopping wet with the gas. Whatever the mission was, I think we accomplished it. Paid boat storage rent or something.

Upon arriving home, I immediately went to the music room, recreated the music in my head, and got it down on my Tascam 4 track.

I added some guitar parts and put rain and thunder underneath it all. Thus, the original Stormbringer was born.

Many of my old 4 track experiments have disappeared into the ether. I still have many of the tapes but no means to play them. That particular tune has lived in my head for decades now, and recently, I recreated it with modern technology and hopefully more talent. For those readers interested in hearing Stormbringer's newest incarnation, it can be found on SoundCloud under Kent Skinner 1

https://soundcloud.com/kent-skinner/stormbringer

Halloweens

You may have noticed...Halloween is one of my favorite holidays! I have always jumped at the chance to dress up and for a few years in college, counted on the money from winning contests to eat and pay rent!

My parents kept a footlocker in the attic with various costumes and props. It was always cool to dig through. My earliest memory of a Halloween costume was, I guess, in 2nd grade. I wanted to be a skeleton. A SCARY skeleton. My mom didn't inspect the package when she bought it and what I got was a GIRL skeleton! It had pink lips on the flimsy plastic skull mask and painted on the cheap fabric costume was a pile of clothes and skin (with pink nail polish) around the feet, along with the words "TAKE OFF YOUR SKIN AND DANCE IN YOUR BONES!!." It was scary, alright. "I can't wear this! It's a girls outfit!" I ended up turning the skull mas inside out and covering the girly stuff at the bottom with my trick-or-treat bag. I think I was scarred for life.

I forget the next couple of costumes, but in th grade, I remember taking some rags and making a monster mask colored with crayons. Scary. The next year, I used the same method and made a Spider-Man costume. I tacked the red parts onto a blue sweatshirt and jeans and, again, made the mask from rags colors with crayons. Again, scary. I'm sure Doc Octopus and the Green Goblin would have been terrified. I started decorating our house for Halloween. Dummies in the windows, lights, etc. I had begun collecting latex masks and figured out how to animate the monsters in the windows with motors and fishing line. I would stand outside perfectly still until the trick-or-treaters decided that I was just another dummy. (Leave it alone, Kevin. Too easy!) Then, I would jump towards them and yell. One teenaged girl told her friend that she had to go home and change her panties.

Our bushes, as well as a few costumes, also suffered from kids jumping away.

When I was 15. Our family went to a Halloween party at the Dallas Yacht Club at what was called, at the time, Lake Dallas. My dad went as Andy Capp, a comic strip character, and I made my mother a giant Winston's cigarette box with boobs. Winston's slogan was "It's what's up front that counts!" I think it was Moms idea. My sister may have suggested that I wear the harem girl outfit from the costume trunk. I borrowed my girlfriend Michelle's long blonde hairpiece and, yes, went in drag to this Yacht Club party. Imagine the teenage boy's surprise when I responded to his invitation to dance with a "No thanks" In a deeper voice than his own.

I acquired a Famous Monsters Of Filmland monster makeup edition that had a lot of very cool stuff in it. I experimented with liquid latex, spirit gum, and a lot of other things. I also was not good at reading directions. This resulted in yanking out eyebrows, a layer of skin, and a few eyelashes and trying to remove a latex mummy mask. Imagine the wax job from Hell. Then the mask shrank and stuck to itself, and it was all a lesson in futility. I did learn a few things and got pretty good at some stuff that fed me in college. This guy was part of a project that I did for a design class, so I got college credit and a meal or two at a Rocky Horror Picture Show contest. I won, though I hadn't realized that I was supposed to be dressed as one of the characters. I hadn't seen the movie. The MC asked me what I was supposed to be. He couldn't hear me through the mask, so he introduced me as "The Thing. From The Ladies Restroom!"

I don't have a picture, but around that time, I made a half-body one-piece latex costume of a Marvel Comics character, Man Thing, a mossy swamp monster. That one lasted a few years before the latex deteriorated. It help us at Camp Kiwanis to cruelly perpetuate the urban legend of "The Bachman Boogieman," terrifying a couple of overnight campers.

Another costume that I have no record of was for a "Come As Your Fantasy" party. I took a very light headboard and footboard and connected them with 18" sideboards, tacked in a satin bedspread and pillows, and hung it over my shoulders with straps. I wore pajamas, and the effect was that I was in bed. Oh yeah, in white paint across the headboard was a tally. You know the image, four 1s, and then a backslash indicating "five." There were dozens of these.

There was a Sixties party at the Co-op. It was the 70s, so it wasn't that far away. I knew that everyone would dressed as hippies or mods, so I went as someone dad. Body shirt, white shoes and, belt, and a paisley tie. I put my long hair up in the same bad men's wig that I had been made to wear at my Pottery Plus job a couple of years before. Black framed glasses and mascara on my mustache completed the ensemble.

I learned a lesson that night. I had commented on how "cute" my girlfriend looked in her miniskirt and 60s makeup and then foolishly told our two mutual female friends that they looked "beautiful!" I learned that there is a scale with "cute" on one end and "beautiful" on the other. Later at the party, a guy showed up that everyone, including myself, knew had a thing for my girlfriend. He started hitting on her, offering her a drink, asking her to dance, etc., until someone took him aside and said, "You know that's KENT, right?" He hadn't recognized me. He disappeared. (No, not like in the movies, he just left the party.) Inspiration: I have lived in a few places that came with unwanted housemates, also known as roaches. Upon moving to Dallas after college and hair school, I made a cockroach costume out of foam. It was pretty detailed and won me some money. A year or two later, I modified the body and added a giant fly head and went as The Fly. More money. The next year, when people asked what I was going to be, I replied, "The Fly." They assumed that I was recycling the previous costume. I showed up as a giant zipper. One drunk guy asked me what I was supposed to be. I told him "Thr Fly and showed him those words on my back. He said, "Oh. I don't get it. I didn't see the movie." That's ok. It wasn't meant for you. I still have a scar on my inner forearm from some hot glue that I used to make some emergency repairs at Club Dada.

The hammerhead shark was probably next. It still hangs in my garage. Foam rubber, contact cement and, spray paint, and lightbulbs for eyes last much longer than latex.

I have done the giant zipper and Baby On Board twice. Mr Hanky, the Xmas poo lingered a few years. Death Warmed Over went over a few alchohol dulled heads. Again, if they didn't get it, it wasn't meant for them.

The most elaborate was my Alien Abductee. It is never the mayor or a congressman that gets abducted. It's always Billy Bob. I dressed accordingly. I had a frame duct taped to my chest inside my overalls that supported two larger than life, fully articulated alien puppets, one in front, one in back. Their hands were connected by dowels that I could move with my own hands and their feet were connected to my boots so that when I waked, they walked. When I danced, they danced. I noticed the front alien danced better than me. Two years in a row, it took so long to get rigged up that we missed the contests! Grrr. It was still a blast. People stopped their cars for pictures, bowed on the sidewalk and my friends and I had plenty of fun.

These last few years, my costume-making has mostly been for my family. One year, Savvy wanted to be a scary green monster. I have reprised my mummy several times but with makeup vs a mask. She wanted to be a headless monster, so I fashioned a torso with a light-up neck and a hole to poke her head through to look like she was carrying it. Glenna wanted to be a running nose. That was fun, although some perverted people thought it looked like a different body part. Zane has usually been easier. His wishes usually involved recognizable icons like Superboy, Angry Birds, or Mega Man. Some were store-bought, some homemade. The Dark Angel wings were my last major effort in a while. I hand-cut, painted, and glued every feather. What was supposed to be an afternoon's work took several days but they have served us well. A lot of the other costumes pictured here were for theme days at the PM school or at karate.

I know I'll probably remember a few more costumes later and hopefully find more pictures. Yes, I may never grow up.

Flight Risks

While I wait for a flight back to Dallas that was supposed to take off at 5:20 and is now predicted to leave Las Vegas at 10:15, I figure it's a good time to write a Flights From Hell story. This one may qualify later. I'll let you know.

So many to choose from. Granted, I have had many more good experiences and I may have to cleanse my psyche with a couple of those after this. In no particular order:

On one Paul Mitchell trip, I had a two-legged trip back to Dallas. My first flight was on a very small plane, and my seat was 2B. No first class, just 2b. We sat for a while before we were asked to disembark due to some mechanical repair needed. That's fine; just put us on another plane. No other plane? THEN LIE TO US! Don't let us think we're reboarding a potentially squinky plane! So we got off and waited, then reboarded, then unboarded again. Finally, they got a different plane. Great. So I got to Corpus Christi and got to my next plane. As I boarded, the flight atyendant asked for my boarding pass. She looked at it and escorted me to a seat in first class."Awesome!" I thought, thinking that maybe I had been upgraded for the previous hassle. I was provided with a complimentary drink and, a snack w hot nuts, and a steaming towel. About twenty minutes after we took off, the attendant asked to see my boarding pass again. Apparently, I had handed her the pass from my previous puddle jumper and was again sitting in 2B. Rather than avoid a fuss and let me finish out the flight comfortably in an otherwise empty seat, she told me that I had to go back to my assigned seat in coach. I did the walk of shame to the rear of the plane and struggled to not yell, "It wasn't my fault! I wasn't trying to pull anything!!"

On another flight and another trip, I saw the flight attendant spill coffee on a passenger who was napping. Naturally, he jerked awake and said, "HEY!!" loudly. The flight attendant snapped back harshly, "Sir! You're going to need to act more professionally!" He paused, still stunned, and replied, "Lady, I'm not the one working here!"

I've had a couple of flight attendants, perhaps sensing a sympathetic soul from another people-pleasing business, deliberately not charge me for drinks. As I said earlier, most of my flights have been pleasant or at least uneventful.

I often travel with a guitar. One flight, my guitar made it on board, and I didn't. Hours later, it was waiting happily for me in San Diego. One flight to an important team training was cancelled. I had to go out to ticketing for some reason, and the man behind the counter engaged me in a conversation about guitars and music. I was issued a ticket for what I thought was the next flight. I waited for forty-five minutes at the gate and started to board when my group was called. I made about ten feet into the boarding tunnel when I heard," Sir! Sir! You're not on this flight!" I assured him that I had to be. On closer inspection, my ticket was revealed to be for the following day! The guitar aficionado at the check-in counter hadn't noticed or bothered to tell me of the cancellation and rebooking! One of my Advanced Academy teammates had gotten bumped, too, but managed to get there on standby. I spoke to a supervisor and at least got reimbursed for time and gas with food vouchers. Grrr.

One time, I had gotten to the airport well over an hour before my flight, but the line was so long that by the time I got to the counter, it was too late to check my bags. I was told that maybe I could carry them on. I knew they were way too big and that I wouldn't be able to. It was the last flight of the day to Salt Lake City. A kind supervisor told me, "We never do this, but I will." and she got me on another carrier that same day! Sometimes, good things happen.

Another time, it was totally my fault that someone's evening got screwed up. My bag was unusual, and I never saw one just like it.....until a trip to Florida. I flew to Orlando, grabbed bags, and was driven to

Daytona Beach, where I checked in to my hotel and started to unpack. " Well, Crap!" I exclaimed. "This isn't my suitcase!" I called the airport and, yes, there was indeed another worried passenger. We drove all the way back to Orlando and, fortunately, didn't have to face the other guy. I did write him a note of apology and included some fine hair product samples from my employer. My bag was there. Doh! I never check my bags at the curb. The time I did check my bags at the curb at DFW flying Delta, the bag man was too busy flirting with a little girl and mislabeled my bags. The flight had a stop in Lexington, Ky, on the way to Louisville. My bags got off in Lexington. I was was to pick up my rent car and drive to my first stop on my education tour and spend the night. I had an 8:30 a.m. class. I was assured by Delta that they would get my bags to me at my hotel in said little town. I didn't sleep well at all. I kept jerking awake thinking I heard the delivery guy. No luggage. I arrived at the JC Penney where I was teaching wearing jeans and yesterday's white shirt. The class was about salon professionalism and first impressions, among other things. They understood. My bags met me at my next stop just in time for my 12 noon class.

My next trip to Kentucky was also messed up. Our flight was delayed and we got to Louisville slightly later than we were supposed to. Usually car rental desks are notified and will wait for passengers with reservations. This time, they didn't. They were closed, as were all of the other agencies. There were also no hotel rooms available because of a hotrod convention in town. I slept in the diner on a vinyl booth seat along with about 15 or 20 other passengers. I arose at 5:00 a.m., freshened up in the men's room, and went down to the car rental desk. Smiling, I said to the agent, "I realize that this is not your doing, but I slept in the lounge last night, and I'm not very happy!" She was kind enough to let me have the pick of the lot. I picked the nicest car they had. I don't recall what it was. Months later, I was talking to Tommy Callahan, the VP in charge of education for Paul Mitchell. I told him that I had been in his neck of the woods recently, remembering that he had lived in Paducah, Ky. He asked, "Why didn't you call me? I live right across from the Louisville airport!"

Airport security is another occasional source of frustration. Again, it was mostly smooth sailing, but one time, I had injured my back in a bike accident a day or two before a work trip to El Paso. I have a cane that I picked up on Mt Nebo that is clearly just a polished stick. There are no seams, metal tips, hidden swords, secret compartments, etc. It's a stick. I was able to get around with the support of said stick and got through the metal detector just fine without any buzzers or bells. The FAA guard stopped me and told me that I had to go back through and, put my cane on the belt, and walk through without it. I informed him that I couldn't walk back without it, but he still insisted. I said, "I will go back through and put it on the belt and let you."

X-ray it, and you can hand it back to me, and I'll walk through a second time without setting anything off, but I CANT WALK WITHOUT IT! I did, he did, I did, and went on my way.

Another time, I was picking up my carry-on after going through with no challenges when the agent asked me, "Are you a wrestler?" " What?" I responded. "You a wrestler?" If I wasn't wearing a very cool white rock star-type suit and he could see my scrawny arms, it wouldn't have been a subject of inquiry. I replied, "No, I'm a hairstylist." He followed with, "You look like...whutsisname...." I'm waiting for " Kerry Von Eric or somebody halfway cool lookin, but the He got it. "Rick Flair! You look like, uh... Rick Flair!" Not a compliment. Flair was one of the oldest, saggy-muscled, should-retired, long-ago wrestlers in the business. "Wow. Thanks."

As an educator in the hair biz, I often travelled with multiple mannequin heads to show or demo haircuts and colors. It could be interesting sending a bag of heads through the X-ray and watching the guards' reactions. "Oh, dey use dem fo wee-igs 'n stuff!" I heard one say to the other.

Well, the flight I was waiting on when I began this story finally got us out about 10:40 p.m., around the time we were supposed to be landing in Dallas. We got to bed about 6:00 a.m. after a very rough and cramped flight. So it goes. Hey, we got a free meal and vouchers for $100 each towards future flights on the same airline from Hell! Yep. Can't wait!

Labels

Please don't label me. I am, like most people, multifaceted. I am liberal, conservative, and moderate. I was taught that those were all admirable qualities. I am not a Conservative, a Liberal, or a Moderate. I didn't join the clubs or drink anyone's Kool-Aid. I believe in conserving what's good, fair, and working, but I am open to improving things when needed. I believe in being liberal in letting people be and live their own lives their own way. I believe in helping the less fortunate and realize that there will always be those who get away with abusing the systems. Catch them and plug the holes. If we save a life or allow an unfortunate to achieve a good or great life, it is worth it. I am for learning and growing and adapting those systems to limit that abuse.

I am at least as patriotic as the next guy, and although I was very fortunate to not have to fight in a war that I could not have understood or believed in (luck of the draw/draft#), I appreciate the ability, the sacrifices and the willingness of our soldiers to defend our principles, beliefs, and ways of life. Notice I said "ways." There are MANY ways of life and that's one of the fundamental pieces of our republic/democracy. We are allowed, in theory, to believe, belong, be employed, express ourselves as we wish. You can identify as (in alphabetical order) an Atheist, Buddhist, Christian, Jew, Muslim, or whatever sect, belief, or even gender you want. You don't have to share those beliefs or even approve of them. That's your choice. Just because you believe something doesn't mean that it's right, complete, or The Truth. The price for this freedom of choice and belief is to accept the fact that there are differences in people and that they have that same freedom.

There has always been division, but it has recently increased tenfold. Sometimes, in the past, people of different mindsets could and would still like and respect each other, eat together, be friends, hang out, and perhaps debate, date, love, and marry.

I may never agree with you, but I want to understand you. You may or may not change my mind about something you believe, but it won't happen by insult, force, hostility, or by insulation. I can like, respect, and love you regardless of your race, religion, political affiliation, etc, as long as you have a good heart.

I have friends who have "unfriended" or been "unfriended" by people they cared about because of their differences. Again, it's their choices and consequences but it's nonetheless sad. I'm not perfect. I still roll my eyes or react without thinking. I still tense up or lose my temper sometimes. Usually, it's in the face of unreason or ignorance. Ignorance is forgivable and fixable. Sadly, deliberate ignorance or intolerance is often unfixable.

Remember 911

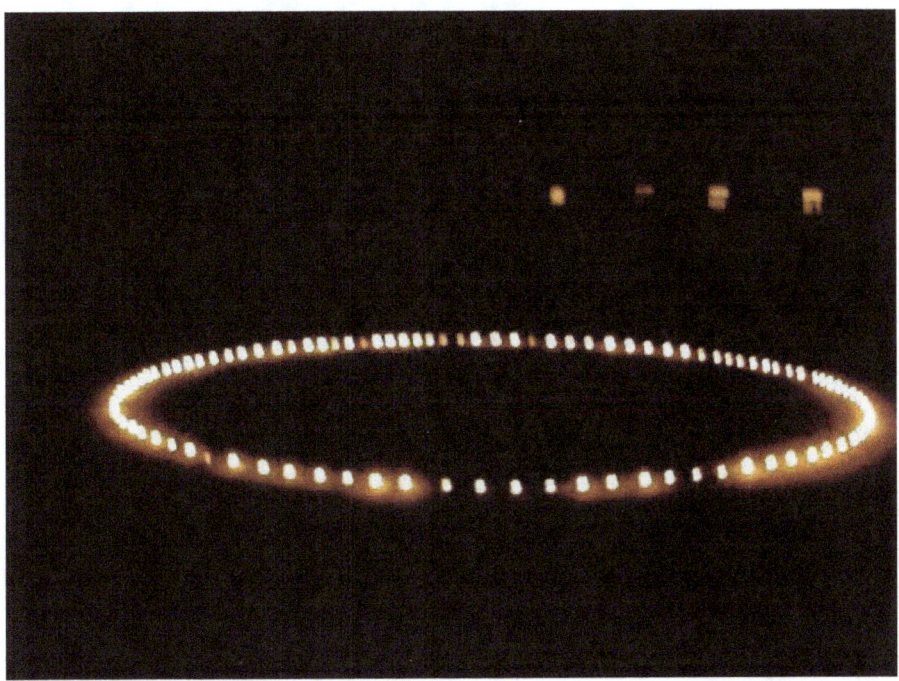

Of course, we remember, but what do we remember? As a species, we have a tendency to heal to forget pain. That's a good thing. If we didn't, no one would go through childbirth twice! We don't need to refuel the horror and the gut-wrenching fear that we felt that day. What we need to remember is the hope, the patriotism, and the unity that we as a country found. We need to remember that no matter how insulated we are from the harsh realities of the world, the hunger, poverty, crime, etc, there really are some bad people out there. Some of them live here. Some of them don't. There really are some heroes and good people out there, too. No matter which side of the fence or wall you live, please remember that we are one country!

I taught a 911 Remembrance/ Constitution Day class in the Paul Mitchell schools. The focus was on remembering the good and on patriotism, no matter what team you play on. I heard many heartbreaking and heart-fulfilling stories. Also, more and more each year, "I remember that school got cancelled..." Remember. Please!

My 911 story is a trifle compared to many I've heard.

On 9/11, I was in Houma, Louisiana, teaching a class for Paul Mitchell in a JCPenny salon. I had just made a point about how it takes only one person to affect the whole atmosphere in a salon when a woman came in crying and told us about the first plane hitting the World Trade Center. I didn't need that strong an example. It had to not be true. If true, it had to be a horrible accident. I managed to finish my class before we all went out into the store and stared at the televisions. It was true.

I tied things up and said my goodbyes. I went back to my hotel and watched TV for a while, and of course, the second plane had struck the towers. This was no accident.

I headed for Beaumont, Texas, not knowing if I would be teaching my next class in the morning. Like everyone else in the country, if not the world, I was glued to my radio, desperately hoping to hear some good news. Maybe it was an elaborate hoax like the Orson Wells War of The Worlds scare in 1938. No, it was true.

I was driving down a long, lonesome stretch of highway, unusually aware of the empty skies around me, when at the last second, I saw I land turtle crossing the road in front of me. Too late. I heard him bounce and bang under my rental car. I'm sure you don't know or maybe wouldn't even have cared in the context of the tragedy and horror happening at that moment but I can't count how many times I have stopped and helped turtles across the road. I know, I know, but it's just something I do. "Oh, GREAT!" I thought. I got about a quarter of a mile down the road and then realized that I was not in any hurry, so I turned back to find that he was all right and was nearly across the road. Doubtless, a bit shaken up, but o.k. That stupid little thing brought me a tiny bit of joy.

I reached Beaumont and, checked into my hotel, and called my wife, Glenna. We decided to share a toast from afar, and I headed down to the hotel bar and ordered a martini. "You want it dirty, hon?" I said,

"No, dry, please." It came very dirty. Fine. She asked, "You gonna sang for us tonight?" I was surprised. "I hadn't planned on it," I replied. How did she know that I sing? Did she think I was someone else? She said, "Well, if you change your mind..." and dropped a big book of lyrics on my table. It was Karaoke Night in Beaumont, Texas. There were some really good singers there that night, including one guy who looked like Newman from Seinfeld and who absolutely nailed the beautiful and very difficult "Unchained Melody." After my second martini, I found myself on stage singing "Yesterday" by The Beatles. Before I could exit stage left, I was joined by everyone and, as was apparently a tradition, had to sing with the group whatever CD they pulled out of the hat. It was "Elvira." Yes, "My hearts on fire, Elvira." I couldn't believe that with all that was happening in the world, I was standing on a hotel stage going, "Oom poppa mow mow!" When it was mercifully over, I left the stage and sat down. They all remained and performed a rough but stirring medley of every patriotic song that was you can think of. There wasn't a dry eye in the house. It was beautiful. I realized that I was in the right place. If I couldn't be home then at least I was with people doing something that they love in spite of the terror and confusion outside. We win.

Birthdays

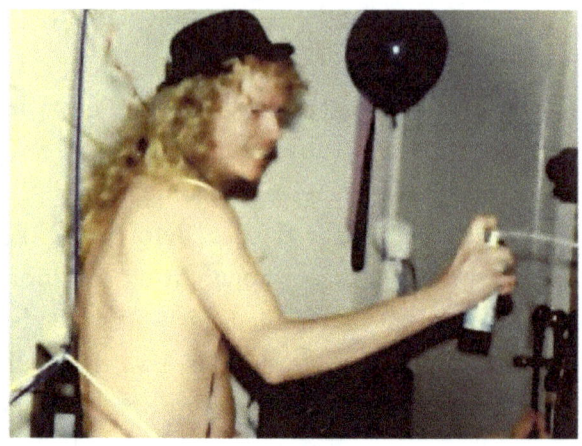

I've had a few. I plan on having many more. There have been a few notable ones that I think will make good story matter.

I'll start with my 50th. A week or so before my birthday, Glenna suggested that I record the song "Pretty Eyes," a sweet song in 3/4 by an old friend, Jeanne Seidner, from my college life days. Glenna has always been good about making plans and keeping them under wraps. This one was very complicated and special. It was my FIFTIETH BIRTHDAY BY GOD, so it had to be special! Of course, something had to happen, but she convincingly downplayed everything and apologetically made me believe that she'd tried, but there were too many conflicting plans, and it would just have to be a low-key celebration. After I spied the limo parked out front, she told me that only our friends Vaughn and Michelle Stockton and Bruce and Pam McRoberts were available. That was o.k. Who else would fit in this awesome limo anyway? Off to dinner, we headed. I did my Di Caprio impression standing in the moonroof of the limo. "I'M KING OF THE WORLD!!" There was some very good single malt involved. We drove all the way downtown and turned east on Ross Avenue. I had no idea where we were headed. We pulled into what looked like an abandoned church and parked. Still no clue. We entered the building to be greeted by easily 150 or more people, including my

|managed to contact or recruit help, contacting nearly everyone that I knew that would care enough to celebrate with me my 50th successful solar circumnavigation! We waltzed to "Pretty Eyes," and I survived a mildly brutal roasting by my long-time friends. There were several " I thought about telling about the time...." and "It's a good thing I didn't mention..." type comments later.

It was absolutely the best surprise party ever!

I had a couple of other memorable ones. On my 40th, I entered the party (not a surprise) in a wheelchair, wearing a bathrobe and pajamas, a bald head wig with straggly white hair around the edges, and thick glasses. There also may have been a bottle of single malt Geretol involved.

The year before, I had heard a phone machine message that I wasn't supposed to. (Remember cassette answering machines?) Anyway, I let myself be set up.

My girlfriend at the time and I went to have dinner with Bruce and Pam at their house. After dinner, the ladies said that they wanted to run and get some ice cream. This was not a normal suggestion, but I knew that it was part of the setup. I remember thinking, "Any minute now, Bruce will say "Hey! Let's run down to your house and grab my guitar." Two minutes later, Bruce suggested, "Hey! Let's run down to your house and grab my guitar." I said, "Sure!" We climbed in his car and headed the few blocks to my house. As he pulled into my driveway, I said, "Go on in. I'll be there in a second!" He stammered.."Uh..Um.." "I repeated, " Go on in. I'll be there in a second!" "Um.. o.k" He went in. I quickly got in my car and stripped down to my green underwear (did I mention that my birthday is St Patrick's Day?) I donned a green derby, my green Doc Martins, and a big green shamrock with the words "Kiss me, I'm Irish!" taped on my briefs (actually, it didn't say "kiss," but we'll go with that) and I ran in the side door spraying everyone with green Silly String. It was truly epic! Somewhere, there is a picture of someone looking astonished, with green Silly String hanging from his gaping maw. There is also this picture generously shared with me on my last birthday by the aforementioned Mr McRoberts.

Of course, there are more stories. They will come. Or not.

Ma:

Photo by Gene Skinner

"Whose turn is it?" "It's o.k. Ma, it's not your turn yet."

This was one of my last conversations with my mother. Playing the card game Bridge was one her favorite pastimes, one that she shared for years with her group of close friends, no matter where she lived. It's not a surprise that in her final couple of days, she thought she was in an ongoing bridge game. On January 5th, it will be twelve years since we lost her to her second bout with cancer. In her 50s, she survived breast cancer and went on to live 30 more good years. Her final battle was mercifully brief. She knew for several months that it was coming, and she was able to take care of business and move closer to at least two of us. We believe that she deliberately struggled to hang in until after Christmas. She did, and she was lucid until her last couple of days.

I've already shared the story of how she had seen a commercial for an Egg McMuffin and thought she might be able to eat one. After being refused at the drive-through, I reined in my anger and frustration with the girl with no authority and went in and explained to the manager, who, without hesitation, fired up the grill and made my mom the best Egg McMuffin he could and would not accept payment.

There are good people. Our mom was one of them.

She always had hopes and expectations for us but was always there to catch us when we needed her. At times, it was hard to feel that we may have briefly disappointed her, but that never never dimmed her love for us or her willingness to help. She succeeded in raising three very unique, good hearted, and in each of our own ways, successful children and had a big hand in a handful of very special grandkids! One of the smartest things I've ever done was to sit down with her and have her tell her life story, often forgetting that I had a video camera on.

There are so many stories. Here's one of my favorites.

"We had sand piles, not sand boxes, and my sand pile was in the corner of my front yard. We had coveralls. They called them Union All's. They had narrow navy and white stripes. Anyway, I had been up, against instructions, on top of this big fence, and I guess a car backfired, and I jumped. It startled me, and I fell! Anyway I went off the fence, hooked a picket on the seat of my pants, and it did not do them any good at all! It sure tore the heck outa my pants, and I went flyin' flyin' in the house and told my mama, "A man shot the hiney outa my britches!" and she spanked me for telling a story! I thought that was wildly unjust! Here she was, not being thrilled that it hadn't killed me, but she spanked me! The man shot the hiney outa my britches, and I had survived, and she wasn't even grateful."

There are more stories, including V.E. Day, of her running across NYC to meet my dad and being hugged and danced with by strangers in the street, rejoicing at the end of WW2. So many more stories. They will come.

She was funny and feisty! Somewhere, I've written of a couple of her "practical" jokes. Actually they were more intended to put someone in their place. The annoying woman at a backyard party who was trying to attract attention by making a big fuss over some guy (maybe my dad? Not sure, doesn't matter.) and standing tip-toe in her heels. My mother's drink ended up in the ladies shoe. "Oh! I'm so sorry! Did that get on you?"

Another time, in a fashion show at the officer's club, there was a self-anointed "fashion model" unaware that my mom was around the corner in silk striped pajamas, corset, turban, cigarette holder, and sunglasses, following her and mocking her every pose. The woman never knew why people were laughing every time she left a room. Ma didn't take crap from anyone! I remember being stunned when we were out buying school supplies, and someone had deliberately or inconsiderately parked over two spots in front of the store. She spit and wrote, "SOB!" In grease pencil on their windshield. Wow. Don't mess wit MY momma!

She bought herself an Opel Manta, a small, supposedly reliable car that I got from her later. It had some mechanical problems, and when the dealer refused to acknowledge her warranty, she walked out to the sales floor and warned the potential buyers. "DON'T BUY AN OPEL! DON'T BUY AN OPEL!" The general manager caught up with her in the outside lot and effusively offered to satisfy her every mechanical need.

A few years after my father's passing, though younger than any of her kids are now, she began to feel old. My sister Carolyn informed her that she was starting to act like her mother, who had successfully decided that she was old. Carolyn's words hit home, and my mother quit smoking (for a while), dyed her hair, and bought herself a brand-new Datsun 280Z. Enough of this "getting old" crap!

My mom loved the candy and nuts conglomeration, Branch's Bridge Mix. One year, she asked for some for Christmas. Everyone in the family bought her cases of it. I'd bet it didn't last as long as you might hope. Once, someone from the warehouse where my mom worked for a while gave her a "funny cigarette." She and her Bridge friends all decided to try it. "I hear it's good for glaucoma!" "I heard it's good for arthritis!" It sat around for so long that it may have lost its potency. No one claimed any effect or benefits for their ills. I'll bet the bridge mix tasted especially good that day. File this under "I wish I'd been a fly on the wall!"

One memory is of her shelling pecans for something to do with her hands while watching TV. She always seemed to have pecans and made the best pecan pie. A guilty pleasure of mine was to steal a handful from the freezer. Yes, I felt guilty knowing her effort, but yes, I did it!

The morning that it was indeed "her turn," Glenna, suspecting that it was Ma's last night with us, had volunteered to spend the night at her apartment. She called me to tell me that she had awakened to find her gone. I remember, still bleary and in shock, for a fraction of a section, saw my mom standing over our toddler son Zane, asleep on the couch. It could have been the light or the sleep in my eyes, but I choose to believe it was her. She would have.

I still think, "I need to call Ma and tell her....." or wish that I could ask her questions that only she could answer. Sometimes, I went a couple of months between phone conversations with her, so it took a while to totally feel her absence and my lack of ability to do so. If I could go back and change things, I would, as my sisters often did, talk to her much more often. Rest In Peace, Ma, though you will never rest in our hearts. You'll live there eternally.

The Big House

Another story that's been brewing for a while that overlaps other stories and is probably part of an even bigger story....(aren't they all?) is of an amazing house that I lived in a for a few months in the mid-70s. It was a 2 story, circa 1920s house on a hill above Northwest Highway in Dallas between Inwood and Midway Rd. If you know the area, you are probably thinking, "Whuuuut? How?" This is some really expensive real estate. It was owned by one of the owners of a big and well-known plumbing company. This will prove to be ironic later. It was surrounded by trees and sat a on a lot with a back yard big enough to play frisbee or to run around laughing and yelling, "Its all a joke! It's all a joke!" More on that later. The driveway was uphill through two stone pillars and was just dirt and gravel. It required a well timed hard right turn off of NW Highway with enough momentum to get up the gravel hill without smashing into the pillars. I was driving my old beat up 65 Dodge van (see "Car Talk" in The Son Of The Return Of Kent Skinner's Stories) so another scrape or three wasn't really an issue. There was also a small orchard at the rear of the property where I buried my sweet doggie Alabaster. My long time guitar player friend, Jim Russell, currently the leader of JR's All Stars, had a girlfriend named Tona Reynolds. She happened to be living in this house with several friends and they happened to need another room mate at the time. I was taking a break from school and had a taken a position with YMCA Urban Services for a whopping $900 a month and needed a place to live. I don't know how they found or secured this house but it was amazing. It was the only house I knew of in Dallas that had a basement. It also had a bunch of hippies living in it, one of whom was me. I got a room downstairs that was actually a long screened and glassed in porch. It backed up to the fireplace in the living room with a big stone wall. It was really cool. Actually, really cold if there was no fire. Not a problem. I had just left way worse in Austin where I was living in the back of a store with absolutely no heat or hot water, sleeping on a cot in the small bathroom and heating this small space with a toaster oven. This was the lap of luxury. I only knew Tona and not really well, though she became a good friend later and was married to my bass player, Ralph Fahrbach for a while. (see Wedding Snafus in Kent Skinner's Stories). I remember a guy named Bill who had The Big Room upstairs, a reward of seniority apparently. There was a girl friend of Tona's and a guy I'll call Ruben. Ruben was one of those kind of fresh off the farm country boy turned hippie that was discovering the universe and considered himself an artist and cosmic guru type guy. He was actually kind of a jerk. He painted big gaudy canvases with poorly executed cosmic visuals. Lots of swirly waves and badly rendered naked people and stars and such. I remember him building a wooden pyramid that would supposedly focus cosmic rays to preserve stuff and him putting a glass of beer inside it. A day or so later he reported "Tastes pretty good! Kinda flat.." I responded "Y'know, if you build an exact scale replica of the Pyramid at Giza and put a dead cat in it, then put it in the freezer, it'll preserve it for months!" He seemed impressed. There was no cooperative organization in the house, just people living messily and bitching at each other. There was resentment over rooms and food and Ruben thinking he was in charge. Being in charge would have included getting the rent collected to the landlord. Gradually, most of the original tenants moved out. Of that bunch from before me, only Ruben remained as far as I recall. One new tenant was Sandi Shore, the sister of an ex girlfriend. She was fun and rowdy and introduced me to my long time good friend, Bruce. I told in an earlier story about road trips with Bruce how initially I had thought him to be a narcissistic dumbass as he was bashing on a piano at a party wearing a cape and a star painted on his forehead when I first met him. One day he showed up with his mandolin and a friend at the house and I learned how smart, creative and talented he is. We have played in numerous incarnations of various bands and are still fast friends. His relationship with Sandi lasted a few months. Our friendship has lasted decades. One day I came home from work at the YMCA tutoring program at Camp Kiwanis and everyone was in a particularly good mood. Someone handed me a tumbler jar of tea and said drink this. He was joined by a chorus of "Kill it! Kill it!" I did my best. It was awful. It was mushroom tea. Of the mind altering kind. Their mood was already altered and no one was thinking quantity or safe dosage. I apparently imbibed much more than they had. I was very anxious about all of this and being told "In a few minutes you are going to get sick but after that it'll be alright." I did and for a while it was all right. My girlfriend Diane came over but did not partake. Sitting on the top of a dome shaped jungle gym, it seemed like the geodesic shape continued up into the stars. That was cool enough. I was calming down and trying to ride it out and enjoy myself. Bruce was running around the back yard yelling "It's all a joke! It's all a joke!" and laughing his head off. It was amusing until I noticed that my hands were going to sleep and tightening up. I tried to shake some circulation into them and ran around a little myself. It didn't work. I ended up in my room with every muscle in my body clenched as tight as they could be. I was glad that I had Diane looking after me and assuring me that I'd be ok. She promised to stay with me and to not take me to a hospital or anything unless I told her to. Throughout this intense and unpleasant trip I maintained enough of a thread of coherence to know if that moment should come. It didn't. When I got to the point that I knew I'd be ok, I sent her home. I suffered only some very sore muscles and an aversion to mushroom tea. Duh. Here's where the story lightens up again. She was living at home with her parents. Pulling into the driveway, she saw that the kitchen light was on. Thinking quickly, she rolled up her jeans and began to water the flowerbeds. Her father came out to go to work and asked "What are you doing up this early?" She replied "I couldn't sleep so I thought I'd just get up and do my chores!" Good thinking! Her name was the title of the A side of my first and only 45 Record. I still have a couple of copies and it showed up on YouTube recently. I have no idea who the person who posted it is. Anyway, at the facility I worked, there was also a runaway program where kids in crisis could have a place to land, get counseling, aid returning home or placement. The director of Urban Services and the director of the runaway center asked if we had room at our house for a kid named Eddie. He was 17 but had been declared an adult by the justice system and couldn't stay at the facility. He was an ok kid that had done some stupid things but was pulling it together. My housemates said ok and he moved into the servants quarter off of the garage. Things went fine until a couple of the runaways showed up at my birthday party. I called the director to let her know that they were there and that there was no illegal activity going on to my knowledge. She said that it was fine but to call if there were any concerns. Eventually, the party died and I went to bed. A few days later I was questioned by the CPS psychologist counselor working with the runaway center and was threatened with contributing to the delinquency of a minor, losing my job, etc. Fortunately the directors stepped up and made it clear that I had only done as asked. It went away. Whew. So did Eddie.

One day I couldn't find Alabaster. I called and searched and knocked on the landlords door on the next lot. When I asked if he'd seen her, he just laughed and shut the door. He had complained about her barking when people drove up. I eventually found her lying by the creek that ran in front. I have no proof but I believe that he knew or had a hand in her dying. She had been sick and there was foamy substance coming from her mouth. I buried her where she had loved playing, in the orchard. Kharma strikes back. The plumbing started going out. The kitchen ceiling started to fall in and the wooden floor started buckling. Calls to our plumbing tycoon landlord were unanswered. He just wanted us out so he could build a tennis court for his rich clients. In retrospect I maybe wouldn't have wanted us there either. He let it get so bad that we couldn't live there and within two weeks of our leaving, he tore the house down. Nothing there. Nothing but memories of that beautiful old house. For years and occasionally still, I have dreams of living there again with it's rambling rooms, sliding French doors and fantastic view. You could sit in the living room at night with the lights off and feel the history and the stories, the echoes of the lives within the walls. Or maybe it was just the tea.

After The Big House

I heard through the grapevine at Urban Services that there was a group of Vista volunteers that had a house on Maple Springs with an available bedroom. Vista is an organization that offers recent college graduates interested in a social work type of field an opportunity to spend a year in the trenches working with the less fortunate while they decide where and what they are going to do with their degrees and experience. Often it led to employment with the agencies that they worked with or had contact with. While I wasn't Vista, I was working in a social work type job so it wasn't a bad fit. Highlights/ lowlights of my brief stay on Maple Springs before going back to U.T. Austin for my final year after deciding I had gone as far as I could without a degree, any degree, include having my dirty dishes placed in my bed (guilty) acquiring a new puppy, Saffron, an attempt to replace Alabaster (impossible) who was run over by a car within 3 weeks (heartbreaking!) oh, and breaking up with Diane. Rather, being broken up with. A bad few weeks.

I heard through a different grapevine that some friends of my younger sister, Barby and my friends Bruce and Sandi were seeking a housemate in Austin. Perfect! They seemed nice enough at first. Soon I heard some references to their previous tenant about how they had to take him to court for non payment or something. Mild prickles of apprehension occurred. Hearing how the female housemate/ landlord had ripped off someone's camera at a concert and seeing her bite her dog's ear gelled my suspicions of "not rightness."

One night I was alone in the house when there was a loud pounding on the door. I opened it to see a large angry Hispanic man demanding to speak to my housemates. Apparently there was an issue concerning a drug deal gone bad. "Look! I don't know anything about this! I'm just renting a room in the back!" I said. I guess he believed me because he did leave. I gave 2 weeks notice the next day.

Then, surprise surprise, having tasted blood with the previous housemate, they threatened to sue me for breach of a verbal contract. I conferred with the student attorneys office on campus and they suggested a settlement. I settled for a months rent and booked. The next news I heard of them was of them finding a great little farm house in the country for a ridiculously low rent, and his buying a new Ford pickup with all the whistles and bells. I remember thinking "Why do good things happen to bad people?" Soon I heard that lightning struck the house and it and everything they owned including the truck went up in flames! Once again, kharma exists!

A good friend from Camp Kiwanis, Mike McGarrity was living in a coop near campus and spoke highly of it. Their sister co-op, 21st Street College House was half a block closer and had a vacancy. It was a very impressive facility. It was solar powered, very modern looking for mid late 70s and absolutely fit my V.A. budget. I think rent was about $190 a month including great (mostly) meals that were cooked by fellow members. That's how a co-op works. Everybody has a job that they do once or twice a week, in most cases, benefitting the house as a whole. My dad had lived in one around the corner in the late 30s. It was home for a couple of years, my final year of college and my year in hair school.

The first person I met when I was just checking the place out was a guy maybe a little older than me who introduced himself as "Aransas Vacilando." I recall him looking at me strangely when I told him my name. He showed me around and explained how things worked. Months

273

later he explained why he had looked at me funny. It turned out that his real name was...Ken Skinner! There was a Kathy Skinner living there too who's brother, Ken Skinner came to visit. At one time there were two Ken Skinners and one Kent Skinner staying under the same roof or roofs as it were. A few months after that someone came up to me and said we're coming to hear you sing tonight! I said "Great!" I was in fact performing that night. He said "I didn't know you sang opera!" I answered, "I don't" He pulled out a program or article that said that I was actually performing an opera recital that night. It seems that there was ANOTHER Kent Skinner attending U.T. who was also a singer.

During my time there I served as lunch cook, dinner cook, room checker (Not like that. I kept keys and checked members in when they moved in and out when they moved out.)

I also served as a co membership chairperson for one semester.

During my short tenure we had our first African American applicant. His race was, of course, not mentioned to the membership committee during considering his application. The most memorable part of that process was after mentioning that he was on the U.T. Wrestling team, he commented that he was "nervous around stranglers." Aren't we all! Some wise ass in the group suggested because of his wrestler stature and his feelings about stranglers that we keep him chained on the front lawn. Still, no mention of his race had been made so the inappropriateness of this supposedly humorous comment was magnified. Those of us who had met him liked him a lot. He was accepted and was a valuable member for some time.

It was the 70s. Drugs, Sex and Rock and Roll! Oh yes, and foosball. Everything you ever heard about those times was probably true. Just saying..for a friend... That's right.

There is probably a whole book's worth of stories to be written about that place. Maybe someday I'll write it. I'll have to change a lot of names. I made so many lifelong friends during that time so I guess the previous living arrangement fiasco worked out for the best. Footnote to this segment: Every year they still have a birthday party for 21st Street

College House in November. I hadn't attended any since maybe a year or two after I moved to Dallas. I heard that some of my old friends were going to be attending a couple of years ago so I drove down that Saturday night. I immediately ran into Paul Baen who had been the house Trustee (or chairman) for a while, we were assigned a guide, a nice young guy who gave us bracelets that entitled us to free craft beer from the special kegs secreted around the co op. We also got access to free liquor from the bar. We were referred to as "The Elder Gods" by a couple of people. When dinner was served buffet style I happened to be close to the front of the "line." "Awesome!" I thought. Not so much. There was no line. It was a madhouse but everyone got food. After dinner, the Trustee gave a welcome speech to the visiting members and when she was done she said "OK!" and the six doors slammed shut. "Smoke 'em if you got 'em! Suddenly maybe 40 funny little cigarettes appeared. I reminded myself that I was in Austin.

Paul and I had been playing a game for our own amusement. It was casting an imaginary "College House - The Movie" "That guy would play Melvin." "She would be Nancy and he would play Scott" etc. I met the kid who would play me. It was very cool to be having a chat with this younger "me" and having him probe me for life advice. How cool would that be to meet the older you and.....Well, maybe it was the second hand smoke.

I visited my old room and the girl that lived in it was willing to let me in and take some pictures. I poked my head around the corner to the room where my girlfriend, Cathy had lived. The door was wide open and I was startled to see a totally naked girl standing there. "Excuse me! Im sorry!" I said. She replied "It's ok." Apparently, my old suite is now the Clothing Optional Suite. Speaking of public nudity, standing in the yard or driving down the street you could not see in the windows because of the reflective mirrored glass. Every morning for months I would go to my sliding glass door and stretch and enjoy the view. Eventually one of my female friends informed me that the reflective invisibility that I was enjoying was cancelled out by the angle and lighting or whatever and that I had a fan club that would sit and enjoy their own view from the dining area every morning! She pointed out that my face was as red at that moment as my underwear! The place is run down now and has seen it share of remodeling and change and it's not solar powered anymore but it's still very cool. It was pretty decadent when I lived there but it's 10 times more so now and if my kids are lucky enough to get accepted by U.T. Austin, I will definitely want them to live....NOT THERE! Probably...Maybe. We'll see.

The Set

Again I think that the co op deserves its own story so I'll move on to my next habitat. My housemates, Mike Williams and Suzy Valentine, named it "The Set." In other words, a place for drama and stories to be acted out. It was an appropriate name for the place. It was a cool ranch style two story house on 6th Street in Austin that is now a law office I believe. Cool ranch, not as in dressing but in an old style of architecture that in this case did not involve central heat or even insulation. Maybe the original tenants were of sterner stuff or had gas heaters in every room. We weren't and didn't. It was bitter freaking cold in the winter even with lots of blankets and gas heaters. You could feel the wind coming through the exterior walls. I seem to recall having a heater in my room that didn't do much. I still spent a lot of time at the co op. I maintained a meal contract that provided me with a couple of meals a day in return for some work. My 65 Dodge van was on its last legs. I got it there and parked it behind the house and as I mentioned in a previous story, eventually gave it to some friends to live in while they built their house.

I also adopted a new dog, a golden retriever I named Bessie, which was short for besame mucho, (kiss me a lot) which she did. She travelled with me some but mostly stayed home with my roomies if I was gone. She hated being cooped up and made Swiss cheese of the back porch screens. After finding her gone for a couple of days, I found her at the city pound. As I passed by several cages of sad doggies hoping that I was there to rescue them I heard a grand ruckus at the back of the facility. Bessie saw me and made sure I knew where she was!

She had a suitor. When she had her first heat a little rat like mutt from the neighborhood decided that she was "The One" and several days in a row, managed to run up the back steps and launch himself through the screen onto the back porch to be with his true love. Well, it was true love on his part but as far as we knew, it was unrequited. We'd come home to find him cowering in the corner with her maintaining a "What are you after little man?" attitude towards him. I'm sure he was heartbroken but the only other golden retriever in the neighborhood managed to win her heart (or whatever) and she had a litter of puppies which we somehow found homes for. I moved from there to Dallas and Mike had friends that lived on a farm and wanted her. I was not sure of my living situation in Dallas and reluctantly but gratefully gave her up.

Date From Hell

For a while when I was single I rented my spare bedroom to friends in transition or need. I had a couple of doozies but that may be another story. One of them was a friend/client Gordo, a recording engineer w two triple platinum records that looked real good on my living He was friends with one of my short term clients "Brenda" That is not her real name but she is in fact now Facebook friends with me. Being recently single and she being cute, I asked him to fix me up. She agreed and invited another girl along as a blind date for Gordo.

Our scheduling was all off as Gordo and I picked "Brenda" up and went to have a drink and a bite somewhere in uptown before time came to pick his date up in Garland. Once the cast was assembled, we were going to go hear some band at a club, but back to dinner. "Brenda" ordered a full meal and ate very little to offset her alcohol intake. I remember her building a small structure in her salad plate with cigarette butts. Hanging in, I drove us all back to Garland to pick up Gordo's date. She and "Brenda" climbed into the back seat and spoke only to each other the whole way back downtown. I don't remember getting more than four words or any eye contact from her all night. We stopped in to another place to kill time before the band played. "Brenda" proceeded to order another meal which she hardly touched but thankfully skipped the cigarette butt castle this time. Finally it was showtime and I soon realized that "Brenda" had some history with the bass player! He was all she could talk about. I foolishly called home to check my answering machine (pre cell phone days) and heard the voice of another female friend who was waaay more fun saying "Kent! Where are you? We are all going out!" I began to pray for a lightning bolt to strike and end this awful date. No luck. I decided that I was just going to chalk it up to being a lesson in character. On the way home I blasted The Potatoes' "Her Head Went Rolling On Down The Road." I didn't care that they didn't get it. That whole night I may have exchanged four sentences with my "date" and I think zero interchange with Gordo's date except "Which house is yours?" She had never been to Dallas and as I recall had never even been outside of Garland! I left Gordo at "Brenda"s house and headed home to sleep that lousy night off. The next morning Gordo called. "I'm sorry man, it's not over." "Brenda" was supposed to catch a bus to Oklahoma that morning and Gordo's battery was dead. I dragged my ass back down to Lakewood and took "Brenda" to the bus station. All the way she was bitching about this, that and everything. "I have to sit on a bus for three and a half hours! " was just one thing. My last words to her were something like "Y'know....If you sit right behind the bus driver I'll bet you'll make it in two!"

More Gigs From Hell

Art Kent Skinner

I may have shared one or more of these before. If I did, they are buried way deeper than you are probably willing to scroll! I attended W.T.White high school a LONG time ago and performed with the W.T.White Folk Music Club. We did a few shows at nursing homes and one time at a home in Waco after the show an old lady asked me how we got away with calling ourselves the White Folks Music Club! Got that straightened out.

I also played in a lot of makeshift bands. We'd do it backwards sometimes. "Gig? Sure!" (Crap! Gotta get a band together!) One was for a church youth group party at White Rock Lake at a for hire facility called The Dreyfus Club. We, Dale Meyler, Steve and Mark Bander and myself, drove around the lake for over an hour and a half asking directions and finally arrived in time to set up and play maybe 20 or 30 minutes. I don't recall getting paid for that one.

A couple of years earlier with at least a couple of the same guys, we played a Boy Scout event of some sort. It went reasonably well until a young hippie chick came into our playing area (concrete floor) barefooted and touched my arm to get my attention. She did. I remember/imagine a 3 inch electric arc leaping between us and her gawking wide eyed at me as if I had done it on purpose!

One more, in later years recollected by my recently passed buddy, Joe Eddy Hines. The Rockin' Devils were using my Altec Lansing A7 p.a. cabinets and someone carelessly left a plastic cup of beer on the edge of one of them. Of course it vibrated off the cabinet and fell to the floor. Miraculously, it landed right side up. However, the impact caused the beer to splash up in a liquid arc out of the cup completely over the small mixer sitting on the floor and landing directly on the power amp (not mine). Fireworks ensued. Gig temporarily halted until a replacement was procured.

Close Call

Art Kent Skinner

I remember going into a club in San Antonio with my friend Delton Childress and a cute young lady immediately walking up and asking me to dance w her. The drinking age was 18 at the time and she looked old enough. She could easily have been 21. I thought "Well o.k.! This is going to be a good night!" I bought her a drink and danced a couple more songs. Then she asked me how old I was. I told her that I was 25 (I think I was) and asked her how old she was. She looked around and leaned in and said "I'm 15." I responded "Ehhh.....I think I'm going to go find my buddy!" The next time I saw her was when Delton and I were leaving. She was on her knees christening the rear wheel of a BMW in the parking lot. Close one. That could have been the rear wheel of my 65 Dodge van.

Elevators

Art by Bill Luchsinger.

Why are elevators awkward? Is it because you have to share a small closed box hurtling through space with little control with strangers, one of whom is wearing too much perfume...or worse ONE stranger? One stranger that feels as awkward as you or worse again, feels obligated to chat for 40 seconds....

Personally, I have fun in elevators. It might have started in college when my friend Lois Leftwich and I spent an evening riding up and down the elevator of her dormitory, playing scrabble on a card table. There may have been wine and cigarettes involved too. Yes, people thought we were crazy. No argument. Most thought it was great. My long time friends Vaughn Stockton, Max Droz and I have shared many, many elevators in hotels and convention halls. A game we'd play was to speak a random sentence to which the other person would pick up and respond as if it was an ongoing conversation, such as, "Really? Ceramic shoes?" "Yes! They are really cool looking but they are kinda noisy and you can't wear them on concrete." Or.. "Did you have to kill them ALL?" "Yes. They wouldn't stop looking at the back of my head!" My favorite might be, "Magnetic cowboy boots?" "Yeah, you don't even have to know how to line dance. They just st move you around the dance floor."

If I'm alone I'm likely to sing or stretch with my leg on the waist high bar around the perimeter. Why is that there anyway? In case the cable snaps you'll have something to hold onto while you plummet to your death?

And....there's that inevitable time that you aren't paying attention and get out on the wrong floor. It doesn't happen when you are alone.

"Oops! Wrong floor!" Not at all awkward.

Wake Up Call

One late night years ago, after more than my share of Deep Ellum

(Dallas's hot music/nightlife scene at the time) I was driving home on 75 when I started nodding off. I remember feeling my car spinning and my doing what I could to change that situation. To the best of my recollection, I spun 360 degrees before coming to a sudden stop. I was jolted wide awake, and after determining that I was, in fact, intact, I jumped out of my pretty little silver Saab and walked around to inspect the damage. My right front tire was about a foot and a half up the concrete wall dividing the highway and the entrance ramp. The car was tilted about 40 degrees. I was astounded to see that there was not a scratch on the car! The tire was ruined but was still inflated. I carefully drove home wide awake, sober, and grateful! From the distance of a couple of decades or so, I won't swear that there was any actual spinning, but it seemed very real, and the impact definitely was.

The actual one and the mental one.

DLMFs.

Everybody knows one or has been one. The DL stands for "Doom Laden." You can figure out the last half. They are usually good hearted people that bad things continually happen to. It's also usually a direct or indirect result of bad decisions made by said DLMFs. This is the story of my tenure as a DLMF. I began my third year in Austin and U.T. sharing a two bedroom apartment on Bull Creek with my old neighbor Delton Childress whom you may remember from earlier stories. Oh, and my faithful dog, Alabaster. Delton had graduated and was seeking employment. That didn't work out so well. We also hadn't noticed that there was a railroad track right behind the apartments and that didn't help my sleep pattern any. So that's why the rent was so low. Today, that railroad has been replaced with or runs alongside Mopac.

Anyway, we had no living room furniture but a couple of bean bag chairs, some huge speakers hooked up to an eight-track car tape deck, and a black and white television. I had an aluminum folding cot in my bedroom for a bed. Actually, it was just the frame to a cot. I tied and spread blankets supporting cardboard to replace the nylon mesh that had given way. I think Delton may have slept on a pallet in his room. These were some sparse times.

I apparently had an outstanding parking or speeding ticket because one day, while I was in class and Delton was home alone, a cop came to the door. "Are you Kent Skinner?" "No sir," Delton replied. "What's your name?" "Delton Childress." "What?" barked the cop. "Delton Childress!" "That ain't no name!" Delton fumbled his drivers license out, and the officer relented. "Well, I guess you couldn't made THAT up. You tell Mr. Skinner to get his ass downtown and pay this ticket, or he's goin' to jail next time I come out here." I did. I hitched down to San Antonio and got the money from my mother.

It was also during this time that I had bought the old 65 Dodge YMCA camp van for $500 and had gotten some good use out of it for a few months before it broke down in West, just north of Waco. It sat there in a church lot for a couple of months until I could afford to have the engine rebuilt. So, I was afoot or riding the bus for a while. I had a friend friend who lived in Dobie, a very posh dorm just off campus. She had a meal plan that included breakfast, which she was seldom up in time to eat, so she gave me her card and at least I was able to have one decent meal a day. One night at a party in her suite I learned a hard lesson about tequila. I disappeared into one of the bathrooms and fell asleep with my head on my forearm whilst worshipping at the porcelain alter. I'm not sure how long I was out but when I awoke, my left arm was asleep. It didn't wake up for a few months. My wrist was completely limp (no hairdresser jokes please) and I had no feeling in it. Needless to say, this put a damper on my foosball game and my true passion, playing the guitar. After a few weeks, it entered the pins and needles stage. That lasted a couple of agonizing weeks. After ultrasound treatments and some degree of patience it slowly returned to normal. As a result of exercising it and practicing my playing improved beyond where it had been before. I was also nursing a relationship with a girl in Dallas who had worked with me at Camp Kiwanis. Being broke, limp wristed and 200 miles away with no car didn't help. I would hitchhike up to Dallas on the weekends with Alabaster and my guitar to see her and play in a band. That's another whole epic. It didn't last. The band, I mean. The girlfriend stuck it out for a couple more years.

As you can read, this wasn't the easiest of times for me, and it actually got worse. We had to break our lease and lose our deposit, not that we would have gotten it back anyway. Alabaster had nearly chewed through the bathroom door while I was at school one day. Delton couldn't find a job, so he moved back to his hometown, San Antonio. My friend, Dale Meyler, was living north of campus with his wife, Keri, and their baby, Deanna. He also was renting a small house on 53rd street where he had a business selling movie memorabilia. I had painted a huge mural on the side of the house of the Marx Brothers, The Shadow, Scarlett and Rhett, and King Kong. He let me move into the back of that house for a decent price, and at least I had a roof over my head. No heat or hot water, but at least a roof. Every night, I set my cot with the blankets and cardboard up in the small bathroom. The tub was full of boxes at my feet. To the right was a small shelf on which I placed a toaster oven, which served the dual purpose of heating frozen meals and heating the small room. Every morning, I would pack it all up so that his customers would have the use of the bathroom. Occasionally, I would hitch over to Dale's house to shower. Two or three times a week, Alabaster and I'd hitch down to San Antonio and shower at my mom's house. She didn't know how bad things really were, and I didn't tell her until many years later. I finished the semester. Vincent Mariani was my painting teacher. In a previous design class with him, he had taken me out to the hall and told me that I was the only person in the class who had earned an A. I mention this because he knew what I was capable of. When it was "show and tell" at the end of the semester, I only had three small paintings done and not well. I didn't earn an A this time. Again, he took me outside and explained that he knew what a hard semester I'd had and that he was giving me, he stressed "giving" me a C in the class. He asked that if I ever did anything that I felt he should see, to please show him so that he could justify his gift to me. I did. I left Austin for a while. I moved in with the my friend Mike's family in Oak Cliff. Mike was another ex counselor from Camp Kiwanis and was a very nice DLMF himself. He was dating Sandi Shore, the younger sister of one of my first serious girlfriends, and was also the future girlfriend of my musical collaborator, Bruce McRoberts. She also was one of my many housemates in the Big House story. Anyway, every morning, Mike's mom would wake me up singing "Love Makes The World Go Round" badly and would make me toaster waffles! This only lasted 2 or 3 months before Alabaster's hair on the couch became an insurmountable problem, and she and I had to seek other living arrangements. I moved in with my lifelong friend Vaughn Stockton and his wife Michelle, my first but short-lived girlfriend. I know, it's a freaking soap opera. They had a cool old house on Bowser near the border of Oak Lawn and University Park. Other than a bad roach problem and an occasional rat, it was comfy. I soon moved into a cabin on the grounds of Camp Kiwanis on Bachman Lake. This may not all be in completely accurate chronological order. Opinions vary. Although perceptions of reality may also vary, reality doesn't, but who cares. At some point, I moved into the Big House, then the house on Maple Springs with a bunch of VISTA volunteers, and then back to Austin, where I returned to UT to finish up my degree. I contacted Professor Mariani and showed him my makeshift version of Jim Allison's crystalume, an instrument on which I'd play a beam of light to create what Jim named music or visual music. He agreed to sponsor me for 6 hours of credit towards my degree, perfecting my instrument and my performance, which I named "Choreoptics." I earned my A this time and did a couple of critically lauded shows for the university.

As you can see, life did get better. In a nutshell, I shed my DLMF mantle, moved to Dallas, took a job with YMCA Urban Services, fixed the van and the relationship, broke the relationship and the van, though not necessarily in that order, and, as I mentioned, eventually returned and got the degree, went to hair school, met Paul Mitchell, etc., etc., etc. blah blah blah. More later if you can stand it.

More Salon Memories

Not an earth shaking coincidence but maybe evidence of a cosmic prankster. One morning, I looked at my books and noticed that my morning consisted of Dawn Franke, Vickie Danke, Gary Shanke (probably misspelled but all rhyming), Marla Finco, and Jim Stanco (close but no cigar). Good enough for a quick, mildly amusing blurb, but here's where it all goes dark and queasy!

Mr Shanke was a good guy, if a little exuberant. He worked for a meat factory and commonly came in on his lunch hour smelling strongly of raw sausage. He told a story of a meat processing plant that he may or may not have worked for.

Here's where the faint at heart might want to scroll on to a post of someone's cat or what they ate for dinner.

According to Gary, the meat plant would collect the blood from the slaughterhouse and it would be dried and stored for selling for other uses. I can only imagine what. Anyway, the powdered blood would get sucked up into the air ducts in the ceiling and would collect moisture, thus reconstituting back into blood. One day, the workers heard a horrific grinding and squealing sound. It was the steel girders bending from the weight of the reconstituted blood! Suddenly, the ceiling collapsed, drenching the factory floor and the unlucky workers in tons of blood and maggots!! O.k. Breathe! I warned you!

I don't think it was the factory that Gary worked at at the time. I can't help though, thinking about this story whenever I see their delicious products on the shelf at the grocery store. Vegetarianism anyone?

Dark Matter

So, this is one of those that I should not be as proud of as I am. However, it was an effective solution to an annoyance and two social wrongs that cost me more energy than they were worth.

I pay a modest fee for the antiquated pleasure of sitting and drinking my coffee (Guatemalan, freshly ground, and freshly roasted) while immersing myself in the Sunday paper. I only buy the Sunday edition of the Dallas Morning News, preferring to get my daily dose from NPR and online sources. I suddenly sound like Frazier Crane in my head. Stop it. It could be worse. It could be Niles. I also live in a neighborhood and city where one is required by law to have your dogs on a leash when outside your property and to pick up their deposits when made. I am less firm on the first and more so on the second if said deposit is on the sidewalk or in my driveway.

Go away, Frazier! No more reruns.

For several Sundays, my paper seemed light and, on further inspection, proved indeed to be minus two to four sections, including but not always the Comics, Metro, Points, and/or Living section, where one can peruse other peoples' problems and marvel at the wisdom of professional life coaches Carolyn and Abby, not to mention, plan ones day according to the position of the stars as interpreted by a stranger if it happens to line up with your expectations. Calls to the Dallas Morning News sometimes but rarely resulted in the redelivery of the missing sections.

There is a family across the street that always seemed a little off. I know, look who's talking. I introduced myself when they moved in. The father seemed confused and just a bit "not right," if not a little unfriendly. I recall, early on, wondering where one of our trash cans had disappeared to. They didn't understand that everyone has their own 2-3 cans and that it isn't a first come, first served situation. The grandma lives with them and has usually been somewhat cordial, though she is a main character in our little drama.

Grandma will sit outside and smoke while their dogs roam free, exploring and fertilizing where they may. My poor dogs regularly lose their shit at the sight of the intruders coming and going where they may. You may know that I have a recording studio in my house. More than a couple of takes have been ruined by the sound of somewhat but not effectively insulated dog howling and barking. More than a few times, I have found dog poop in my driveway or on the sidewalk in front of my house. I'm sure there has also been plenty in the grass that I haven't noticed.

Anyway, without any real evidence, I wondered if the lady across the street had been guilty of "borrowing" parts of my paper. One of the drawbacks of a good imagination is the likelihood of believing ones possible scenarios. Real or not, I came upon a solution for both of my problems.

I shared my idea with my wife, Glenna, and though she advised me to not stir shit up, I did it anyway. I saved the previous week's paper and folded it up neatly. Included was some days-old dog poop from the sidewalk, just barely on my property. In retrospect it should have been the "Business" section. Oh well. I got up early and, picked up the new paper and, substituted the tainted one, and went back to bed. A while later, I was awakened by my not-too-happy spouse. She had gone out to get the paper and was sadly the unintended victim of my revenge. After apologizing very profusely, I hardheadedly reloaded my landmine. I didn't see it happen, but I later saw the paper still in the driveway with some dark matter lying a foot or two away.

The dogs still roam free, occasionally fouling my concrete but my paper has arrived and remained intact for several weeks now. My coffee is still delicious and my astrological guide, when read, is still sometimes coincidentally spot on.

Best Of Kent

Art by Harry Knights

BEST OF KENT SONGLIST W COMMENTARY

Here's a song list in no particular order.

VIRTUAL LOVE: written by my music partner in crime, Bruce McRoberts. A son of passion and possession sung to the user by her computer. I am providing the vocals.

FALLING OUT: by Bruce McRoberts. Performed by Marc Mydill and me. A beautiful, sad song of bad communication. Originally done with Jack B. Quick. Reworked here as a more intimate lament.

ROUND AND ROUND: written about and dedicated to some friends that fought and loved frequently and passionately.

PHANTOM'S THEME: from the movie Phantom Of The Paradise.

Written by Paul Williams. Pretty much my personal theme song.

Instrumentation by Marc Mydill and myself.

CONVOLUTION: started out to be about relationship ended up about EVERYTHING. By me. Instrumentation by Marc Mydill and myself.

THE CONQUEROR WORM: poem by Edgar Allen Poe. Music by me.

Instrumentation by Marc Mydill and myself.

RINGS MEDLEY: words by JRR Tolkien, music by me. I wrote the music in high school and while backpacking through Europe, I attempted to see Professor Tolkien with hopes of playing it for him. Needless to say, without an appointment, the guard at the gate of his estate kindly denied me entrance. He explained that even if he could let me in, that the professor was pretty much living in Middle Earth at that point. Instrumentation by Marc Mydill, David Mills on viola, and myself.

DIE FOR YOU: my sappy 90s rock ballad. It began as a simple chord progression I stumbled on playing with my Roland keyboard back in the late 80s. The sad lyrics that eventually emerged were representative of my mood at the time due to an unfixable romance.

Instrumentation by Marc Mydill and myself.

LUCKY MAN: by Emerson Lake and Palmer. My vocals, Mike Maulsby on guitar. Towards the end you can hear a very out of place noise. While I was attempting to lay down some earnest, heartfelt vocal harmonies, Marc Mydill, who was engineering my part, suddenly squawked in an attempt to throw me off. Wise guy! Before we could fix it, his computer crashed, losing the originals. The only surviving copy immortalized his joke.

THE FEAST: by Bruce McRoberts, performed by our old band Jack B.

Quick: Bruce, Mike Maulsby, Ralph Fahrbach, Jerry Kelley, and me. BIRDS: by Neil Young. I heard a friend perform it in high school. I went backpacking thru Europe that summer and, without ever hearing the original, learned it from memory. Upon returning to the US and hearing the original, realized that I had pretty much rewritten it.

Instrumentation by Marc Mydill and myself.

ANYTHING: By me, inspired by a couple of failed romances. Yes, again! Instrumentation by Marc Mydill and myself.

BLACKWIND: By Bruce, performed by Jack B. Quick again. You could call it environmentalEnviron-metal...

UNCLAIMED CHICAGO was inspired by a sad story of unclaimed bodies of homeless people in Chicago that the city buried identified. Bruce McRoberts read the story and, after getting the author's permission, used the article almost verbatim as the lyrics to this complex, almost baroque electronic piece. Again, I provide only the vocals.

HEADLONG DOWN THE STAIRS: fun song about a serial killer with a basement full of bodies by Ronnie Hall of Lost Souls Inc., with whom I frequently shared a stage. I played it quietly at a wedding reception once. No one was paying attention! "Oh, how pretty!" Instrumentation by Marc Mydill and myself. Max Droz May have played bass guitar.

GOOD FRIEND AND LOVER was a toss-off, almost satirical country song by Hal McDonald. Bruce and I used to perform it, and I eventually added the middle verse and tried (failed) to improve the original lyrics. Hal said, "Do whatever you want with it." I love Marc's production and guitar solo. I dislike my vocals immensely.

Instrumentation by Marc Mydill and myself.

PRETTY EYES: by Jeanne Seidner, a friend from my Austin days. Her audience was largely smitten college guys, and this was one of her standard heart melters. she did it much better than I did. Instrumentation by Marc Mydill and myself.

THE HUNT was a never finished song about my clubbing days as a wild and crazy single guy. It's a better instrumental. Instrumentation by Marc Mydill and myself.

MT NEBO SUNRISE: My favorite soul-cleansing getaway place. On my too infrequent visits, I will sit on the eastern edge of the mountain and serenade the sunrise. I have another piece that I play on the other end of the mountaintop for the sunset. Instrumentation by Marc Mydill and myself.

WANDERING is, in my opinion, the prettiest and saddest song I ever wrote. I will do a better recording someday.

PUNKSTACY is a blatantly sexual rocker. Recorded with Mixcraft. Some guitar work by me. I intended to get Marc to replace most of the guitar parts but fell in love with the working version as it was. CITIFIED Once again, I recorded the basic tracks with Mixcraft. I visualized someone leaning in the doorway to their New York City apartment, watching traffic, drinking coffee, and enjoying a morning cigarette as it begins to rain. I loved the original no guitar version but after sending it off to Marc, suggesting something Santana-ish, I can't hear it without his amazing playing!

STORMBRINGER: It was late eighties, and my friend, Richard Watts, asked me to tag along while he ran an errand out by Lake Lavon, where he kept his boat. He arrived at my house late morning while I was trying out some new music equipment. He asked, "What's up?" I replied, "New toys!" "Let's see!" "O.K.!" So, I turned on my new digital delay, Roland drum machine, and Juno 106 keyboard (which has since bitten the dust) and hit an a minor chord, tapped out a drum rhythm, and I grabbed my flute. I just sort of improvised for a couple of minutes and liked what was happening. It was kind of an ominous tune with a martial, driving beat and the trailing echoes of flute lines and trills, and it impressed us both. With that sound track in my head, we headed out to the lake. I remember that the rain was pounding down in sheets and I do remember Richard's fancy custom van running out of fuel in the middle of nowhere and watching him stomp off in the rain to the beat of the tune in my head to get gas. As I waited in the comfort of the van and with that tune driving and echoing in my brain, I was suddenly startled out of my reverie by a bolt of lightning striking a tree no more than 20 feet away from me! It f—-ing exploded! The images of lightning striking as portrayed in movies or, drawings, or still photography don't do it justice. The explosive thunder was instantaneous and instead of a forked flash of light hitting and vanishing, it instantly appeared at the tree and hovered and writhed for a moment before shattering and fragmenting in the air. The fragments shimmered for a fraction of a second before wriggling off like a fantastic fireworks display! Rich returned a while later, sopping wet with the gas. Upon arriving home, I immediately went to the music room and recreated the music in my head and got it down on my Tascam 4 track. I added some guitar parts and put rain and thunder underneath it all. Thus, the original Stormbringer was born.

Many of my old 4 track experiments have disappeared into the ether. I still have many of the tapes but no means to play them. That particular tune has lived in my head for decades now, and recently, I recreated it with modern technology and hopefully more talent. The flute is unplayable, so I played some of those parts with guitar. I left the room in the first half, actually a separate piece, for Marc to add some magic. Even without Marc so far, I like it. All instruments, with exception of percussion by Mixcraft, by me.

FLOTSAM AND JETSUM

Art Kent Skinner

Yes, I've written a lot of downbeat sad songs. This isn't one of them! I played almost all of the guitar parts and produced this happy anthem with Mixcraft.

SORRY, WRONG GALAXY! Same story as before when I loved the original version just fine until Marc added his guitar work. Can't hear it without it

Skynergy

ETHER WAY begins and ends w some surreal wind sounds. I see a futuristic post-apocalyptic scene with a steampunk road warrior-like couple hiking/ skipping down a highway, happy in spite of the devastation surrounding them.

WACKJOB I picture a lurching cartoon Frankensteinian steampunk beast with one take lazy guitars.

PUNKSTACY is a blatantly sexual rocker. Recorded with Mixcraft. Some guitar work by me. I intended to get Marc to replace most of the guitar parts but fell in love with the working version as it was.

SORRY, WRONG GALAXY! I loved the original version just fine until Marc added his guitar work. Now I can't hear it without t!

JUNKFUNK, I like the catchy, funky, wackawacka rhythm with the clean and sexy Peter Green-like guitar underneath, which gradually takes over towards the end of the song. It's kind of like a fun night ending in seduction.

TRAFFIK I hear a European, perhaps Eastern European city with its chaotic downtown traffic and colorful ethnic mix of people and market sounds and smells.

STORMBRINGER: It was the late eighties, and my friend, Richard Watts, asked me to tag along while he ran an errand out by Lake Lavon, where he kept his boat. He arrived at my house late in the morning while I was trying out some new music equipment. He asked, "What's up?" I replied, "New toys!" "Let's see!" "O.K.!" So, I turned on my new digital delay, Roland drum machine, and Juno 106 keyboard (which has since bitten the dust) and, hit a minor chord, tapped out a drum rhythm, and I grabbed my flute. I just sort of improvised for a couple of minutes and liked what was happening. It was kind of an ominous tune with a martial, driving beat and the trailing echoes of flute lines and trills, and it impressed us both. With that sound track in my head, we headed out to the lake. I remember that the rain was pounding down in sheets and I do remember Richard's fancy custom van running out of fuel in the middle of nowhere and watching him stomp off in the rain to the beat of the tune in my head to get gas. As I waited in the comfort of the van and with that tune driving and echoing in my brain, I was suddenly startled out of my reverie by a bolt of lightning striking a tree no more than 20 feet away from me! It exploded! The images of lightning striking as portrayed in movies or, drawings, or still photography don't do it justice. The explosive thunder was instantaneous and instead of a forked flash of light hitting and vanishing, it instantly appeared at the tree and hovered and writhed for a moment before shattering and fragmenting in the air. The fragments shimmered for a fraction of a second before wriggling off like a fantastic fireworks display! Rich returned a while later, sopping wet with the gas. Upon arriving home, I immediately went to the music room and recreated the music in my head and got it down on my Tascam 4 track. I added some guitar parts and put rain and thunder underneath it all. Thus, the original Stormbringer was born.

Many of my old 4 track experiments have disappeared into the ether. I still have many of the tapes but no means to play them. That particular tune has lived in my head for decades now, and recently, I recreated it with modern technology and hopefully more talent. The flute is unplayable, so I played some of those parts with guitar. I left room in the first half, actually a separate piece, for Marc to add some magic. Even without Marc so far, I like it. All instruments, with exception of percussion by Mixcraft, by me.

STEAMPUNCTUAL he image of a steampunk Noah's Ark seen on a stranger's desktop screensaver fit this wild piece with all it's interlocking and interworking parts.

JAZZERWACKY A free-form piece starting out kinda creepy and jazzy and morphing into more rock with crazy rhythm and scat singing. I picture a bunch of friends, maybe Alice In Wonderland characters, singing around a table. Probably wine and kazoos involved.

TERRORBYTE I had a recurring abstract nightmare as a kid, repetitive alternating scenes of peaceful fields and sudden immersion in a dark stream. There was a large piece of machinery half submerged in the muddy stream and an immense feeling of dread and loss. This captures some of that. I got a good case of the creeps listening to the final version of this.

TRANSAMBIENT: I needed to do something airy and pleasant after TERRORBYTE. I like the multiple layers and the humanizing heartbeat.

BREATHE springs from my Celtic genes (jeans?) A carefree jaunt ending in a secret.

HAGGISAURUS is another Celtic-based rocker. Just a fun mashup. Maybe it could use some AC/DC vocals.

TIPTOE reminds me of the painting "Sunday Afternoon on the Island of La Grand Jatte" by George Seurat, with all of its interacting and non-interacting characters entering and exiting the scene. I picture a puffy gentleman passed by two pretty ladies passing, two little girls skipping and holding hands. A hesitant fellow stops and ponders the scene. Hipster dude enters semi-jiving from another direction. Two old women chat and muse.

ISLANDIA sprang from a rewrite of another of my 80s 4-track instrumentals. It took on a life of its own and only vaguely resembles the original. I see an island with its varied life forms going about their usual routines and beginning to scatter and seek shelter from on oncoming storm.

ICARUS chord progression is from another old piece where I pictured an aerial view of driving around coastal mountain hiways. I also remember being very worried about my mother's first bout with cancer. The new version takes me to my dreams of flying, of soaring high and spiraling back to Earth, hopefully on my own and not like Icarus, who flew too close to the sun! Version one is all me except the percussion. Version two has Mike Maulsby adding soaring and dramatic lead guitar tracks. I love them both!

SAXUAL MISCONDUCT Catchy drums lead to a tentative, unsure feel. Sax enters, coaxing and seducing, eventually having its way with the music.

CITIFIED Once again, I recorded the basic tracks with Mixcraft. I visualized someone leaning in the doorway to their New York City apartment, watching traffic, drinking coffee, and enjoying a morning cigarette as it begins to rain. I loved the original no guitar version but after sending it off to Marc, suggesting something Santana-ish, I can't hear it without his amazing playing!

FIRST FLIGHT was my first piece using Mixcraft. I tried to capture the chaos and craziness of an airport.

MARTIAL BLISS Very War Of The Worlds inspired. Peaceful nature sounds suddenly interrupted by punishing futuristic war music, only to be followed by nature emerging victorious!

KENT SKINNER'S STORIES BARES ALL

Tequila Mockingbird

Back in college, briefly sharing an apartment with Delton Childress, my ex-next-door neighbor from The Brownlea apartments (a whole bunch of stories already told here), while watching tv, I found myself unconsciously rubbing the base of my right index finger where a wart had decided to present its small but annoying face on the seam of my jeans. Before I realized it, I had rubbed it raw, and it was bleeding slightly.

Being a poor college student, I had no first aid kit available, so I went to the kitchen and found the only antiseptic liquid in the apartment, a bottle of Jose Cuervo tequila! I dabbed a bit on my tiny amputation site and suffered through the burn. Then I thought of salt to maybe cauterize the wound, as I'd seen in a Civil War movie. I bit down on a leather strap and....o.k., there was no strap, but I would have if I had had one. I went to bed. I typically sleep with one hand under my pillow, and all night, I kept hearing this tiny voice asking.....

"Where's the lime??"

Ok. It's all true except the last part! At least the wart went away, which I totally understand, having dabbed myself with tequila more than I care to remember. You see, you do one shot, lick the salt, bite the lime, kiss the woman, etc., once, and you think, "a well, that was good! Hey barkeep! Let's have another!" And...another! The thing is, the first one hasn't really hit you yet, and you have two more waiting in the wings, ready to kick your ass!

John Paul Dejoria, CEO of Paul Mitchell and Patron Tequila, once said after doing 2 handstand push-ups on stage at a celebration for several Paul Mitchell Associates, including me, having attained the rank of Senior Associate being held at the House Of Blues (in which he also was a partner) "I'm not encouraging you to drink, but if you do, DRINK THE GOOD STUFF and follow it with 2 ounces of water for every ounce of alcohol because the reason you feel bad the next morning is that you are dehydrated!"

I understood but didn't listen. In my celebratory state, I asked a pretty redhead to dance, which led to a couple of shots of Patron and a couple more dances. "Iiiimm married," she slurred. " That's cool. I'm only dancing!" I responded, quoting David Bowie. After a third shot, I pulled my famous disappearing act to the upstairs bathroom to hide in the handicapped stall to sober up somewhat. "Thiiis izzz nice! I could ssssstay hear a whiiiile.!" I did and eventually slipped out and caught a cab back to my hotel, where my buddy and roommate for the night, Max Droz, held my hair out of the toilet as I had done for him on a previous occasion. I hadn't paid heed to John Paul's sage hydration advice.

The next morning at our training, I dragged in a few minutes late and was called on immediately by Tommy Callahan (VP in charge of education for JPMS) to answer a question in front of a hundred of my peers. I don't recall the question or my answer, but it was apparently inadequate. Lesson learned.

My red headed dance partner was nowhere to be seen. I heard later that hotel security had found her asleep in the bushes. I saw her briefly at lunchtime, looking a bit green around the gills. I know that she had ignored the 2 ounces of water advice, too. I never saw her again. Did you ever read or see Kurt Vonnegut's "Slaughterhouse 5" where Billy Pilgrim is unstuck in time and lives his life in random order? That is what this story looks like. I think I'll keep it that way.

Another barely remembered, if not memorable, tequila story...and you'd think that there should only be one, was one Halloween while still in college at U.T. Austin, I attended a friend's birthday party (if being unconscious in a bathroom for an hour counts as attending). I only recall doing one shot of tequila, but that would award me the title of "Lightweight," so there must have been more involved. When I woke up with my head on my arm, kneeling before the porcelain alter, I realized that my arm was asleep. I assumed incorrectly that it would wake up sooner than I had. It didn't. Six weeks and several ultrasound treatments later, it went into the agonizing pins and needles phase, which lasted another 2 weeks or so before eventually returning to normal. There was no guarantee that it would. It did, though, for a while. Being limp-wristed really put a damper on my foosball game and my guitar skills.

The first time I ever drank tequila was with my buddy Vaughn and his eventual wife, Michelle. We had shared a cool old apartment in Oak Lawn when it's reputation was being "the hippie part of town." long before its current status. I got the bedroom, and they had a leaky king-sized waterbed with no frame in the living room. I'm reminded that this story took place at their next apartment in Lake Highlands. We sat on the floor and took turns with the salt/shot/lime ritual and did a fair amount of damage to the bottle of Cuervo. Yes, before the night was over, I found myself in the bathroom spinning on the toilet (you're welcome for that image), calling for Michelle to bring me a wastebasket. She declined, thinking that I was going to crap in it. I won't swear that these are the only lessons I should have learned the first time. Sometimes, it takes a few awful mornings after, wet ponytails or loss of limbs to get it.

Toby Or Not Toby

I've worked with a lot of interesting people in my life, particularly during my time with Paul Mitchell The Schools. Some I didn't see eye to eye with and still loved and respected, and some not so much. While I was there, I strove to make it a fun place and was, I confess, responsible for more than a few practical (and some not) jokes.

I found a realistic 7-foot rubber snake at JoyToy in Austin. I got to work early and rigged a system of hooks and fishing lines that would make the snake uncoil and lunge toward the door of the staff bathroom. I was politely asked to not do that again by a very pregnant employee. "So, Timmy! Tell us the story again of how you were born in a bathroom 3 weeks early!

"Well...."

I used to get new hair products to try out and give feedback on from Paul Mitchell. One day, the owner of the school had just gotten his hair cut. He picked up a jar of slime, you know, the kid stuff, with a blank label that had appeared on the station. He dipped in and rubbed it into his hair. "I don't think I like this!" He said. Not a happy owner.

There was/is a...I don't know what to call him..facility coordinator? Anything involving maintenance, construction, and repair was his responsibility. Handyman doesn't do him justice. Anyway, I found a large washer, a three-inch metal disc with a hole in the center. I then googled lederhosen and printed out a picture of a jolly German man in leather shorts. I cut it out and glued it to the disc. When I told him that the washer was on the Fritz and let him get all the way to the laundry room before handing him my little token of joy, he responded, " Actually, the fritz is on the washer!" Technicalities.

They got me sometimes. Students jumped at me out of lockers, the clothes dryer, etc. It was a fun place to work for a long time until it wasn't.

The best one was an act of revenge. There was a cocky little —— I'll name Toby. Toby Green. He was a teacher but had never worked in a salon. He fancied himself to be a rapper and producer, having grown up in the poverty-stricken streets of Frisco, Texas. (For the unaware, there ain't nothin' poverty about Frisco.) I'll admit that 90 percent of the time, I liked him, but to me, he looked like a hip-hop wannabe young Woody Allen. I guess it worked some of the time because he was eventually let go for "fraternizing" with a couple of young, pretty students. Anyway, he had started working out and imagined himself a lot more macho than he was. (remember Woody Allen) he happened to come around the corner at the same time I was going the opposite direction. He bumped into me and said snidely, "Watch out, Santa Claus!" I thought, "You little ——..." Revenge is a dish best served cold. The next day was the first day of his vacation. Cold enough. Heh heh heh...

There were two phones in the teacher's office. One was for the Cosmetology department, and the other one was for the Esthetics teachers. The Esthetics teachers never used it, and its number was unknown to us. "Someone" used it to leave a message on the Cosmo line.

Altering their voice's pitch and ethnicity as best they could, said "Yessss, this is Lawanda Jackson. I need to speak with a Toby...Toby Green. See, he's my daughter's baby daddy, and since he's running' that place (he wasn't), he can afford to help my daughter out. See, my daughter only have one leg, and she need an attachment for her wheelchair to pull the baby buggy. Please have him call me as soon as possible!!" Someone heard the message that afternoon, and it went viral. Several people asked me if it was me, and I flat-out denied it and asked to hear it. It sounded nothing like me. I should play more poker. "Toby" was gone for the rest of the week, leaving the story to ripen and fester. When he returned, he was baffled. "I don't know anything about this!" I believe that he had to have figured out who was responsible but couldn't prove anything. The recording mysteriously disappeared. He never spoke of it to me, nor should he have.

I didn't just wink. It was a twitch.

Acts Of Dog

Well, I've written about many milestones in my life ways to identify time frames. I've written about friendships, houses, jobs, cars and guitars. Hopefully, my attempts to link up the segments of my life have been entertaining to you, the reader, as they have been useful and therapeutic to me. This story is about the many fur babies I have lived with mixed in with a couple of non fur bearing babies. You'll laugh! You'll cry!! You'll ask yourself, "Why did he think this would be interesting??" Hopefully not. "Asking" not the "interesting" part.

Every day on Facebook, I read of someone's dear companion "crossing the rainbow bridge". I think it may be a Norse mythology reference. Thanks, Thor. I feel for their loss, and I know that when the time comes that my big girl passes that, I will also receive both genuine and obligatory condolences. The first few pets I recall are a blur. I remember two sequential Cocker Spaniels, both named.

Taffy, I think. I don't know why a new name wasn't offered Taffy #2. According to my sister, Taffy 2 was a bad momma. She would have a litter of puppies and abandon them, usually ending up at the dog pound. This happened several times with fines. Finally, she was found by an old guy who raved about how pretty she was. She went home with him. The last we heard of her was when he called and said she had had a litter of puppies and disappeared. He was advised to check the pound. I think they were followed by another Cocker named Blackjack and a Beagle named Lady. I have no memory of their personalities. During that same time period, there were two cats named Pedro and Pancho, a grey tabby and an orange one. Pancho got smacked by a car early on, but Pedro stuck around for many years. When we moved from Ohio to Burlington, Massachusetts, my mother fell in love with a baby Boston Terrier, and we named him Button. I think it was inspired by his little black nose. Actually, his full name was "Sir Button of Burlington." Within a year or two, he gained a companion, another Boston named "Skinner's own Candy Barr" (after the famous stripper) or just Candy. We had Ratan furniture with open backed seat frames, and Button and Candy would crawl underneath and hang out while my parents watched tv. They got used to hearing the Dallas news come on at 10 and would jingle and crawl out from under the chairs and make for the patio door. They would respond to my fathers commanding, "OUTside!!" Another key word was "Go." they'd be dancing at the side door in a flash. They were trained to not go in the formal living room or our bedrooms. Occasionally we'd hear the jingle of tags sneaking down the hall, and then they would haul ass back down the hall when busted or occasionally leaving a tootsie roll-like offering when not. While they were both friendly and affectionate with us, they didn't put up with rowdiness or horseplay. Like me falling out of a tree and being carried by my sister Carolyn's boyfriend and now husband, Allen. In addition to hurting and having the wind knocked out of me, I also suffered elongated bite marks from two Boston Terriers dangling from my back and ankles. Too much tomfoolery!!

Another vivid memory is of Button getting "amorous" with Prissy, a full-blooded Brittany Spaniel that we had briefly. Picture a medium-large red and white hunting dog running around the back yard with a small black and white bug-eyed, tongue-wagging Romeo attached to her from behind. Every four or five of her steps, one of his feet might touch the ground. upon witnessing this breach in purebred breeding protocol, my mom flew out to intercept with the garden hose and improvised a Summer's Eve intervention. Yes, that's what I mean. I don't know if Candy was aware of his indiscretion. I never told her.

A serendipitous happenstance added years to Button's life, according to our veterinarian. A playground ball found its way into our back yard. We would marvel and be entertained watching Button mount the ball with his front legs and run backwards around the yard! I remember the ball being pretty nasty. I just didn't know why. Until much later.

"......Ooohhhhhh!" Things you realize much later. The vet said that it was the best thing that ever happened to him. Again, Candy was oblivious or perhaps silently grateful.

They moved with my mother to San Antonio after my father's death, where they grew old together and, like many elderly soul mates, died within a few weeks of each other. In the mean time, I was given a puppy by my girlfriend, Carol. She was at least part Cocker, Beagle, and maybe Golden Retriever. I named her Alabaster after her hair color, which almost perfectly matched my own. Unlike my girlfriend and I, we were inseparable, which cost me a couple of living arrangements. We went through times of hardship and poverty together, often sharing a cheap bag of lunch meat for our daily sustenance. I've written of her before of how she would wait for me outside the buildings at U.T. Austin while I was in class and how she had more friends on Campus than I did. Someone crocheted her denim bandana, which went missing for a couple of days, only to return to her neck with her initial boldly displayed. I never learned who was responsible. I got picked up while hitchhiking to Dallas more than a couple of times because the driver recognized her! Once, while waiting outside of the auditorium where she was taking a music history class, she began to howl and bark whenever the instructor started playing the piano. Embarrassed, I went outside and scolded her. "Hush!! I'll make a hat out of you!!" I returned to peals of laughter. The whole auditorium had heard my threat. Another time, during a winter rain, I had left her in the foyer and told her to "Stay!" I was in a painting class on the 5th floor, and she came running into the classroom excited that she had found me. I picture her going down the hall of each floor, poking her head into every classroom, looking for her daddy!

I'm pretty sure she was poisoned by my landlord at The Big House on NW Highway and Inwood, another story.

I tried to fill her place with another puppy, this time a golden retriever I named Saffron. I only had her a couple of weeks when she got out and was hit by a car. I was soon given a little black puppy, believing it to be a lab mix. I named her Sombra, or shadow in Spanish. If she was a Lab mix, the other half was toy poodle. I left her for a few minutes in my unlocked van (yes, I know now), and she disappeared. I saw her a few days later in a nearby yard playing with a bunch of kids and decided that she would be happier there than with me. (And then there was that poodle bit...)

After living in the Coop for a couple of years and moving into the house on 6th Street, we called "The Set," I acquired another Golden Retriever. I called her Bessie, which was short for Besame Mucho or "Kiss me a lot," which she did. I'd leave her on the semi spacious screened in back porch while I was at school. We had not formed the inseparable bond through isolation and starvation that Alabaster and I had, so taking her to school with me wasn't an option. Also. I was taking the bus to campus. She broke out one time and was picked up by Animal Control. As I passed many cages with sad but hopeful-looking doggos praying that I was there to save them, I heard the unmistakeable cry of "HEY!! HEY!! HERE I AM DADDY!!! I'M HERE!! SAVE ME!!!" except in Dogglish. We went home, and I secured the porch again. When she had her first and maybe only heat, a little brown rat-looking terrier managed to get in by propelling himself through the screen of the porch. She wasn't impressed. He, however, could not get a long enough running start to escape, so he had to hang out in the corner until I got home. He was gone like a bullet. The only other Golden in the neighborhood did manage to get lucky. She had a litter of pretty little gold puppies that all found good homes. I decided to move back to Dallas and pursue my career there. My housemate Mike Williams had friends living on a farm that really wanted her so with my future living situation unclear, I sadly gave her up. I had no business owning dogs since none had been around long enough to challenge the Alabaster connection.

I moved back to Dallas and didn't take on any pet responsibility until I got involved with a cat person. We had at various times a calico Manx that was apparently pregnant and vanished to have her babies. Then we got a white kitten and a tortoise shell kitten at the pound. Tragically, the tortoise shell kitty crawled into bed with us and got smothered. It was awful. The white one, "Peru" (as in flake) grew up being called "Fuffawhite" but escaped from my friend's back yard while we were out of town. He thought the fence would keep him in. He got turned in to the pound. We were too late to bail him out. They didn't keep cats around more than 3 days. Another one bites the dust. It has been said that you have to go through a few cats (and women) before one sticks. Merc was a Russian Blue and he hung around for a while before disappearing. He would wrap around my neck and let me carry him around the house like a heavy fur scarf. Mikey (short for MyKitty) was an orange Tabby with a big "M" on his forehead. He and I had had a good relationship. That relationship was ended by someone driving too fast down Brand Road thinking he was out in the countryside. I guess. Grrr. Enough sad cat stories.

I'm allergic to them now as is my daughter, Savannah. Cats, that is. Not the stories. I guess I could have thrown in a couple of other brief dalliances with nature during my childhood and adolescence. Sparky, the hamster, had the nerve to expire on my watch. Who would have thought that not feeding him for three days would lead to such tragedy? "Ooo, that smell! Can't you smell that smell?" I wonder if I inspired that Lynard Skynard song. Probably. They were always hanging around begging for ideas.

I wasn't the weird kid in class (yeah right) but one day the #1 weird kid brought some baby opossums to school. I took one home and tried to domesticate it. Nope. Ugly bastard bit me or tried every time I was close enough. I had imagined walking him downtown on a leash. Me and my possum Opie! That didn't happen. I figured out later that my folks had pulled the old "He must have gotten out of his cage" routine. Oh well, at least I still have all of my fingers. BTW, Opossums eat ticks and don't get rabies. Opossums are your friends. Ugly friends. Mean friends. But they eat ticks. And fingers.

I may be responsible for the demise of the last horned toad lizard in Texas. I have not seen one since this one. I tied a string loosely around his neck before going to school. He tried to escape by going straight away from where the string was anchored. Horned toads may not be bright enough to realize that just chilling or going backwards would loosen the tension on the string. When I got home he was standing on his hind legs with the string taut. Then there was the pet salamander. "Is that a piece of jerky on the bathroom floor?" No, it was Sir Issac Newton having escaped his fishbowl via the branch sticking out of the water. Sorry Issac, no reentry without paying the cover.

Y'know, all of my life I have considered myself an animal lover and have never deliberately taken a life. Reflecting here, I am beginning to feel like the Son Of Sam of the animal kingdom. Anyway, I mercifully let up on my contribution to natural selection for a while after the cats and cat lady went away. I eventually accepted a Chow/Shepard mix puppy from my next door neighbor's daughter. Seemed like a good way to get to know her. Didn't work. "Charlie" became "Bananahead." I actually loved the name Soleil, French for "the sun" which I hoped to name a daughter some day. It didn't stick. When I came home every day, she'd go bananas and I'd yell "Bananahead!!" so that became her name. I did, in fact eventually name my daughter Savannah Soleil Skinner.

There was a short lived residency by a hamster named Mr Yamster by my girlfriend at the time. He lived in a fishbowl with a spaghetti strainer that happened to fit on top so he had a distorted view of the world. Bananahead would sit and stare at him without any obvious desire or malice. We decided to introduce them once, I held Mr Yamster carefully and brought them face to face. Bananahead lunged faster than I had ever seen her move and instantly all one could see were two little kicking legs sticking out of her mouth! I quickly grabbed her jaws and retrieved a very startled Mr Yamster from certain death. Oh yeah. To a dog, anything smaller than your head is potential food.

Bananahead was very sweet but not too bright. She never got the gist of "Fetch." I'd throw something and she'd go sniff it and ask "Why? That's not food!" We lived above a creek w it's an unobstructed view....until someone built a two story house inn the way. Grr. Bananahead loved the water and constantly rowed under the fence to go swim and explore. She also met her baby daddy in the invading neighbor's yard. He never paid child support. Bananahead begat "Thud" and "Squirt." Thud was named such because of her brawny shoulders and her tendency to knock things over and bust out of fences. "Screw burrowing. I'm bustin' outa here!" She would literally bust through fence boards to get out. I could not pet three demanding dogs simultaneously so I blessed my friend Richard with Thud. She eventually disappeared after busting through Richard's fence several times. She would occasionally show up with a herd of puppies and he'd welcome her home only to have her bust out again. She was a free spirit and would not be contained. She eventually stopped coming around. One day, sitting in my vet's waiting room i was leafing through a photo album on the table. There was a picture of a dog that looked just like Thud. I asked the girl at the desk if she knew who's dog it was. She replied "He's right here behind the counter!" Thud Jr stood up and it was amazing! He looked just like his momma! She said someone had brought in a litter of puppies found at a park under a tree. The momma had escaped capture. I know she's long gone now but I know that she led a life of freedom and adventure..and promiscuity!

As for Thud's sister Squirt (Squirty), you can imagine how she got her name. She was sweet and needy and lived to be 14 years old as did her momma. Bananahead slipped away in her sleep in my house in Garland. I had her cremated and I scattered her ashes in her beloved creek below our neighbors house. Squirt moved with Glenna and me to Wylie with a short stay at Glenna's mom's house where we lived while our house was being built and Savannah was being born.

Squirty stayed over our good friends Bruce and Pam's house while we were at the hospital having Savannah. She must have inherited some of the genes that drove Thud to playing Houdini. She broke out right away. They lived on the edge of the countryside that now surrounds the Bush toll road so she had a huge area to explore. Every day they and we would drive around yelling "Squirt!! Squirty!!" I'm sure the neighbors had questions. After 3 days of this, sleeping at driving to and from Medical city to Garland I had a good idea. After 3 days, my shirt smelled an awful lot like me so I tied it to their fence. Upon coming home with the new girl in my life, the McRoberts showed up at grandma's house with our sweet Squirty! She had smelled me from afar and found her way back to their house! I had been simultaneously celebrating the birth of my daughter and lamenting the loss of my doggie daughter. All was well and she lived a good life. A few years later after bringing her home from a groomer, she didn't seem right. I asked if they had sedated her and they denied it. A couple of days later she passed while I was out of town working. Glenna took care of her and we had her cremated. Again, I spread her ashes in her and Bananahead's beloved creek. As I scattered them in the water, I heard jingling like the sound of dog tags approaching. I believe she and her momma and maybe Thud are forever romping in their eternal swimming hole.

I (perhaps fortunately for them) had nothing to do with the acquisition or naming of our current furry housemates. I was out of town again when Glenna was told of a young yellow Lab that was being disowned, having unwrapped some Christmas presents without permission. Her name was "Susie" but I came home to a happy young doggie renamed "Sunny" for her disposition. My being gone a lot, we had discussed getting a dog again for security and company. Young Labs are known for their good nature and for chewing and tearing stuff up. You must accept that you will lose some things if you decide to own one. For example, my glasses. Sunny is the smartest and most communicative dog I've ever known. She expresses herself vocally, if not verbally, very well. If her squirrel friend is out there, she'll cry, "OOOoooooOO!!!" We have come to realize that she has an arrangement with the squirrel. She will let him strip our pecan tree bare if he will let her pretend she rules the yard. They have come face to face without any drama or bloodshed.

They have sort of a laissez-faire arrangement. They let each other look good when being watched.

Sunny also has a rare talent that few have witnessed. She can walk on her hind legs like a little dog does when she wants to see what is on the counter or table. She got busted eating our fish, standing on the table. Even after being scolded, a few minutes later she was back on the table. This is a full grown Labrador Retriever! On our dinner table! The other night I foolishly walked away from my plate of Mexican food for a minute and returned to see her nibbling gently on the side of my grilled avocado. "If I just take a little from the side, maybe he wont notice!" I yelled "NOOO!!! BAD GIRL!!" She looked shocked and hurt! "Well YOU left it on the coffee table so I thought it was fair game!" She stared at me with that sad hurt look. I felt bad for days. She says volumes with her eyes and eyebrows. And her head in your lap. And her wet nose on your elbow. And her drool on your pants leg.

I have a long faint scar on my forehead from a bramble that caught me in the face while I was chasing her through the woods by our house. Yes, she gets cabin fever and as a younger dog, she loved to bolt out of the house at any opportunity. One time she ran by the basketball courts. I pursued and after catching her, returning her home, grabbing my bags and heading out of town for work, a couple of young men showed up at our door. One of them claimed that she had chased him and he had lost his iPod (not true). Glenna asked "Well what do you expect me to do about it?" He wanted her to pay him. She declined and suggested calling the police and they left. As a result, we soon followed our kids into Karate, so Sunny could be indirectly responsible for Glenna's four World Champion trophies and my State and District titles!

One day, sunny's perfect world was disrupted when she unwillingly got another room mate. Glenna's mother, Delia, decided that she wanted a Chihuahua. It had to be male, fixed, and housebroken. Right. It seemed like a good idea at the time, her being 86 and living alone. Glenna went to the Wylie animal shelter and brought home a young fixed male named Bruiser, that was supposedly housebroken. Right. The only broken thing about him was his left front leg. It was broken and went unset while he was apparently living on the street for a while. Delia renamed him "Pepe." That morphed into "PuttPutt" later. Funny how that happens. You just don't always know what they are like when you first name them. "Demon Spawn" has probably been taken. Life with Grandma Delia lasted 2 weeks before she announced, "This is not going to work! I think he has gender issues!" I assumed that she was referring to his having to squat when he peed since he couldn't lift his hind leg without tipping over. No, she was correct in that he did not like men. At all. The first time he was handed to me, he nearly took my finger off. So, PuttPutt moved to Wylie rather than go back to the pound and to certainly be put down. Who wants a broken Chihuahua? As soon as he moved in, he made our dining room his cat box. Thousands of dollars later, we have beautiful stained concrete downstairs. I also own a carpet cleaner for upstairs. He, like lots of small beings, believes he is bigger than he is, and he doesn't like disturbances in the force or whatever his status quo is. If I get home or someone knocks or a bee farts or.....ANYTHING!! He barks himself hoarse. We have finally made peace, though. I discovered that we have a mutual taste in beer. I'll dip the fingers of my right hand one at a time in my Real Ale Devil's Backbone and let him lick them off. No double dipping. I'm not fond of Chihuahua saliva chasers. After 5 fingers, I'll cut him off. It mellows him out just fine. These days, he won't go outside to pee in the morning until I bend down and pet him. He's got me trained. He and Sunny get along fine outside. Not so much indoors where the possibility of food or affection exists. Sunny will come scratch at the door and stand there waiting for him to come out and pee. She then has to re-mark "her" territory. She is, in fact, Queen Dog of Skinnerville. She is around 12 years old now and hopefully has a few more good years in her. As hard as it was losing Alabaster, Bananahead, Squirty, and all or at least a few of their fellow interlopers when Sunny joins them across that Rainbow Bridge, I know she'll be in good company. I will be devastated, and worse, I'll still be stuck with this mean little —— of a Chihuahua!

Update: Sunny made it to 17 years. Unheard of for most large dogs. It was extremely hard on this family.

That reminds me of the story of two guys walking their dogs. The German Shepard's owner says, "Whew! It's hot! Whaddya say we pop into Louey's for a beer?" The other guy says, "They won't let us in with these dogs!" "It's cool! Follow my lead!" He starts to enter Louey's, and the bartender says, "Hey! You can't bring that dog in here!" He replies, "But this is my guide dog!" The bartender says, "Oh, I'm sorry, I didn't realize! Come on in!" The other guy starts to follow, but the bartender stops him. "Sorry! You can't bring that dog in here!" The other guy says," But I'm blind, too! This is my guide dog!" The bartender retorts, "They don't use Chihuahuas for Guide dogs!" Guy#2 exclaims " THEY GAVE ME A F—ING CHIHUAHUA???"

The Special Shampoo

Another early pre Rembrandt/Hair Odyssey story. Maybe a repeat.

There was a newspaper article concerning some local stylist that was arrested for offering his upscale female clients a service that he called "the SPECIAL shampoo." This was a source of some amusement. The owner of our salon at the time was Richard Watts and that day he had a lady client in the shampoo bowl that he knew well and also knew was a good sport. He asked her if she wanted "the SPECIAL shampoo" and she said "Sure." To her surprise and amusement, he climbed up onto the shampoo chair straddling her and began to shampoo her. Laughter ensued. Again, another stylist who will remain nameless unless he responds thought this was pretty funny and tried it on his next guest. "You want the "SPECIAL shampoo?" he asked. "I guess so," she replied. He too mounted the chair. Laughter did not ensue. Screaming did.

She was a first time client. He didn't work there much longer.

Date From Hell 2

Set the Wayback Machine to mid to late 90s again. Back when I was a single (in Steve Martin's voice) a "wild and crazy guy," I was in my early makin' the scene in Deep Ellum phase, when Deep Ellum WAS a scene. I met a tall, pretty girl at a friend's party That I'll call...Emily, not to protect the innocent, but because I have no recollection of her real name. Please don't let her name actually be Emily. Emily was a professional working actress. I only spoke with her briefly at the party but managed to get her number. That's probably best. I shouldn't have been talking to anyone. My friends and I left early and continued a night of legendary debauchery. Deep Ellum was known for its artistic crowd often attired in black so I usually wore all white to stand out from the crowd.. except for my black hipster "cowboy" boots. I use parentheses because a real cowboy would not have been caught dead on them, silver toes and all. They had seen much better days, their soles repaired multiple times with cardboard and duct tape inserts. Anyway, I called Emily and set a date. I picked her up at her apartment in my pretty silver Saab which I've mentioned in a previous story or two. Nice car....except that my reverse gear had gone out and I couldn't afford to fix it. Saab story. Therefore if forced to park in a head in parking place, I had to put it in neutral, push it back, jump in and brake before proceeding. Picture me, blonde hair down my back, white outfit and black "cowboy" boots, shifting, pushing, jumping, braking and proceeding as if nothing were unusual.

I think we went to the Art Bar, a coffee shop/bar on Congress directly behind and connected inside to Club Clearview. We had a couple of drinks and chatted about lots of things. My biggest mistake, besides my outfit and a car I couldn't maintain was to pontificate and share my shallow thoughts on the fine art of Acting. My acting experience was limited to having been in a high school musical and senior play. Oh, and 1 semester of Drama in college, but I had OPINIONS! I spoke of noticing times when it appeared to me that the actor didn't quite get the author's intention, maybe because of an awkward phrasing or expression. She argued that the actors interpretation was at least as important as the authors mere words.

I also predicted that Michael J Fox would be looked back on as one of the finest actors of his generation!.... Big sigh. Well, he was really good in Back to the Futures 1-4!

I didn't convince her or maybe even myself on either point. When the conversation dried up, I drove her home in the pounding rain, at least I had parallel parked and didn't have to shift, push, jump, and brake this time. We arrived at her apartment, and we made a mad dash for her building. I walked her upstairs, said good night, and got a passionate "sideways hug." Ok, well, a hug.

I walked outside and immediately dropped my keys in an ankle deep puddle. The rain had not let up the least bit. Fortunately, these were standard manual keys, not electronic. I fished around for a couple of minutes, my cardboard and duct tape repair job boots taking in the maximum volume of water possible. Did I mention that it was probably 40 degrees out? I prayed that she wasn't watching from her warm, dry upstairs apartment. I found the damned keys and plodded squishing and splashing out to my car. My nifty white outfit and down my back blonde hair were drenched, matching my mood perfectly.

I got to my car, shifted, pushed, jumped, cranked the heat to MAX and proceeded to my warm, dry house in Garland.

I think I drove home in just my underwear.

Life story in a nutshell for High School Reunion Newsletter

Well... 2 days after we all graduated from WTW, I was in merry old England for a couple of weeks and then in Europe for 2 months where I made some lifelong friends, went to the beach with Miss Portugal, had lunch with Major Knut Haugland, famed WW2 resistance fighter and explorer on the Kon Tiki, discovered my Scottish roots, experienced world opinion of the U.S. and found my lifelong love of good beer. Upon my return, I attended Eastfield College and then U.T. Austin studying Commercial Art, something I fell quickly out of love with. I worked on and off for YMCA Urban Services running a tutoring program and a summer camp. I had way more responsibility than I was responsible enough for!

I finished my degree at U.T. standing there on the edge of my future, knowing I didn't want to do commercial art, (I was destined for Rock Stardom you know..)I was notified that I had 9 months of money available from the V.A. My best friend, Vaughn Stockton had quit college and was making a good living as a hairstylist with Vidal Sassoon and was supporting his family comfortably. At that time it took 9 months to complete hair school if you went full time, I figured I'd have 9 months of income while I worked on becoming a rock star! During that 9 months, I met Paul Mitchell long before there was a product line. I began to think that maybe this hair thing wasn't so bad it was certainly a great way to meet women! I eventually became a Paul Mitchell Associate and National Educator. I loved traveling and doing shows and classes for a couple of decades. I owned a successful salon for many years.

After a few long and short term relationships I married one of my favorite clients of 17 years, a lovely Physical Therapist by the name of Glenna. Glenna was also a state and national powerlifting champion. She had her own cable network workout show and I had always had a thing for her. She showed up to one of my music gigs without a boyfriend or tagalong friend one night and I kissed her and said "We should talk." A couple of weeks later she called and asked " Are you ready to talk?" We did.

We have an 18-year-old daughter, Savannah, and a 16-year-old son, Zane. We got them into Tae Kwon Do as kids, and they both had their 1st degree in Black Belts before Glenna and I decided to sign up. We both enjoyed competing in state, national, and world tournaments.

Glenna has 4 world titles. I have some State and District (4 states) Champion titles and placed 9th at Worlds.

I still play and produce music. When Shawn Phillips comes to town I get to open for him. We have become good friends. I also opened for Robert Fripp of King Crimson. I have become friends with and shared both music and hair show stages with most of my heroes. I have learned from the greatest. I should also be much better than I am.

Jobs I have held and/or lost:

- Bus Boy
- Snack Bar Attendant
- Warehouse worker
- Magician
- YMCA Camp Kiwanis Camp Counselor/ Bus Driver, Assistant Director/ Director
- YMCA Tutor Program Director
- Commercial and creative artist
- Hairstylist/Salon owner Rembrandt The Salon & Kent Skinner Hair Photographer
- Paul Mitchell National Educator/ Senior Associate/Task Force member
- Artistic Director for Seventeen Spa/Salon
- Education Director for Paul Mitchell The School Dallas

- Paul Mitchell Advanced Academy Haircutting Team (responsible for PM Cutting System, training and certifying teachers in 100+ schools)
- Author
- Owner of Kent Skinner Education
- Part-time stylist; retired.....sort of.

Tommy

"Is life so dear or peace so sweet, as to be purchased at the price of chains and slavery? Forbid it Almighty God! I know not what course others may take; but as for me, give me liberty or give me death!"

I had heard of Tommy Callahan, the legends and horror stories of this intimidating man who did not suffer fools gladly, that held exceptionally high standards and was the last person you wanted to certify in front of, but this was the first time I had seen him in action. He had opened his presentation with this speech by Patrick Henry. There wasn't a dry eye in the house. I sat in a crowd of Paul Mitchell Associates with chills running up and down our spines, not just from the words we had just heard but from the power of the presenter. He then continued his presentation on…presentation skills. He gave a brief introduction of what he'd be sharing and then asked us to suggest a topic for a five-minute speech. Someone pointed at the decorative potted tree at the side of the stage. Tommy turned around, plotted silently for maybe two minutes, turned back, and gave a fascinating five-minute speech about the tree. It was amazing. I learned more about presenting in that brief workshop than I had in all my previous years of being an educator. I introduced myself and awkwardly complimented him on the class. For a long time, that was a common feeling for me when I was around him. Over the years, the occasional nod of approval, comment, or compliment from him were very meaningful because I knew that he was a straight-shooting, no b.s. Kind of guy.

One winter at one our Art and Business trainings in Denver I found myself having to present to him. It was not one of my best presentations. Fortunately the following week in Atlanta, I again found myself presenting the same material to him. This time however, using the coaching he had given me the previous week, things went much better and he told me so. That meant a lot to me. As I donned my long yellow leather trench coat he said "That is a beautiful coat! Is it a _____?" I don't recall the brand he mentioned and I honestly had no idea if it was. It wasn't. I found it on a sale rack in a store near the Mexican border. I often receive compliments on it.

Tommy is one of those people that I don't like saying "I don't know".

Later that day I was walking through the lobby of the hotel wearing my famous coat and Tommy said "Hey! A few of us are going to get some barbecue later. Want to join us?" Was he kidding me? Of course I wanted to join them! I dragged Max Droz, a fairly new Associate along. I don't remember for sure who all was there but I think that Tony Promiscuo, Memphis, Shannon "Bugsy" Hyde, Wayne Bishop and Nick Ortega were there. It was quite an experience to hear their war stories and talk of legends. Hell, to us, these guys were legends themselves! I learned of

Tommy's escape from addiction, his faith and healing and many personal stories and interactions with the greats. Later, we all went to Bugsy's salon and got an up close haircutting demonstration by Tommy and Bugsy. It was greatness in action.

Though Tommy enjoyed his whiskey, he strongly encouraged us to limit our alcoholic intake to two drinks the evenings before our trainings. It was good advice though I took guilty pleasure in buying him a third glass of Makers Mark one night. One hard morning when I had not obeyed that 2 drink directive (we had celebrated our new Senior Associate status at the House of Blues the night before), I walked in to our training a few minutes late, thankful that the auditorium was dark. Still, Tommy saw me and called on me to explain the value of the Color Bar. I improvised some answer. Tommy didn't comment. Sometimes, not saying anything says the most. He immediately called on someone else who recited the official version. On one of his many birthdays, I gave him a pendant that I designed decades ago and have given to friends and mentors over the years. It's a sterling silver smiling baby's face, at least the nose and mouth. It was my way of FACEing him. (FACE= Find, Acknowledge, Celebrate, Enjoy} I don't know if he ever wore it, but I only give them to very special people, and he deserved it. He also complimented me on a recording of a song that I wrote, "Convolution." Again, those spare compliments always mean the most.

Doug Christensen, a good friend and former Advanced Academy cutting team member reminded me of a hilarious story. Doug had excused himself from our meeting to answer Nature's call. He found himself standing next to Tommy at the urinal. As I mentioned before in a different context, sometimes saying nothing is best! Doug, for some reason felt obliged to say "It's an honor to be peeing next to you!" Tommy didn't say anything. He just washed his hands and walked out. Later as an opener to his presentation Tommy said something like "The weirdest thing just happened to me...."

I remember sitting with him and discussing the new (to me) concept of Multiple Intelligences. It was fascinating and intriguing. Without my having taken an assessment, Tommy gave me a detailed breakdown of what were likely to be my dominant MIs. He was spot on. I eventually became pretty well versed in the subject and using it greatly improved the effectiveness of my classes.

On one trip through the southern states doing classes for JCPenney salons, I landed late in Louisville Kentucky. Usually if flights are delayed the car rental companies will make some arrangements to stay open later to accommodate the passengers with reservations. That didn't happen this time. I had no way to get to my first stop on my little tour. There was also a huge car convention in town and there were literally no hotel rooms available. Several passengers and I spent the night on the Naugahyde benches in the airport lounge and washed up in the bathroom before politely expressing my displeasure to the nice lady at the car rental the next morning at 5:30. She gave me the pick of the lot. I include this story because the next time i saw Tommy I shared it with him. "Why didn't you call me?" He asked. I said "Well, I thought you lived in Paducah." I replied. He said "No, I used to. I live right by the Louisville airport!"

Oh well.

So many stories and good (mostly) memories about and inspired by a great mentor!

Misty Mountains!

Art Credit: Zane Skinner

Once, as a result of an inept and incompetent sales rep for the major hair care brand that many of you know I worked for decades, who was responsible for booking my educational classes in El Paso, having not actually booked anything for me to do and after having flown there and slept in a mediocre hotel and awakening, expecting a full day of opportunities to share my knowledge only to be dumped at a mall while he scrambled trying to throw some classes together to keep me busy and failing miserably, I found myself with a whole day with nothing to do before my flight home. (Yes, I got paid anyway) I think I just broke my record for run-on sentences.

I drove over to Juarez and poked around for a while returning with a bottle of Almondrada, a delicious almond liqueur not available in the U.S.

I still had about 4 hours to kill, so on my way to the airport, I noticed a bar by the name of Foxy's. I'm not excusing my choice, but it sounded like an interesting way to blow a couple of hours and likely a couple bucks before my flight home. I was met at the door by a disembodied voice telling me through an intercom, "5 dollar cover, 5 dollar drinks, no alcohol, no refunds." That should have been enough. I imagine there must have been a problem with their liquor license or something. I paid my 5 dollars and entered the dark club. There was no one on stage and almost no one in the club. I took a seat near the back and ordered a 5-dollar Coke. The waitress encouraged me to move to a table that was closer to the stage and said that someone would be right up in a moment or two. I sat, sipping my barely carbonated 5-dollar coke and batting an annoying fly for about 5 minutes, and was about to leave when the DJ came on and announced in his best gentlemen's club DJ voice, "GENTLEMEN!! FOR YOUR VIEWING ENJOYMENT..... MIStyyyYYY MOUNTAINS!!!

A mid-40s Mexican woman who looked like she'd had a few kids ambled out onto the stage and performed an embarrassing striptease. Not wanting to hurt anyone's feelings, I endured her performance. Did I mention an annoying fly that showed a persistent interest in me and my 5-dollar coke? After she was finally done, she came straight to my table and asked if I wanted a table dance. I politely declined and said I just wanted to finish my 5-dollar coke before I had to go. She said, "That's ok, Baby. There will be some new girls up in a minute." I sipped my 5-dollar coke, swatted the persistent fly, and dubiously awaited the "new girls." After about 5 more minutes, the DJ, in his best gentleman's club DJ voice, came on and announced, "GENTLEMEN!! FOR YOUR VIEWING ENJOYMENT......MIStyyyYYYYY MOUNTAINS!!!" I

334

downed the remains of my 5-dollar coke, bid adios to my persistent winged friend, and bailed.

Several months later, we did a hair show in El Paso. It was a huge success and after we were done, the owner of the distributorship sponsoring the show said to me "Mike (the sales manager for said distributorship) tells me that there's a great club that he goes to when he's here called Roxy's...or Foxy's...?" I relied "I know this place. Uh uh. Nope!" He responded "Well, Mike says it's great!" I acquiesced, willing to either laugh hysterically or be surprised. Well, Foxy's must have ironed out their TABC issues because the place was packed and rocking. A decent time was had by all. There was no sign of MIStyyyYYY MOUNTAINS!!!

Grounded!

Art Credit: Kent Skinner

Having a teenaged son, who, by the way, is a lot like me in many frustrating and rewarding ways, I am reminded of some of my own experiences, similarities, and decided differences in my own father's responses and expressions in discipline. Grounded

Grounded: according to Wikipedia, "Grounding is a form of punishment given to older children, preadolescents or adolescents by their parents (or teachers or headmasters in a school setting) for bad behavior and poor performance in school or other duties." In my house, grounding meant:

- No friends over. This hurt them more than me. We always had the best snacks: Charles Chips. Delivered chips, pretzels, chocolate covered graham cookies, etc.

- No going anywhere unsupervised by a parent or teacher.

- No radio. This was way before FM much less XM or Sirius radio.

- No Monsters! This included my monster models, Famous Monsters Of Filmland magazines, cards and whatever.

- No comic books! This explains a few gaps in my much neglected collection. My idea as a kid was to save them for my future son....(he couldn't care less!) maybe some day.

- No TV! Restriction from all FOUR CHANNELS!!

- Maybe worst of all, no guitar. How was I to grow up to be a ROCK STAR without practicing on my Sears Silvertone acoustic and later Olson's Electronics Zeno electric guitar which i earned by learning my parent's favorite song, "Laura's Theme" from Dr Zhivago, better known as "Somewhere My Love" I eventually nailed it.

The longest I was ever grounded was for 3 months. My good friend to this day, Dale Meyler's 15th birthday, March 16, happens to be the day before mine. He had a small party, and at its conclusion, several attendees agreed that we would reconvene later, around 1:00 a.m. My also lifelong friend, Vaughn Stockton was spending the night at my house. Mike Bayles (R.I.P.), the brother of Michelle Bayles, who I was dating and Vaughn later married (another story previously told), had little restraint, parental or otherwise, and joined us later. Dale, his sister Vickie and her friend Cheryl (?) Dodson also joined us.

We really didn't do anything much besides roam the streets around our neighborhoods and enjoy the thrill of being out late without the permission or knowledge of our parents. Mike did steal a flashing barricade from a construction area and place it behind someone's car in their driveway. That was pretty much the extent of our juvenile delinquency that night. Soon after, we were just walking down the street when a car pulled up behind us. We ran. About a block away, I felt a firm grip on my shoulder. It was a cop. "Hold it right there!!" He caught both Vickie and me. Mike got away as did Cheryl but since she was spending the night with Vickie, she had to circle back. Dale came back since they had caught his sister. Vaughn stayed by the car as directed. The officer asked "If you weren't doing anything, then why did you run?" One of us replied "We thought you might be hoods." Laughing, the cop said to his partner "They thought we was "hooks!" One of them asked if we had any weapons. Dale replied "Only my switch light!!" shining his flashlight into the officer's eyes. Not wise. We were driven to my house and my parents were awakened. Dale, Vickie and Cheryl were delivered to the Meyler house where they were lit upon by a very enraged parental unit. My dad was unhappy and disappointed (much worse than angry). We spoke the next morning which, as I mentioned was my own 15th birthday. I was allowed to have my party which, due to the previous night's adventure was pretty sparse. Vaughn and Michelle clicked that night (why did I initiate...(was it me?) playing Spin The Bottle?) 50 +/- years later they are still married and I have had SO many adventures that I never would have if my party hadn't turned out the way it did.

Anyway, this story is about being grounded. I was for 3 months. My dad decided to take a look at my school notebook. I had not cleaned it out from the previous semester, so there was much to inspect. In addition to whatever new homework I was being assigned, I was to rewrite anything messy, was graded as unsatisfactory, or had doodles or unnecessary drawings. This was my life.

About 6 weeks in, as a result of my focus and efforts, my dad eased my restriction. Vaughn was allowed to spend the night. Aaaannnnd guess what we did. We snuck out and toilet papered Michelle's house. This was not viewed by many as an act of vandalism at the time though her parents were shocked and disappointed. They didn't get the mindset of 15 year olds at all.

After completing our late-night clandestine mission, Vaughn and I were a half block from my house when we saw headlights coming up behind us. "Get in the car!" ordered my father. He had had a "hunch." After Vaughn and I cleaned Michelle's lawn the next morning under the sad and confused eyes of her parents, I served the rest of my sentence. I did get my comics, radio and TV privileges, monsters, friend access, and guitar back. Still working on the rock star part.

Mallified

It was like a scene from a post apocalypse science fiction movie! Glenna and I walked out of the Sears store at Richardson Square into the mall. It was dark and cluttered. I think there were tumbleweeds. Maybe. All of the stores were gone and nothing living stirred. Only the ghosts and memories flitted by. She and I had both worked there in the eighties though we never met until years later. Glenna worked at the ice cream place in the middle junction, at a sporting goods store and a department store. More on this mall later.

My first hair styling job was at a high dollar Alamo Heights salon and lasted a day! The owner was a very busy, tense and terse German stylist that had no time to work with my lack of experience, me having just gotten my license and having much to learn. Having moved to San Antonio specifically for that job and committed to house sitting for my sister Carolyn, I went ahead and took a job at Regis in Ingram Park Mall for two or three months before returning to Austin. During that time I met the regional supervisor, Suzanne, who makes a brief, important appearance later in this story. One day Suzanne called me to the back and said in her heavy Austrian accent "Rrrudy and I have a little bet. You don't have to answer if you don't want to......Are you gaaay?" That caught me completely off guard. Astonished (and not gay), I replied "No!" She walked away towards "Rrrudy" and said "He isss. I can tell!" That would probably be grounds for a lawsuit today. I recall one odd day running into two old friends from high school there in the mall in separate incidents. Gary Davidson was the drummer in a band I played in. It was nice to reconnect. Later that day I glanced up from the haircut I was doing and saw another familiar face at the front desk. She was making an appointment with me. I had a small speaking part in a high school show where we were acting as if we were attending our future reunion. I was paired with Marvelle Muntzell, a girl I knew in real life but not well. The woman in the mall booking the appointment ten years later was she. When she came back for her haircut, I approached speaking my lines from the high school play, "Marvelle!.... How nice to see you!" She had not recognized me until then. I think it took some reminding her of our stellar stage performance for my lines to connect. We are friends again these days on Facebook. One last Ingram Park Mall story. A local Radio Station teaming up with a suntan lotion company held a " Show Us Your Tan!" contest in the mall. Contestants when called would step forward and pull off the radio staion's t-shirt and show off their tans revealing a little bit of untanned skin for contrast. One poor teenaged girl got a little too exuberant pulling her t-shirt off and took her bikini top with it. Lots of contrast! Boy was her face red!

After leaving San Antonio and my first two salon jobs, I returned to Austin, moved into the old house on 6th Street with Mike Williams and his girlfriend Suzy Valentine. We named it "The Set" for its cast and drama and it has its own story.

During my first year or so in the hair biz I worked in three Austin Salons. I will insert them here for the sake of chronology although there were no malls involved. The first was named, "Looking Good." Joe Eddy Hines (RIP) and Denise Hill were two of my Vogue Beauty.

340

Schoolmates who had been working with a salon owner named Glen in Lakewood Hills near Lake Travis an area with a lot of new money. They were moving the business to the University Of Texas campus area. Glen rented a building that had been a free-standing drive-through fried chicken restaurant. We laid parquet flooring, painted, and made it into a nice looking salon! The mirrors, sinks, stations, and furnishings all came from his former salon in the hills. The only thing missing was business sense! We had a great staff, cool place, open bar....maybe not a great idea... Glen was upbeat and generous. He once treated us to an all-expense paid San Antonio hair show trip, and we stayed in a very nice hotel on the river and drank plenty of Bombay Sapphire. The salon couldn't afford this. Glen had the great idea to call ourselves Expression Consultants rather than hairstylists. I once handed a card to someone at a party and they looked incredulous. "What is this? What do you do?" Being in a rather creative state of mind I replied "People come to us that want a total image makeover. We sit and sketch while we interview them. At the end of the consultation we present them with four or five radically different profiles each with suggestions including wardrobe, hair, possibly plastic surgery, lifestyle coaching and speech therapy if needed! He replied "That must get REALLY expensive! What if someone doesn't pay?" I said "We send a couple of black belts to interrupt their dates. Not to threaten the client, but being karate experts for their own self protection. They ask "So, how's the toupee working out?" and such."

I left him speechless thinking to myself "Hmmm! This isn't such a bad idea!"

It was at Looking Good that I discovered that I had a knack for doing long hair styling. It fell to me to blowout and style Glen's business partner's daughter's calf length hair every week. I learned a lot. Everyone had something that they enjoyed and were good at. Joe was a terrific hair cutter, Denise was well rounded and Glen was a mostly old school hairdresser. He could not cut his way out of a paper bag but he could make a bad haircut look like a million bucks. That was good. Some of his guests had a million bucks.

The newest, greatest product line in the industry was Jhirmack. Jerri Redding, having sold his own name and line had started and built Redken with his wife Paula. She took the company in their divorce and he started Jhirmack. We and thousands of salons helped build Jhirmack's reputation up as the newest and best in hair product technology only to have him sell out to an over the counter manufacturer like Playtex or Conair. I forget which. This put it on the drugstore shelves and it was no longer exclusive to salons. When our poor Jhirmack sales rep next showed up at the salon, Glen physically removed him out the front door. It wasn't the first or last time Redding pulled this.

All was well until the paychecks started to bounce. Glen had a "friend" that he frequently gave cash from the drawer leading to insufficient funds for little things like..oh, say, bills... and paychecks. One day I showed up to his nice apartment door quite angry and told Glen that if he wanted me to keep working for him that he was going to have to pay me in cash from then on. He did until the salon folded soon after.

Joe and I then went to work at what seemed to be a cool concept salon, Solara. It was in a nice old house with wooden floors. The owner didn't like noise so there were no loud blow dryers. We used hand held heat lamps with quiet fans in them. It took FOREVER to dry and hair but our prices made up for the time loss. We also use wooden rods for our perms. Very 70s Austin. It took much longer to rinse the porous wood than it takes with traditional plastic rods. Again, prices should have made up for time. The owner was also very fussy about music. He had a great stereo and a reel to reel tape deck with which he meticulously planned our aural and audial experience. I made the mistake of introducing some Pink Floyd to the experience. "IT'S TOO JANGLEY!!" He exclaimed! He also had a thing about shoes needing to be shined. I had a very comfortable and not cheap pair of deer skin loafers that when tended to properly looked very nice. He pointed out to me their lack of polish. I had no polish with which to exhibit that niceness so until I could take care of business, I opted to wear a funky pair of red, white and blue patent leather bowling shoes the next day. Sitting behind the front desk, I had kicked them off for a minute. They were very uncomfortable and hot. Boss man reached his limit. I was out on the street again.

Next came The Mane Event, a salon near campus owned by two Turkish brothers, Najate' (probably spelled wrong) and maybe George. Najate' was a gregarious womanizer who kissed every female client entering and leaving. They loved it! It probably doesn't work as well without an accent. I fit in pretty well there and enjoyed my brief time with them.

We would hang out, smoke and joke behind the salon between clients and I remember telling a particularly funny and vulgar joke to his brother, (George?). I won't repeat it here but might share it with you privately sometime if asked. It was actually one my mother told me. He laughed and went in to tend to his elderly guest. While combing her roller set out, he thought of that joke and began to grin. The grin begat chuckling which led to laughing out loud with tears running down his face. He had to lean on the wall shaking with laughter and of course could not explain his mirth to his sweet old lady!

I mentioned The Set earlier here and in previous stories, the house I shared with Mike Williams, Suzy Valentine and sometimes a young lady named Erin. Erin was a seventeen year old freshman at U.T. and I think officially lived at the 21st Street co op. I must have done her hair at The Mane Event because Najate' was infatuated with her. "I'm having a party at my house Saturday and you must all come! And be sure to invite Erin! My girlfriend and I, Mike, Suzy and Erin all went. As I recall, Cathy, Suzy and Erin were the only females in attendance at a party of maybe 30 Turkish men. The food was incredible and Najate' had apparently been somewhat of a pop star back home. There was a large poster of him on the wall of his living room. At the request of some of his guests, he sat on the floor with a metal tray on his lap and played percussion with it and sang. All of the men chimed in at the right places. It was pretty fantastic! Even young Erin was impressed but not to the point of becoming Najate's romantic conquest.

Eventually I left Austin for the final time to pursue my plan to work with and eventually own a salon with my buddy Vaughn, whose fault it was that I had gotten into this business to begin with, thinking incorrectly that I could maintain my faltering relationship with Cathy long distance. It was not to be. You live, love, sometimes lose and hopefully learn.

In Dallas, I was originally hired at Samson and Delilah, another Regis owned salon in Valley View Mall. I only worked there a month before transferring to Richardson Square Mall to work with my buddy Vaughn. I remember a couple of stories at S&D that are maybe worth telling. One is of a newly elected Dallas sheriff wanting his mustache "frosted" to match his salt and pepper hair. Fortunately I had nothing to do with this fiasco. Facial hair is generally coarser than the hair on your head and can be harder to lighten. His perfectly acceptable natural mustache color would not lift past orange. After several different attempts, they just dyed it back to black. Lesson learned by all participants. The other story is of a job applicant. He was a hairstylist of the more flamboyant breed and had informed the manager of his special wardrobe that included a gold lame' jumpsuit with feathers, a purple sequined outfit that had to be sewn on each time he wore it and another jumpsuit made of clear vinyl that he wore hot pink hot pants underneath. He assured us that his presence would draw plenty of media attention, him being the celebrity stylist that he claimed to be. Not hired. I heard later of his working with a friend of mine at another salon and showing his portfolio of stars that he had supposedly done. The pictures were all cut out of magazines. He was fired after offering to share his stash of amyl nitrate with his clients. "It'th perfectly legal!!" That didn't last long. Anyway, back to Richardson Square. I transferred there to pick up on Vaughn's and my plan to eventually open a shop but first I needed to build a clientele. I got lucky in that I could and enjoyed braiding, thanks to my weekly long hair workout at Looking Good. Bo Derek had just made the white girl corn rows popular in the movie "10" and I was the only stylist there that could or wanted to do them. I made a deal with the manager to do all of that in exchange for not doing little old lady shampoo and sets. Best for all because I wasn't any good at them having only done one on a live person in school and at my state board test. I did a couple of Bo Dereks and several No Derek's. The stylist who did Bo's braids was quoted as saying "It may make a 10 out of a 9 but it won't make a 4 out of a 3." One of the successful ones became a lifelong friend, Lori, the inspiration of several stories yet to be written, probably with new names.

I think I've shared the Coolhand story, but I'll do it again. Because I was working with my best friend Vaughn, I typically ate lunch with him. Apparently, some of the stylists thought that I thought I was too cool to hang out with them, I guess because of the braiding deal or something. Every day, I'd come in, and Denise Van Deusen would ask, sneering, "How's it goin.......COOLhand?" Eventually, she and the others realized that I was o.k., although the nickname stuck. To this day, when Denise sees me at my Dallas salon, she says, "How's it goin' Coolhand?"

The mall had a very diverse population. I suppose they all do, from the high school socialites working mostly in the classier department store of the three, to the party element, to the self important mall security guards including the too old to be hitting on the high schoolers perfectly feathered salt and pepper haired guard, the mall walkers, slime balls, rednecks, head necks, hippies, new wavers, etc. etc. etc. and of course many, many nice but normal people. I have imagined writing a sifi novel/movie about a post apocalyptic mall sealed off from the radioactive world and its inhabitants forming their own social structure and government. It would probably be a "B" movie at best with all of the stereotypes mentioned above. It's surely been done.

Another story that comes to mind was told to me by a friend. Strangely, my friend Pam McRoberts, the woman I think I remember telling me has no recollection of it. She told of stopping by the Chic Fil-A in the Richardson Square and ordering sandwiches for her kids and herself. When it was time to pay she realized that she had no card and was 10 cents short of her ticket. Rather than saying "Oh that's okay, don't worry about it!" or digging a dime out of his own pocket, the manager of unsubstantiated foreign origin took the lettuce off of her sandwich! Problem solved! Cheese! Actually, no cheese.

My run in with Santa's helper over a parking space took place at Richardson Square Mall. While momentarily facing off with a van for a rare parking spot close to Christmas, a little white compact car shot in between us and stole it like a chihuahua on a meatball. I left a merry Christmas note on her car and by chance, locked eyes with her later in the mall. She was one of Santa's elves. She looked panicked. I mouthed "Merry Christmas," probably with an evil grin.

Another memory. I didn't witness it but as some kind of promotion, Spider-Man made a dramatic appearance at the mall. He was lowered in by a helicopter and was to drop amongst a bunch of awestruck kids. Something went wrong and he fell from too high up and was injured whilst striking said awe. He wasn't seriously injured, at least not physically.

It's a good policy to avoid dating your clients. How many disappeared when things didn't work out? I never listened. One failed long term relationship began with "Would you like to go see Jethro Tull with me?" Her reply: "I'd rather see Bruce Springsteen." That was a sign. Right there. Shoulda listened.

One day one of my young clients asked me how I might respond to her friend, also a client, asking me to take her to her senior prom. She had already bought her dress the tickets and rented a place for a party when she and her borfriend broke up. I replied, "Wow. I'm flattered, but...I'm a little old for that!" I was 27. Two more of her friends, and finally, she approached me with the same question. The "I'd rather see Bruce Springsteen" girl who I was dating at the time said, "You should take her! It'd be fun!" I did. I did people's hair all day and didn't mention my going, and when I showed up at the prom, some of them asked, "What are you doing here?" I answered, "I got a 911 hair emergency call! Have comb, will travel!" It was all on the up and up and I did indeed have fun. I also never heard the end of it from my girlfriend. "I can't believe you took that little girl to the prom!!!" "You told me I should!" Another sign. Right there. I shoulda listened!

There was an in salon training with one of the Regis educators. He was a wise guy and a pretty good stylist. It was a color method training and he suddenly asked "Does anyone have some KY?" One of the more flamboyant stylists replied "I have some in my truck! Do you want me to go get it?" The trainer answered "No. I just had a feeling you did!" Bwahhaha.

I worked at that salon for a year and a half. One of the things that helped me build my clientele was a cutting method that I learned from Paul Mitchell himself. He called it Volumetric Layering. It was a time of spiky topped rock and roll hair and this method could be used very effectively for that. I still use it for longer looks. One day I was at the salon for a meeting. A girl who I had been using this technique on called to see if I could cut her that day. I explained that I wasn't working that day but could help her the next day. When she asked if someone else could cut it I told her that someone else would do something different because no one else was using that particular method and suggested that she wait for me. Well, she came in later and the bosses pet, a brown nosed troublemaker aptly named Patsy took her. Whatever conversation actually took place, she told the manager that I had said that there was nobody working there that was any good and that I wouldn't even get my own hair cut there!

The next day when I arrived the boss told me that she had to let me go. I told her the true story but she had already called Suzanne, the regional supervisor in a panic and was told to do what she was paid to do. "I hirett you to mek decisssionsss!" Rather than sort it all out and admit she'd jumped the gun, she saved face by following through. I drove across the street to Belt Line Hair Design owned by Richard Watts, the subject of some of my early stories where Denise V was working and started a 20 year tenure. So, sometimes what seems unfair ends up being a good thing. No more mall for me! I made many life long friends and clients there. Many of them still come to me as do their kids and grandkids! I owned the salon for over half of that time before selling it during the post 911 crunch having married my long time client and crush, Glenna. We had started our family and were building our house. I had no problem selling it and took what was supposed to be a terrific job as Artistic Director for Seventeen Salon and Spa. That's another story and nightmare!

Nearly all of the malls where I have worked or shopped are either gone or are wastelands without anchor stores and with transient businesses, empty slots and warning signs. I guess the current trend of open area shopping malls is a trade off of air conditioning and weather protection for open space and skies. It is fresh and open. It also gets very hot, cold and or wet! Richardson Square was torn down and replaced with several chain stores with outside entrances. Sears was the only survivor and recently announced its closing. I've always said that every choice we've ever made has led us to where we are. Perhaps different choices would have led me to writing, producing and shooting the B movie "The Mall" in Richardson Square, it would still be standing and we'd be having Mojitos right now with Quentin Tarantino.

Oh well. There may have been a sign. Right there. Mighta shoulda listened.

Mall Addendum?

I am at the point with all of this story telling biz where it gets fuzzy as to whether a new story is an addendum to an older one. They cross paths, sometimes with two or three other stories.

Anyway, this one is connected to my Santa's Elf story but also involves a Christmas tree, Richardson Square Mall and my Terminator sun glasses...whatever.

Again, as many of my stories begin "Many years ago.." I was stopped at a red light at Plano Rd and Belt Line pointed east sitting in the far right lane. My light turned green and I paused as one should do before proceeding. I began to pull into the intersection when a Ford Mustang with two punks in it ran the light and cut across three lanes, laughing and flipping us off. I slammed on my brakes, almost losing the Christmas tree I had tied to the roof of my Montero. Looking right, I saw them pull into the Sears parking lot at Richardson Square off of Plano Rd, so I turned right into the same lot off of Belt Line and stopped at the end of their row, blocking them in. I jumped out of my truck wearing the same black leather jacket, black leather cowboy hat, gloves, long hair and Terminator sunglasses I was wearing when I had my encounter with Santa's elf in the previous story...and this was also the same parking lot.... hmm. I had no idea what I intended to do besides scare a couple of punk teenagers. In my mind I picture me wielding the old guitar neck that I used to keep in the car but I don't think I really was. The driver rolled his window down and yelled "What's your problem?" "YOU!!" I replied. He suddenly realized that I was one of the people he had endangered and his buddy had flipped off. Both sets of eyes went huge and the passenger yelled "Let's get outa here!" The driver threw his car into reverse and hastily backed out of the isle swerving and burning rubber and tore out of there after nearly crashing into a couple of cars.

I got back in my truck thinking, "Well, that turned out alright." Then I went home and put up my Christmas tree.

Mensa Mania

Art Credit: Zane Skinner

My sister Carolyn and I are very different in some ways and very much the same in others. She has been an active member of Mensa, a club for people with high IQs for many years. She found a place where she felt like she belonged and made many lifelong friends. She found her extended family. For a long time she encouraged me to take the test and join the club. I had my own extended family in Paul Mitchell doing what I love and really didn't have the time or interest. I finally relented and agreed to DJ and perform at a Mensa party. I had a big sound system and my Crystalume, a visual music instrument that I have written of previously. I imagined that an audience of intelligent people might appreciate a visual interpretation of my original music. I hauled it all and set it up in the ballroom and did a decent performance. There were some polite claps but mostly confused befuddlement.

I proceeded to switch hats and just play music. I had been told to play a broad range of music to entertain people from 19 to 75 years of age. I brought all kinds of music, sire that I would make everyone happy. Not so much. During the first song, something reasonably contemporary, an older man came up to me and asked, annoyed, "DO YOU HAVE ANY DANCE MUSIC? I MEAN LIKE GLEN MILLER?" I did and I put some on for him. Immediately a kid, probably the 19 year old is asking "DONT YOU HAVE ANY NEW MUSIC?" I did and pulled something out for him. This went on for a few songs and then a middle aged woman said "I CAN GO GET MY BIG CHILL ALBUM AND BRING IT BACK HERE IN 30 MINUTES!" I said "WHY DONT YOU DO THAT?" and continued pissing people off that only wanted to hear music that suited their own tastes. Big Chill lady showed up with her album and I left her in the booth. "I'M NOT GETTING PAID TO DO THIS!" she yelled. "NEITHER AM I!" I replied and went to the bar and ordered a scotch. I just let her play her record and soothed my temperament with single malt. Soon the older and younger crowd thinned and when the 2 hrs was up I packed and left with nary a thank you, not that I needed or deserved it having abandoned my post.

Lesson learned: Just because someone has a higher IQ doesn't mean they have broader horizons!.

Twenty-One Pilots

'Twas a cold winter's evening. Ralph, my old friend and bassist for the legendary (in our own minds) Jack B. Quick called me at my hotel room in Milwaukee and said "I have free tickets to see some band tonight. I don't know anything about them but hey! Who knows? It's free!"

I said, "Sure. Why not? It's free!"

I was in Milwaukee a few years ago doing a Haircutting training for the staff at the Paul Mitchell school in Waukesha, Wisconsin, a beautiful place, but..not a lot going on at night besides Netflix and cheese curds, both of which can be pretty satisfying on a frigid Wisconsin night! So, what the hell? It was free.

Ralph picked me up and we went into Milwaukee to what had once been an Eagles lodge but was now a large nightclub broken into several smaller venues. Our room couldn't have been more than 12-1500 sq feet with a decent stage and sound system that was being misused by some local cover band playing to tracks of other people's electro-pop music and sharing clever between songs banter like "GOOD EVENING MILWAUKEE!!!" and "ARE YOU READY TO ROCK?" Yeah. Rock me with your prerecorded tracks of other people's music. There may have been 30 people there. We got a beer and settled in to be less than impressed. Fortunately, we had missed some of their set and it was over fairly soon. Hey, it was free.

Then the headliners came out. It was just two guys. One was a muscled, tattooed, and mohawked drummer. He was terrifying...and I mean it in the most complimentary way. I mean, he was astonishingly good! The other guy was a little kinda Ed Grimley-looking piano/keyboardist singer who was really, really animated and versatile. At one moment, he might be crooning into the mic behind the piano, and the next, jumping on said piano rapping, his rapid-fire, staccato words like a verbal, emotional barrage/cascade of descriptive and gut-pounding emotion, then perhaps sitting on the edge of the stage laughing and chatting or both of them might be pounding big steel drums in the middle of the electrified crowd of perhaps by now, forty people.

That may win first place in the official semi-annual Kent Skinner's Run On Sentence awards. If you get the impression that I was blown away by these guys, you are, of course, correct. When they were done, we went side stage (there was no backstage) and introduced ourselves. Both of them were as nice and unassuming as can be. I remember telling them how much we'd enjoyed them and saying something like, "I'm sure you hear it all the time, but I've known or played with a few people that were destined for greatness before they made it, and I definitely have that feeling about you guys!" They both were humble and appreciative of the small following that, had braved the bitter cold to come out and hear them. Of course, I bought their CD. By the way, they are called Twenty-One Pilots. And it was free.

Last week, my 17-year-old daughter said that her friend's parents had bought tickets to see them in Fort Worth and asked if she could go. We agreed and drove them and picked them up. The $25 dollar parking lots were completely full. We had dinner and waited nearby, tucked into a gated entryway to the botanical gardens. They were closed, and we were safe and somewhat hidden. I was playing Words With Friends while Glenna crocheted. Suddenly, there was a loud rap on her window. She screamed as it it was Jason with a machete! The security guard jumped to and then, laughing, told us that they were about to open the gates to let some guests out. We obliged and went back to the arena and parked at the foot of the stairs. The girls came out soon amidst a flood of happy, mostly young people. They were ecstatic.

Attendance at that show was around 13,000 people. I would have loved to see them myself (and sneak backstage and say "I saw you in..." yeah, right!) but floor tickets that night were going for $300-$500 apiece. Revenue was $845,836. We saw them for free.

Concerts

Art Credit: Kent Skinner

Having just written about my having seen Twenty-One Pilots for
free before they were famous, recalling my Beatles story, and Vaughn
Stockton's and my experiences at the Texas International Pop Festival, I
thought recalling a few more great concerts might be fun! So, yes, I saw
the Beatles in 1964. I bought my (still) good friend's ticket for 5 bucks,
much to his perpetual dismay. You can find that story way back on the
Kent Skinner's Stories page. My next concert was Paul Revere and the
Raiders. I took my then-girlfriend, Michelle. She and Vaughn are still
married. Another buried story. Happy digging!

Next was Cream's farewell concert! I recall Eric Clapton stopping
in the middle of a solo, reaching down to the stage, rising back up, and
saying something like (thick British accent), "Dropped me f—-ing pick!"

Not quite sure who was next or for that matter the specific timeline for the next zillion concerts. Maybe Hendrix at SMU, a mind boggling show, or more likely the Texas International Pop Festival which was right after Woodstock, where Vaughn and I saw Zeppelin on their first U.S. tour, Grand Funk Railroad, Ten Years After, Sam and Dave, The Incredible String Band, and a couple more that played on the one day we were able to attend. Look that story up too if you're interested.

We saw The Allman Brothers too. I know how wrong this is, but somehow, we got caught up in a long-running inside joke that involved a lady friend of a friend of Vaughn's who had been set up on a blind date with a guy who happened to have a cleft pallet. Not his fault but he had said several strange things to her like "Thaaay baby! I thee your length!" And "The other night we that up thome thick... Hyoooooey! We thure with high!" I know it was cruel, but for a while, we made an occasional joke mimicking this poor sap. At the Allman's show, Vaughn said to me in that voice, "THITH THURE ITH A GOOD CONTHYERT!!" Then, for real, a harelipped woman turned around in front of us and said enthusiastically, "NO THYIIIT!!." Ouch! Busted! When Jethro Tull was touring and promoting their "Aqualung" album, I invited a girl that my oldest Dallas friend, Dale Meyler, had gone out with briefly. Dale was fine with it. A couple of days after accepting, she called and told me she couldn't go, needing to tie up some loose ends in another brief and passing relationship. We did end up dating for a couple of years. So, I asked Dale's sister Vickie, a future Miss Denton, to go. She accepted. She had never been to a rock concert before. I arrived to pick her up wearing jeans, sneakers, and probably a concert t-shirt. She answered the door in a lovely white semi-formal dress, white sandals, and, I believe, white satin gloves. Today, I might have responded, "Well, alrighty then!" and swung back by the house and put on my tails, but I was maybe 18. Not cool. I survived. Anyway, Tull was phenomenal. So was the opening act... The Eagles! "Hey, man! I don't mean to get political or anything, but if we all could get our heads together, we could take country music away from the rednecks!" That didn't happen so much. Instead, Rock opened its multi-tendrilled arms and welcomed it. Thus was born Southern Rock and eventually New Country. Listen if you like or can to The Wolf for a few minutes and imagine an R&B, Rock, or Pop singer replacing the Country artist. It's all poured from the same spigot today.

I saw Jethro Tull many times. One tour, I saw them on consecutive nights in Dallas and Houston and realized that Ian Anderson's seemingly random and wild stage antics were actually well-choreographed. Of course. One of the most dangerous and stupid things that Vaughn and I did was to drive straight through from Dallas to Albuquerque, eat dinner, see Tull in concert, and drive straight through back to Dallas. I was hallucinating from highway hypnosis and swerved to avoid a giant goat skull in the road. We're lucky to be alive!

The Moody Blues are one of my favorites too, but they often suffered from sound engineers not knowing who focus on as they frequently switched from one singer to another. Every other concert was either amazing or badly mixed.

I saw Alice Cooper's "Welcome To My Nightmare" concert. It was fun, but the opening act was a leather jumpsuited bass-playing cutie named Suzi Quatro. She sang bad girl anthems like "Your Mama Won't Like Me!" I bought, loved, lost, and sought her album, finding it again years later at a flea market. Some albums can weather the storms of time. Hers didn't. So many concerts and shows are a blur now. I know I went, but have few memories of it. Wonder why?

More greats: Dire Straits last tour. I'm glad I didn't miss that! I tuned in late, but I am still a huge fan of Mark Knopfler. The Who, The Cars, The Doobie Brothers, Aerosmith, Heart, Lyle Lovett, Tom Petty, Elvis Costello (he borrowed my guitar to sit in with The Skunks after his show). Alex Chilton borrowed the same guitar. David Bowie, Bruce Springsteen (I asked a girl to see Jethro Tull, and she said, "I'd rather see Bruce Springsteen. It was an omen that I ignored and wished I hadn't! Not because if Bruce...he was great!) The Runaways (post Cherie Currie but featuring Joan Jett). I met them at a meet and greet at Inner Sanctum Records. They looked like they'd rather be anywhere else. The Ramones, Tangerine Dream, Sugarcubes w Bjork, 10,000 Maniacs, Leo Kottke, Yes, Several Times, Chris Isaak, B52s, Bonnie Raitt, J Geils, Beach Boys,

Leon Russell, Three Dog Night, Foghat, ZZ Top, Sarah McLaughlin, Spin Doctors, Lightning Hopkins, B.B. and Freddy King... Michael Jackson (gf won tix. Great show.) George Strait (again, free tickets). I saw Shawn Phillips in the 70s at the Majestic never imagining that I would open for him regularly in the future. I also opened for and was awestruck by Robert Fripp. And, of course, a few times, The Rolling Stones! I recall an awful one-time date where she was falling down drunk before we even got there. I think it was her Keith Richards impression that sealed the deal. Great show, though! Keith should have hired her to make him look good. I took another one and only date to see Joe Cocker at Moody Colosseum. He was so wasted he was incoherent. Even more than usual.

Back in the 80s, Electronic music pioneer Jean Michel Jarre, the city of Houston, and NASA collaborated on a spectacular show. The whole downtown skyline was draped and lit with giant projections and lasers. The sound system was devastating! One of the astronauts on the Challenger was supposed to broadcast his saxophone solo from space to the event. We all know how tragically that worked out.

Todd Rundgren played at a large club/ small concert venue called The Agora. He truly killed it. Two nights later he was sitting next to me at the Peter Gabriel show at the same place with his mouth wide open. Peter TRULY massacred it!

I saw Pink Floyd several times. Always mind-blowing! Quadraphonic sound at McFarlin Auditorium. The laughs on Dark Side were coming from all around us.

Linda Ronstadt...I hitchhiked to the Armadillo World Headquarters, got in early, and stood right in front of the stage. She looked me right in the eyes and sang "Love Has No Pride." You could have literally stuck a fork in me.

I saw Bare Naked Ladies in Dallas. (I've actually seen quite a few, but in this case, I'm referring to the band!) They were a lot of fun, but it was the opening act, Frente!, that stole my heart. It was just a guy on guitar and a singer named Angie Hart doing quirky and personal, well-crafted songs. At first, I thought, "Okay, another breathy little girl-sounding songwriter, yeah, yeah..." but when she called out some inattentive, noisy non-listeners, commanded their respect, and proceeded to bedazzled us all, I was hooked. I was in New Orleans the next day and saw that they were playing at the House Of Blues. I mentioned John Paul DeJoria, one of the co-owners and CEO of Paul Mitchell and Patron tequila, and copped a box seat! I promptly bought everything Frente! had on disc. Come to think of it, my pal, Tim Stephens, and I met a couple of very pretty women that bitter cold night in Dallas and, upon exiting the club, discovered that someone had broken into their car and really screwed up their electrical system while stealing the stereo. We waited until they were safe and mobile, froze our butts off, and said, "Good night!" Talk about a buzz kill.

Long before he was famous, Vaughn and I hitched down to Austin to see Stevie Ray and Jimmy Vaughan in Blackbird and Crackerjack. Vaughn was friends with them and several band members. Back at their house, one of them showed us some nasty-looking black stuff in a baggie that was in the freezer. It was psilocybin mushrooms. No, we didn't do any. We still had to hitch back to Dallas, an all-night journey, probably mentioned in an earlier KS story. One story that I have told several times incorrectly as having starred Stevie Ray was actually featuring Kim Davis, later of Point Blank. Vaughn and I drove down in my 52 Chevy to a little club by Fair Park in Dallas. It's not the safest part of town for a couple of underaged white kids from North Dallas. As soon as we got out of my car, we witnessed an intoxicated old black guy literally being thrown out of The Famous Door Club, doubtless named for the original and more famous Famous Door Club in New Orleans. He was holding a harmonica and slurred, " I wiz jus tryin' ta jam wit da band!" We scooted around him and into the club. Kim was already doling out some serious licks with the band and we realized pretty quick that he and we were the only white folks in the club. It didn't matter to anyone. Some old guy came up to us and said, "You boys got coolness! I'm gonna buy you a beer!" We are grateful accepted our big, cold bottles of Schlitz and kicked back to enjoy some terrific blues! Good music can knock down all kinds of walls, real or imaginary!

A few years ago, I surprised Glenna with 10th row, center section seats to see Stevie Nicks. It was a phenomenon show. I've always appreciated her but that show made me a fan. I'm sure that many more memories will come back to me after I publish this, and I'll say, " I should have included...!" They may make the hard copy edition.

I once saw a T-shirt that said, "I may be old, but I saw all the good bands!" Shoulda bought it. Iearned it, for sure.

Old Green Teeth

Before there was a Rotten Rubber Band, Stymie (Johnny Tubbs) Dennis Wall, Jim Russell, Troy Potts, Nancy Holt? and I played in a loose knit band that tried on several different names. There was a Juan E. Lizard involved too. I would hitch hike up from Austin (school) every weekend with my guitar, amp head and sometimes my dog Alabaster. This wasn't sustainable nor was I as good as the rest of these guys. I wasn't fired or so much replaced but I gently phased out of the band. Hard to play with a band you can't rehearse with. No hard feelings. After one fair night at some biker bar we headed back to the old 2 story house (long gone now) that the band rented on McKinney Ave (or maybe just off of. One of the guys, had brought some biker chick home but had sobered up enough that he had a change of mind and decided to head out of town leaving her unattended. An alternate band member (no names) awoke from his pile of sofa cushions to someone crawling under his covers. So the story goes, after a brief, embarrassing tryst he immediately almost sobered up. "Baybee, Git me a cigarette!" That sobered him up the rest of the way! He jumped up and hit the bathroom, and scalded and scrubbed himself sterile. I don't know what followed except that for a few weeks the guys would tease him "Old green teeth came around looking for you!" Peals of laughter ensued. Supposedly no STDs were acquired.

Turtles

Art Credit: Kent Skinner

Don't think me strange…okay, if you know me you probably already do. I dream of turtles. No, not constantly, yes that would be weird but they occasionally show up in a dream. I don't know why. According to various sources it can represent long life, coming out of one's shell, or according to one book of dream interpretation, breasts. Yeah well, I think that particular author may have his own problems to work out.

I cant count how many times I've stopped to rescue a turtle from traffic. On one of my road trips for Paul Mitchell, I was headed north to Oklahoma and was dismayed to see dozens of turtles or rather, terrapins lying shattered in the road. It was kind of surreal! As I continued for miles I watched hoping to be able to save some. Mile after mile, dozens and dozens of unlucky migrants. It was like lemmings drawn to the edge of a cliff! I must have stopped a half dozen times only to see each time that I was too late.

Finally, at last I saw one just starting his probable final crossing and I pulled back over. I scooped up my confused travel buddy. "Let's go pal! You're coming with me!" I resumed my journey while he (I assumed without reason that it was a he) crawled around the passenger side floor. I kept my eyes peeled for more travel companions but alas, nothing but many more unfortunate pilgrims lined the road. "Well, I guess its just you and me bud!!"

I arrived in OKC and not wanting to leave him in my rolling toaster oven, I took him in to the salon. They were kind enough to give me a cardboard box to keep him from tripping somebody's grandma. I taught my class and we headed for Tulsa. He was a hit every where we went. A year later, upon returning for more classes, several people asked about him. I told them that he was doing quite well in the terrarium I had improvised on my return home. My girlfriend cleverly christened him... Mr Turtle. Hey, she named her hamster..Mr Yamster. More on him later. I cant talk. I named my dog Bananahead.

A couple of years later, my old friend, Dale Meyler who was living in East Dallas very close to downtown called and said that he had rescued a turtle from the road and asked since I lived closer to open country, if I wouldn't mind letting it go away from the city traffic. I naturally agreed although, I didn't follow through with the intended request.

When I arrived home, we decided to see if the new guest and Mr Turtle would get along. We put them on the kitchen floor on opposite sides of the room. Any questions about Mr T's sexuality were quickly dismissed. He stuck his neck out as far as it would go and I swear, it was like a cartoon. His legs turned into wheels and he burned rubber haulin' turtle ass across the floor! He was on her like a bun on a Whopper! Again, I'm assuming she was a her! Now, consider the physical logistics. Flat stomachs, round backs. They're not stackable like Tupperware. His hind legs grabbed on behind her rear flap. She retracted her legs and closed the flap, locking is legs in. Turtles may have multi purpose tails or something because that little appendage was poking and probing, trying to find a way in. The only contact his abdomen made with her shell was about an inch up the curve. This left most of his body elevated about 45 degrees from the floor. His front legs flailed in the air and in my mind I see his tongue hanging out of his mouth and as she dragged him wild eyed

362

around the kitchen using her front legs I think I heard him hollering "Yippee Ki Yay!!!"

Well, it was obvious that she wanted no part of this. I picked them both up and she wasn't about to open the flap and risk getting knocked up. He couldn't get off of her unless she did. I took them to the sink and tried the cold shower routine. Nope. It then occurred to me that if I turned her upside down that she would need all four legs to right herself. It worked!

Later we put them in the terrarium together. It was large enough that she could have her space and they did get along once they got used to each other.

My girlfriend and I eventually ended our romantic relationship but remained friends. We decided that it would be best to let our terrapin pals live their lives in their natural habitat. We took them deep into the woods by my house and put them on the ground. He sat there for a second to orient himself. She, however saw her chance and booked! He watched her go and being the Turtle Whisperer, I sensed sadness on his face! It was kind of heartbreaking. She got about twelve feet away and stopped. She stopped, looked back, turned around and came back for him! They went off into the woods together! I hope they stayed clear of the road.

Music History for blog interview

Like many musicians my age, I was inspired by The Beatles to pick up the guitar. My first was a Silvertone acoustic from Sears. I think the first song i learned was All My Loving. My dad found the lyrics and thought I'd written a love poem to some girl. Not yet.

I formed a combo with Dale Meyer, Vaughn Stockton, Kyle Evans and a couple of other kids rotating in and out. We were called THE MYSTERIANS. That got quashed when? and The MYSTERIANS stole our name. Various bands came and went with Dale, Mark, Steve Bander, and a few other guys.

Just out of high school, I backpacked through Europe and played constantly for $$ and food. Through college, I played with a few of local notables and notables to be. After graduating, I met Bruce McRoberts a prolific songwriter/keyboardist that I played with in several bands and recording projects, the most notable though greatly overlooked Jack B. Quick. We had plenty of good local press and a vague nod in a Rolling Stone article after South X Southwest. After a few years of beating our heads against the walls playing only original music in a Prog/Art rock vein (think Tull/Genesis) in an age of New Wave and later Alternative Rock, JBQ went on hiatus, I, newly single, hit the open Mics and free stages and built a following as a solo artist, playing often in Deep Ellum and Lower Greenville. I shared stages with Sara Hickman, Josh Allen, Rev Horton Heat, New Bohemians, Lost Souls Inc., and more. JBQ eventually reformed, though I, enjoying my solo thing, had declined signing back up. I shared a gig with them and sat in with them on vocals on a New Years Eve gig. I fell back in. We shared a few stages with National touring acts and played every club in Deep Ellum during its heyday. After a few more years, a couple of irreplaceable members moved away and JBQ was history again. Bruce and I recorded a few more tunes that can be heard on SoundCloud under Kent Skinner1 and Ned Nefarious.

Rewind... Mid 80s, pre-JBQ, I recorded my first record, Diana/ Home To You. Yes, a 45! It made it into a few jukeboxes and was a minor hit in Guadalajara of all places. It got played on Q102, and a few copies resurface here and there occasionally. A friend called me excited, saying that I was on KZEW. I ran to the stereo and turned on....not me but Justin Hayward's Forever Autumn. I had to take it as a compliment.

Anyway, post JBQ, doing solo gigs, i was asked if I'd like to open for Shawn Phillips at Poor David's Pub. I eagerly responded affirmatively. Shawn was one of my early influences along w Jethro Tull, Moodys etc. 10 days before the big night i cut my left middle finger badly on a hair cutting razor in my travel bag. I tried everything people suggested, vitamin E, aloe, positive visualization whatever,,,and it was coming along nicely when an ex gf i ran into...BIT IT and busted it open! This all led to a decade long collaboration with the husband of a client of mine, Marc Mydill a terrific guitarist, who sat in that night and filled in what I couldn't do.

I met Shawn that night and have opened for him more times than I can count or remember. Another notable stage sharing was with Robert Fripp, one of the most highly respected guitarists in the world. (King Crimson, League of Extraordinary guitarists, etc) I had a 5 piece band, and we actually could not share that stage because Mr Fripp's band took every square inch of it. We played on the floor in front. A year or so later, at a Laurie Anderson concert, a guy I was squeezing past in a row a seats stopped me and asked, "Didn't you open for Robert Fripp?" I said that I had. He replied, "You guys were great!" I don't necessarily agree, but it's nice to be remembered.

In the 70s I'd hitchhike from Austin with my guitar, amp and dog to play gigs in Dallas. These days, I mostly play in "shut up and listen to the music" environments. Hauling heavy equipment and playing all night in bars and restaurants where the audience didn't come to hear what I want to play doesn't appeal anymore. I do the occasional live benefit and stay fresh doing virtual concerts and open mics. I still open for Shawn when he hits Texas. I love spending time in my studio experimenting with electronic music, recording new songs, and rerecording some of my early pieces many of which I gladly share on request.

Unifried.

Having grown up though not active in what some people outside of our church would consider a fringe religion I have always been interested in other groups take on The Truth. I've said in the past, I might not agree with you but I do wish to understand you. This story has little to do with that.

A couple of years ago I got a call from a very nice lady who had seen Glenna and me performing at Poor David's Pub in Dallas. She was an event coordinator for her church, a Unity church in Oak Cliff and she invited us to perform at their Winter Solstice Celebration. I have several friends that belong to the Unity Church and I was curious to see what their celebration might be like. We agreed to perform and were asked to do a 30-45 minute set but not to include any Christmas music. I thought that their way was to include all sects but that was fine. We prepared our set and looked forward to the show. I somehow got the wrong idea that we would be performing on an outdoor stage with and the fact that we weren't was also fine seeing as how it was mid December!

The show took place in the main chapel (?) and the altar served as the stage. There were two or three acts before us that included some Native American chanting and some kind of moon goddess worship music I think. Interesting enough. We set up quickly. I use a reasonably complicated rig that includes two convincing digital vocal harmonizers so that Glenna and I can, if desired, sound like six people. Also in the gear are a couple of synthesizers that read my guitar and produce orchestral and /or choir accompaniment. Because of the complex set up, I have it pre wired and only need the sound man to accept two lines out into his mixer. Easy as pie. Well, the grumpy sound man had a taste for more complicated pie and wanted to twiddle and have more control. The result was an imbalanced stage mix and the house and outdoor mix only got me. No Glenna. Not great. Friends in the front row who could hear Glenna's unamplified voice said that we sounded good in spite of the bad mix. The next two acts were pretty impressive, a folksy, mostly acoustic band with nice harmonies and good musicianship and a solo multi instrumentalist playing mostly electric violin. They made the long drive worthwhile. There was also a candle lit maze and a big bonfire in which to throw sticks you had written your problems on. Interesting. On the whole, it was a fun if not musically satisfying (to us) evening.

Lionel Returns!

Art Credit: Kent Skinner

"OH..MY..GOD!!"

"What?"

"Curtis just threatened to kick Lionel's ass!!"

I can't think of a better way to continue the saga of Lionel, the lost soul lawyer that I introduced a few years ago. So much more has happened, some funny, much sad, some very wrong. I was mixing color in the color room of the salon when Ashley, my assistant came around the corner and exclaimed the above. So, Lionel, typically oblivious to the possibility that there might be someone present that is just as passionate about their own political stances, which did not jibe well with his, was loudly pontificating about Hillary and Trump whilst having his hair shampooed. Curtis, the husband of another of my guests, while waiting for her to be finished, had finally had enough and stormed back to the shampoo area and told Lionel to "SHUT THE F—- UP OR I'M GOING TO KICK YOUR ASS! NOBODY WANTS TO LISTEN TO THIS S—-!!" Lionel, somewhat shocked, backed down and stuck a cork in it for the moment. Unfortunately, or maybe best, I missed the whole exchange. In a while, I explained to Lionel that although Curtis had been over the top, that he was at least partially right that no one comes to the salon to listen to political rants and that it is likely that good people with differing opinions will be present. On another more recent occasion, he got going, and though his time was up and I had begun another guest's haircut, he continued to espouse his political opinions. Before I could stifle him, my guest, a very conservative, level-headed woman, spoke up. We need to stop this RIGHT NOW!" He apologized and went on his way.

I still consider him a poor lost soul. It's been suggested that he may be on the autistic spectrum. That could very well be true. He is often completely unaware of how he is coming across to people and at the same time desperately seeking acceptance and an audience. A couple of years ago in October, another of my clients who went to school with his daughter told me that his ex wife, the love of his life had died. When I saw him a few days later I said "Lionel, I am so sorry! I heard the news." He replied, "What news?" I answered "About Robin.." He asked "What about Robin?" I hesitated and replied "I.. may have heard wrong...." His face darkened. He said "I know it has to be her son (in law?)! He's telling bulls—- and...well, she was in the hospital but she got out and she's fine! He's always trying to cause drama!" The following April, Lionel showed up for his haircut stunned and devastated. He had just heard that the preceding October, Robin had, in fact died. She had been released from the hospital but had been taken right back in and had indeed passed away.

He only found out because the stepson called and wanted Lionel's signature on some documents in order to access her estate. During those seven months, nobody had told him that the woman that he still loved dearly had died. Needless to say, he was destroyed. I'm glad he came to me, his, as he had called me on several occasions, best friend. Sometime soon after, having gotten access to bank information, the stepson wiped out Lionel's savings. Lionel had held on to the dream that they could reconcile and their finances had remained linked. Another episode that I'm a little fuzzy on involved him falling outside and being very overweight and slightly injured he was unable to get himself up. It was extremely cold and he had spent the night crawling in the cold only to be rescued the following morning. The EMT told him that he should be dead. He refused to go to the hospital. Too hard headed and warm hearted to die, I guess.

One night, after losing his savings he asked if by chance I had an old blow dryer he could have. I happened to have one in the car. It was an old dryer from the school that I had repaired. Lionel happens to drive an old Corvette, bought in better times. I said I'd trade the dryer for his car. He said "Sure! Anything ever happens to me, it's yours." Nothing in writing. It'll probably end up in stepsonny's hands.

The most recent visit at the time of this writing, Lionel lurched in to the salon on crutches wearing white gym shorts, flip flops and a slightly bloody bandage on one knee. The skin of his legs looked like he had been rolling in cracker crumbs. There was not as much political discourse this time. There was some, but he kept it between us. He reiterated how unique and special a person he thinks I am. Shortly after my color client, Lisa had come and seated herself at the next station, we finished his haircut. As he rose from the chair with great effort, he pointed at a small puddle on the floor. "Oh, there's a small puddle. Don't worry. It's just lymphatic fluid. It's not toxic or anything." YES IT IS!!!! YOUR LEG IS LEAKING!!" I didn't say that out loud. We settled up and booked his next appointment. He gave me his traditional stinky hug and departed. Lisa started to rise and come to my station. "STAY THERE!" I said.

"I'm cutting you there!" "OHMYGODTHANKYOU!!" She said.

I got out the bleach and sterilized EVERYTHING. We laughed. Inside I was screaming, "I will call him today and see how he is doing." I don't think I want the Corvette.

Us vs Them

Art Credit: Kent Skinner

Since the dawn of mankind (great way to start a rant!)....people have had a need to band together. For food, protection, companionship, recreation, procreation, shelter etc. Then at some point this band or tribe discovered another tribe just over the hill or just outside the boundaries of "their" territory. Thus began "Us vs. Them." "We don't know them. They're different. We don't like them." Sometimes the strangers had something that they desired. Sometimes they had something that the strangers desired. Sometimes they traded. Sometimes they merged. Many times the stronger tribe just took what they wanted. Food, supplies, slaves or whatever.

This mindset of "Us vs. Them" never went away. It lives today in our politics "Libtards vs Trumplodytes." It lives in our race relations: Black vs. White vs. brown. It lives in our lifestyles: Straight vs LGBT... I notice when you capitalize the words they suddenly become tribes. It lives in our religions. Christians vs. Jews vs. Muslims vs. Hindus vs. Buddhists vs. Wiccans vs. Mormons vs. Baptists vs. Atheists (not really a religion), Cowboys vs. whoever (kind of a religion) and so on. People die at British soccer games because they sing the wrong fight song. People die because they call God by other names. Within each of these faction there have always been charismatic people who climb into leadership roles and many people follow and perpetuate their tribal mindset. These leaders always had their own spin on the truth. BTW There is only one truth but countless perceptions of it.

It's much easier to blame someone else than to admit ones shortcomings or lack of understanding. It's easy to demonize someone who is from a different tribe than it is to delve in and try to understand them. Understanding does not necessarily mean agreeing.

Its easier to buy into a seemingly impressively researched conspiracy theory and feel like you have "the inside poop" on the moon landing or 911 or Obama's citizenship or chem trails or 5G or whatever the scoop du jour is than to accept the possibility that another tribe might be right about something you don't totally or even want to understand. Again, understanding doesn't mean agreeing.

There is so much division today for many reasons. With social media as convenient and insulating as it is, bullies and asshats have awarded themselves license to print whatever they want regardless of other's feelings. I have recently seen good people hurt, reputations damaged and careers ended because of gossip and groundless cyber bullying. TAKE A STAND! Not for your team but for the good of mankind! Don't buy into the unbelievable because it's convenient or shocking or more exciting than reality! Is there stuff going on that we don't know about or understand? Of course there is, was and always will be but just because you and I don't get it doesn't mean that it is a plot or hoax by "Them." I think I need to put on John Lennon's Imagine right now. It will take more than just imagining.

Sam And The Tigers

Art Credit: Zane Skinner

We live in a world where due to increased sensitivity, awareness, media and public opinion, one has to watch one's words. What used to be funny is now often considered not. This was funny to everyone involved at the time and may not fly now but I think it still deserves sharing. My old friend Nancy had a little girl named Page. She still has her, she's just not a little girl anymore. They were sitting in the waiting room of her doctor's office and Page was "reading" out loud from the popular but since then banned children's book, Little Black Sambo. Google it and yes, you'll see a stereotypically racist caricature of an African kid. Actually, Google almost any kid's book and you might see caricatures of kids of every race. Except for the name "Sambo" having been often used as a slur since the original story, I don't think there's really anything racist about the story itself. Also, tigers are not native to Africa. They originated in India and further east. The original author, Helen Bannerman lived in India in late 1800s and the early 1900s and had in fact, placed her story there. Somehow it was changed to Africa by the publishers. A newer less potentially offensive version is titled "Sam and the Tigers."

The story I tell here is still as funny as it was then to all involved.

Page was 2 and a half, maybe 3 years old and was too young to really read but Nancy had read it to her enough times that she knew it by heart. So Page is "reading" out loud with exaggerated inflection. Well, there happened to be two older African American women also sitting there in the waiting room. Nancy realizes that Page had memorized the book exactly the way she had heard it read to her so many times, complete with the exaggerated expression and inflection she herself had used and had probably heard as a child! She was red faced with embarrassment!

Happily, both women were laughing out loud and responding, "Now.. what'd that little black boy say again?" Page gladly repeated," Puleeeeease Mista Tigah! Please don't eat me up!!"

More laughter ensued followed by "One more time! What'd that little black boy say?"

Sometimes You Can Smell It....

Art Credit: Zane Skinner

One job I had while in my early college years was delivery guy for Webb Chapel Florists. It was owned by Wanda Stockton, my friend Vaughn Stockton's stepmom. To give you a taste of her demeanor, once after telling Vaughn's dad that she wanted to go dancin' and being told that he was too tired, she retrieved his 45 and shot 6 holes in the bed around him. He took her dancin'.

Delivering flowers would be an easy enough job, you'd think, but people want their flowers delivered on time, to the right address and not wilted. That's a given. It's hard to do when the flower orders are mixed up and especially hard to deliver them fresh in Texas in a van with no air conditioning! I drank my share of Mr Pibb that summer and listened to my jam box as I drove. Yeah, no radio either.

One day when I wasn't there, Wanda arrived unexpectedly and sniffing disapprovingly snapped "Billie Jean!! I smell POT in here!" (I guess she knew what it smelled like.) Billie Jean, the flower arranger replied wide eyed, "Well..... Sometimes you can smell it...and there dont even be's nobody been smokin it!" Hands on her hips, Wanda responded "If there "DON'T EVEN BE'S NOBODY BEEN SMOKIN' IT, then HOW AM I SUPPOSED TO BE SMELLIN' IT??" I don't know the rest of that conversation, my not having witnessed it personally but I'm sure there was more sarcasm involved.

A couple of memories that come to mind involved funerals. I remember Billie Jean saying, "Now, Boogah! (her nickname for... everybody) You be sho to git dese flowers to dis funeral home by 9:30 and dese to the other one by 10:30!!" I got to the first funeral home way early. When I arrived at my second stop early, according to my schedule, people were already filing out from the service. I had to deal with angry and disappointed family members that didn't see their flowers at the alter. I felt bad for them and embarrassed. (Please don't shoot the delivery peon!!) Billie Jean had screwed up my schedule. Musta been the pot that nobody is smokin'. At another funeral home, I walked in the front door and was greeted by a grouchy old fart in a black suit. He said, "Flower room's around back!!" I replied, "I know, but I was specifically told to get someone to help me carry the coffin spray in because the mums are very fragile...." "FLOWER ROOM'S AROUND BACK!!" He interrupted. "Yeah, but I..." "SOMEBODY SHOW THIS DUMBASS WHERE THE FLOWER ROOM IS!!!" No one responded. Charming guy in the black suit met me at the back and offered no help. Listening to his grumbling and cussing, I carried the large, fragile array of mums in the back door by myself and paraded them past a couple of bodies on tables with tubes in them. "BRING IT IN HERE!" he said. I entered the viewing room to see a half-open casket with the corpse of an old man lying in it. "GO ON! STICK IT ON THERE!" he barked. I did and left past the other two unlucky stiffs out the back amid fading obscenities. There was an Arby's or Roy Rodger's next door. I later imagined knocking on their back door wearing a black suit with a friend on a gurney covered by a sheet and saying, "Our air conditioning is out. Would you mind if we borrowed your freezer?" Musta been the...

Once a pawn a time...

Michelle: "Do you even have a savings account?"

Me: "There's pawnshops I've never even been in!"

It's another one of those conversations I have no recollection of but was reminded of years later and absolutely believe took place.

This is also one of those stories that will overlap and probably repeat parts of my other stories. Such is the nature of a life fully lived. Mine includes an addiction to other people's misery. That's not true at all. Just the results of what might have been bad choices somewhere in their lives. I've certainly made my share.

Part 1: My earliest pawn shop victory that I can recall was in an old place on Red River in Austin. I had just received an amended check from Uncle Sam, having been shorted some for a semester's V.A. benefits. I was actually looking for a tape deck and after asking if I could listen to one that was way up on a shelf, the shopkeeper snapped, "You gonna buy it?" I asked "Can I test it out?" "IT WORKS!" He barked. The concept of sound quality and signal to noise ratio were obviously beyond him. I decided to pass. Then I noticed two large black boxes facing each other. I separated them and realized that I was looking at two Altec Lansing A7 "Voice of The Theater" speaker cabinets. At the time, they were worth at least $500. I just looked on eBay and I can buy them now for around $4000. I asked Mr. Customer Service "How much do you want for these?" "Them old git-tar boxes? I'll take one seventy five." I told him "I gotta hook them up." I told him I needed two cords, an amp and a microphone. He brought me the crappiest mic he had but I made do and hooked them up. I handed him the mic and said "Talk." "Wuh.. wuh...whut do I say?" I said "Say anything." foreshadowing the title of an 80s movie. "Say your ABCs!" I suggested. He did. "N..Now what??" He stammered. I said "Start counting!" He did. He was sweating by now, not used to hearing himself amplified. He was mine. I drove off minus

$125 with two large friends that brought me decades of enjoyment. I used to use pullies to raise and lower them off of my balcony at College House in Austin. They took up a large portion of a couple of very small apartments in college. They were so efficient that my small Panasonic cassette stereo and my Craig slide mount eight track deck would power them adequately. They also fit perfectly side by side right behind the front (and only) seats of my 65 Dodge van, astonishing more than a couple hitch hikers. I loaned them to several notable artists over the years. Elvis Costello sang through them as did Alex Chilton, John Dee Graham and Jessie Sublett. Jessie, playing with Standing Waves borrowed them and dropped one off a dolly onto the cement of 21st street resulting in my first repair. The next was when 1000 watts of dc power popped both voice coils with cool flashes and smoke. Another night, doing sound for the incredible Jeannie Seidner, I tied them to the top of my Opel Manta and drove them a couple of miles to Dobie Mall. Pedestrian's jaws dropped. Sara Hickman's voice later graced their cones and coils. I'm pretty sure that Joe Eddy Hines and the Rockin' Devils also pushed them to their limits at one time or another.

Years passed, and I transplanted the works into slightly smaller, though not much lighter, JBL cabinets and left the empty boxes at our rented practice studio in downtown Garland, intending to pick them up later. A couple of months passed. I happened to be running by there one evening, and luckily, I saw them in the alley behind the studio. I finished my race and came back for them later that night. I guiltily drove them home, nonverbally apologizing to my old, abandoned buddies. Eventually, technology caught up with us, and better sounding, self-amplified, MUCH lighter and smaller speakers became available. I succumbed. I did find a home for them with a fledgling garage band who reloaded them with lesser speakers. At least they live on! I hope they are doing well and bringing someone joy.

A Murder Of Grackles

Art Credit: Kent Skinner

AAAAWWWK?!!!...AAAAWWWK?!!!.....
AAAWWWKAAAWWWK?!!!....AAAWWWK?!!!

I parked under the tree behind the salon the other day. The tree was full of grackles. I mean full! I know that many crows = a murder of crows. A group of grackles is a pod, flock, or flight. I think murder sounds better. Anyway, they were all making exactly the same sound. Saying the exact same thing in Gracklese or whatever they call it. Oh yeah, they call it "AAAWWWK?!" It was as if Mother Nature had taught them the same song. "Okay! Now, everyone start on the same note...Edgar! Open wide! Same note..." Edgar: "But I identify as a raven!" "No Edgar! We all start on the same note and go up in pitch slightly..."

Anyway, I think I saw Edgar walking on the ground in front of my truck, oblivious to a mass of grackle poop on his back and tail. Or maybe not. Maybe he wanted to leave the pod of like thinking grackles to pursue his life as a raven. Chances are, most of that flock had some poop on them!

I did see another bird, I think a mockingbird, fly into the tree and quickly exit. Too many birds singing the SAME song, and an unpleasant one at that.

I suddenly thought of a dear friend... She has always been fun, outspoken, sarcastic, and intelligent, though of a totally different political and religious mindset than me. I love her anyway. She regularly posts inflammatory and often false propaganda mined from extreme sources and exclusively responded to by those of a similar frame of mind. It has nearly cost her the friendship of at least a couple of people that I'm aware of. People who care enough to turn a blind eye or at least forgive her blatantly incorrect and insulting "fake news."

I then thought of some of my friends on the exact opposite side of the fence and how they, too, flock together and ignore truth, good or even middle ground from the "opposition."

I also thought of people I grew up with, partied with, lived and worked and played with that have flocked to one extreme or the other, and I lament the times gone where we could just love or like one another despite our inherited or chosen politics.

In a nutshell, flocking without regard, without truly understanding (perhaps believing) and singing the same song as everyone else in your pod can lead to great personal loss and strutting around oblivious to the load of poop on your own tail! Aaand later I drove way with grackle poop all over my truck.

Soda Jerk

Art Credit: Kent Skinner

Two soda fountain memories:

First, my sister would drop us off at Sunday school and would supposedly park the car and go to the adult service. She actually spent that next hour having an ice cream soda and reading magazines at the Highland Park drug store. This went on for years.

Second, after getting fired from my snack bar job at Target for making joke announcements, rather than tell my parents of my stupidity, I hung out at the Preston Forest Skillern's Drugs and read comics. The seedy soda jerk/ "assistant manager" asked me if I needed a job. I jumped at it, thinking it'd be easier to tell my folks that I had just made a "career change." He and I smoked a couple in the back "kitchen" and would open and close whenever we felt like it. We never cleaned or mopped but would go through incredible amounts of Lysol spray to hide the odor. After almost two weeks of giving him a ride to work and random hours, I found out that he wasn't really the assistant anything, and I wasn't really on the payroll. It got sorted out somehow, and after taking a polygraph test that I was not old enough to legally authorize, I opted to quit rather than go through the embarrassing and likely job-ending process of a second and legal parent-approved test. Skillerns was owned by the Zales Corporation and one of the Zales daughters worked at that particular store. In my shallow 16-year-old mindset, I couldn't see past her prominent proboscis and did not respond to her flirtations. Foolish and unkind me. Zales money can buy all kinds of surgical modifications if desired. I could be sitting on a much nicer toilet writing this story on a much nicer and smarter-than-me smartphone. I did get paid my $1.50 an hour for my 2 weeks, though.

By a very odd coincidence, my parents met the Target general manager at a dinner party and heard all about my exit story and p.a. shenanigans. They were just waiting to see how long I would pretend to go to work at the snack bar before admitting to my dumbassedness. I think they had ESPP- extra sensory parental perception. I may have inherited it.

Linda And Me

Art Credit: Grayson Perigo

Years ago, my older sister, Carolyn, gave me a t-shirt for Christmas that read "I Choked Linda Lovelace" on it. Really? My sister? So I wore it that morning. A little later, she asked me if I wanted to go to church with her, and I declined, saying that I didn't have anything appropriate to wear. She said, "Just wear what you have on. It's a very open-minded church!" I replied, "Well, they must be!" It turned out that she had misread the shirt when she bought it. She was aware of my musical crush and thought it said, "I Chose Linda Ronstadt." Yeah, I skipped church that morning.

I mentioned in an earlier story how having hitch hiked to the Armadillo World Headquarters in Austin to see Linda Ronstadt (not Lovelace), I stood at the edge of the stage while she sang "Love Has No Pride" smiling and gazing right into my adoring eyes. Well. At least, that's how I choose to remember it.

KENT SKINNER'S STORIES KNOWS ALL, SEES ALL

Art Credit: Kent Skinner

Accidentally On Porpoise

You may be surprised to know in another life I was a marine biologist. Yes, there was always something fishy about me! Anyway, I received a large grant to study a subspecies of porpoises that apparently had zero mortality rate. They had been living so long that there was no procreation either. No need! I brought a few of them back to The United States for study, but to my great dismay, they began to fall ill, and I nearly lost a couple of them! I was in a panic! I didn't know what to do! They were too weak to make the return trip home. Then, by a weird fluke, I discovered that it had something to do with a symbiotic relationship they shared with a rare breed of seagull. Not just any old seagull. Again, I had to go to the coast of Africa to try and retrieve some of these birds in the hope of saving our amazing sea brethren.

Luck was with me at first, and I located and corralled some of these birds who, missing their fishy friends, came willingly. Our return trip to the airport was stalled. In order to get to the plane, we had to travel through some dense jungle, and at one point, our path was blocked by a huge, majestic lion asleep across the trail! There was no way around on either side so I realized that the only way was over him! We cut down some bamboo, and with the caged birds strapped to my back, I pole-vaulted over our fierce, slumbering obstacle. Immediately, I was surrounded by the Jungle Police! "You're under arrest!" they exclaimed! I asked, "What for? What are the charges?"

He replied, "For transporting gulls over the stately lion for immortal porpoises!"

Ghost Stories

Well, it was suggested that I share a couple of true ghost experiences here. The first of several was about 4 years ago. I am a semi-retired hairstylist, and one Sunday, I was at the salon alone and awaiting a guest/friend that I was doing a favor for, coming in on my day off. While I waited, sitting in my styling chair, suddenly, crystal clear, and as if someone was leaning close and whispering loudly in my right ear I heard my name, "KENT!" I got up and investigated. There was no one in the building. The shops next door were also closed and empty. Later, I asked the owner of the building if he had ever experienced anything unexplainable, and he said he hadn't, but there used to be a funeral home a few doors down. I doubt it had anything to do with this. As far as I know, I never knew anyone that had been through there.

The next one needs a little backstory. When my mother passed about fifteen years ago, we removed her rings before she was taken from her apartment. My brother-in-law, a completely trustworthy and good man, put them in his jeans pocket for safekeeping. Later, he discovered that they were gone. We searched every square inch of everywhere he had been that afternoon with no results. I visited pawn shops and gold buyers for weeks and still keep my eyes open for the distinctive rings. My sister and brother-in-law were devastated. About two years ago, we moved my wife's mother in with us. Having just remodeled, we let her have our master suite downstairs, and we turned my music room (biggest room in the house) into our new bedroom. One morning, as my wife was preparing for work in the spare bedroom next door that we call "the get ready room," I had just stepped into the hall, and I heard a woman's voice say clearly, "I'm looking for a ring." I asked my wife, "What did you say?" She responded, "I didn't say anything." "You didn't just say "I'm looking for a ring"? "No. I haven't said a word." Then I realized that I had just passed my mother's portrait hanging in the hall. I hope she finds it. I'll keep looking.

Men With Hats

On the first day of our honeymoon in Jamaica, I threw my back out! No, not that way! We stayed at a beautiful all-inclusive resort called Swept Away in Negril. They offer all kinds of water sports, great service, nice accommodations, and terrific food. On that first morning, we were scheduled to go scuba diving. I brought my own gear, and I knew that there was a tiny non, life-threatening leak in my vest, and to be sure that it hadn't gotten any worse, I lifted it into a big tank of water to check it. Being married to a Physical Therapist, I should have known to use good body mechanics but in my haste, I didn't. Ouch! It wasn't the on,y time I'd hurt my back, but it was the worst. For the whole time in Jamaica, I could barely walk. Of course, walking down the beach, local entrepreneurs were glad to offer "local medicine." "Yah, mon, I got anything you need!" "Have you got Ibuprofen?" "No, mon, sorry!" I didn't take him up on his other suggestions. I did end up buying a cool walking stick made of some local wood with two odd-angled branches serving as handles. It was brightly painted and ornately carved. It had a couple of comical men's faces with beards and wearing hats. It served me well that week, and by our last night, I was able to slow dance with my bride.

Anyway, over the years since, I've needed it at least a couple more times. One of those times, I had hurt my back in Tae Kwon Do and was using it to get around at work at the Dallas Paul Mitchell school. Robert Cromeans, the Global Artistic Director for John Paul Mitchell Systems, was visiting, and I was back stage supervising a few students who had volunteered to help prepare models for his presentation. He noticed my walking stick and asked about it. I told him I'd hurt my back in Karate and was nearly better. He looked at it a little closer and asked, "O.K., but do you think it's a good idea to be walking around the school carrying a cane covered in d___s?" "WHAT??" I responded. Upon closer examination, I realized that he was right! Those little smiling men wearing hats......those weren't hats! In all those years, gratefully using that cane when needed to get around, it had never occurred to me what was really carved into it! I quickly went back to my office, and using a black Sharpie pen, I augmented the artwork enough that it wasn't as obvious what the intent of the artist was! In the mean time, I'm still grateful to have it and have needed it more than I wish.

23 years later, we have just returned from our second trip to Jamaica and, by sheer luck, ended up at the same resort, though neither of us could remember the name when we booked it. It was much more fun this time, not needing that stick!

Stand Up Comedy

I'll preface this story with the fact that my mother-in-law is a retired nurse. I found this first part out later after a bizarre exchange involving my inquisitive toddler daughter and my incredulous wife. So, apparently, grandma was in the process of changing my baby boy's diaper when his 2-year-old sister had questions. Grandma, being well versed in her medical anatomical terminology, was gladly willing to answer her granddaughter's queries. "What's that gramma?"

"Well, that's the…"

Anyway, fast forward. I was in my own bathroom, standing in front of the porcelain receptacle doing what it was designed for, when a tiny voice behind me asks, "What are you doing?"

I quickly turned away from her and replied, "I'm GOING to the bathroom! Would you mind??"

Probably unaware that standing is a viable option for males and, I guess, females too, though less accurate, she responded, "No, you're not! You're playing!!" and exited quickly. Moments later, Glenna arrived, looking VERY concerned. "What's going on??" "I'm trying to take a leak!" "Savvy just came and told me, "Daddy's playing with his rectum!" "I'M NOT PLAYING WITH ANYTHING!! I'M JUST TRYING TO PEE!!"

Apparently, grandma was not as thorough in her geographical explanation as she was in her terminology. I held on to this story until I decided Savvy was old enough to hear it. She was appropriately mortified but thinks it's hilarious now, as do I.

Leaf It To Me..

In addition to my years as a marine biologist/ surgeon/ superhero/ rock star etc. I also spent some time as an anthropologist. Here's one of many tales.

Working for a major Texas university with a strong interest in plants, I was given a grant to study a particular tribe in the Amazon. I was asking for more money, the subject matter being even more fascinating than I originally thought and I was asked to present my findings to the committee.

"We have already granted you a small fortune!" they said. "Just what is it about this particular tribe that you think warrants us giving you more?" "Well, they have a fascinating natural herbal medicine system!" I replied. The chairman said "They ALL have some kind of herbal medicine System. What so special about theirs? I answered "Well, for example, they take the leaves of this one palm plant and roll them up and use them for suppositories!" The Chairman replied "Well, while I'll admit that while this is rather unusual it hardly justifies the amount of money you are asking for." I countered "You don't seem to understand! With fronds like that, who needs enemas?"

Zaneisms

Photo by Glenna Skinner

Many of you know about our kids, Savannah and Zane. Here are some of the things they, mostly Zane, said as he was growing up.

Zane: "Dear God, Thank you for all the things that you made and all the food and please don't litter or you have to go to court. In Jesus name, amen."

New Zane ism: I ate a orca! Hey! I thought they were supposed ta be black and white, not green!"-Zane, enjoying his first bowl of gumbo.

Zane: "I need to find the potty." Me: "See that bush across the street." "No! Then the streets would be all slippery, and cars would crash each other!" "Oh, then I'd better take you to the bathroom."

Zane- "I know what would be a good show...America's Funniest No Whining Videos! And I would be on it!" Me- "I'll let you know when they start auditioning."

1st Law of the mind in action: Me: "Zane, I asked you to take your clothes upstairs and hang them up!" Zane: "I'm chewing gum!" Me: "Better stay off your bike then."

Zane- "I have finally comprehended the theory and mechanisms of quantum physics!" Everyone ever- "you're so smart, bro, haha." Yes, Zane just got hold of the iPad.

Zane, upon FINALLY mastering potty training...well, almost.

"I went poopie...I went peepees. I went.....I went BROWN!!

Zane: " My 5 best wishes are...#1 ..lots of food. #2 to be with you all the time. #3 Three more hour of sleep... #4 Any good games that are not girly...#5... I'm still working on that one." I'm right there with him!

Zane: " Why is it called your bottom if your feet are at the bottom?" I don't know. "Ask God. He knows everything." I'm sure he has nothing better to do.

Took the kids to Six Flags. Me: "What was your favorite ride?" Zane: "I liked them all....especially Mr Fabreeze!"

Zane:" I love Indian food, Mexican food, Jimpanzee food......"- much laughter on our part. Supposed to be "Japanese".

Zane @ King Fu Panda 2 in 3d : "WOH! TOO CLOSE! BACK OFF CHINA LAND!"

Zane was worried about his impending extraction. It was so tiny it was hard to get hold of. Then I was inspired to action by the immortal words of Mr. Nicholson. "You want the tooth? YOU CAN'T HANDLE THE TOOTH!"

Me: "And the atmosphere is made of oxygen, hydrogen, nitrogen..." Zane: "and Richardson?"

I have several special names I use for my son.

Me: What's your favorite nickname that I use for you?

Zane: Either Cheesefritter or Mitten. I've never used either.

New Zane ism: The other day, Glenna was lifting Savvy's pack into the car and asked, "My Gosh! Who do you have in here?" Zane, to the tune of "Do You Want to Build A Snowman"

"Do you want to hide a body?" That's my boy.

Zane: "Every time I dream, you're in it 'cause you come in my room and jump into my dream cloud!"

Zane's latest: "There's a song in my tummy that makes me not be in bed."

Zane: "I need to find the potty." Me: "See that bush across the street." "No! Then the streets would be all slippery, and cars would crash each other!" "Oh, then I'd better take you to the bathroom."

Me: "What do your rooms look like?" Zane: "Mine looks kind of like a square."

Zane- "I know what would be a good show...America's Funniest No Whining Videos! And I would be on it!" Me- " I'll let you know when they start auditioning."Zane to Glenna, "After I ate spaghetti and I didn't brush my teeth yet, I tried to play your flute, but the spaghetti smell wore off now, and it doesn't smell like it anymore." Glenna, "Ack...ack.."

Me: Do you even know who John Wayne was?

Zane: No, but I know who Mayo West is or whatever.

Me: "No, son. That's not a freckle. It's a mole." Zane: "You mean moles ated you?"

Me: "How did I end up with all of you on my lap?" Savvy: "It's like a magnet between our bottoms and your lap!"

Zane-ism of the week: "I think I need one of those mattresses so I can make my brain work."

Glenna: "Does it sound like the kids are in bed ?" Me: "I think They're asleep." Zane: "I'M ON FIRE!!! MY PANTS ARE ON FIRE!!!!! Did you see my butt?" Us: sideways, in tears.

Me: "Why didn't you do what your mom asked you?" Zane: "I didn't hear her. My ears are too short!"

Me: "You kids ready for our nature walk?" Zane: "I've already been walking a LONG time. I was walking around my room."

Zane- "When we were in the pool and splashed water on each udder..." Me- " There were cows in the pool?"

Zane, re. being nice to everybody: "I try to be good at girls, but my brain won't let me!" I totally get that.

Zane: "Why do I have to don't do anything because my tummy is hungry? I don't have time to do stuff. I have time to eat because my tummy is hungry."

Zane: "I'm tired of sleeping. I'm all out of it, and my nose is stuck."

Zane: " My 5 best wishes are...#1 ..lots of food. #2 to be with you all the time. #3 Three more hour of sleep... #4 Any good games that are not girly...#5... I'm still working on that one." I'm right there with him!

Savvy @ the Thanksgiving table: "Are the girl ones chickens and the boy ones turkeys?"

Zane: "Who tooted?"

Me: "Now, don't start getting smarty pants with me." Zane: Well, "I try to listen, but I keep saying it too fast!"

E.E.Skinner (My Dad)

'Twas a cold winter evening, the gang was all leaving, O'Riley was closing the bar. When…he… turned and he said to the Lady in Red, "Get out! You can't stay where you are!" She…shed a sad tear in her bucket of beer as she thought of the cold night ahead when..a…gentleman dapper stepped out of the crapper, and these are the words that he said, "Her… mother…never told her the things that a young girl should know about the ways of Air Force men and how they come and go.

The years have taken her beauty, and life has dealt her ajar So remember your mothers and sisters, boys….And let her sleep under the bar!"

One of my early memories of my father was him teaching me this Air Force drinking song so that I could surprise my mom and grandparents. It worked. For some reason, he edited the word "crapper" out and substituted "cloakroom." THAT DOESN'T EVEN RHYME!! We sang it wrong all of my life driving on family trips. Who says "cloakroom" anyway? It wasn't until a few years ago that I figured that out.

My dad was a remarkable man. When I speak of his accomplishments, I sometimes wonder if the person I'm speaking to suspects me of making stuff up. I'm not. I'll start early, though, just to give you an idea of his character.

Born in 1919, he was the middle of three kids, surrounded by his older brother, J.C. (Jake), and younger sister, Norma Jean (Jean). To avoid the confusion of having two kids named Gene and Jean, my dad was called "Skeet," as in skeeter, as in skinny as a mosquito. My cousins Laurie and Steve still remember him as "Uncle Skeet."

Skeet would come home from school each day and sit on the porch with his little sister, Jean, and teach her what he'd learned. I'm sure that this exercise worked for both of them since sharing knowledge is a great way to retain it yourself. They were both very intelligent people. From what I've heard, Jake was the wild card. I have little memory of him since he died when I was very young. In pictures that I inherited somehow, he appears to be in Cambodia in the mid-1950s. I'm no expert, nor is my cousin Steve, who speculated that since the US was not officially in Cambodia during that time, that perhaps Jake's supposed heart attack in Hawaii might have been of "other causes" and elsewhere. In other photos, its very obvious that he had a good sense of humor and must have been quite a character. It's a shame when one's life disappears into the ether with no one to tell your stories. He and his wife, Ollie Mae, never had children.

Their father, Frank Skinner, died in an oil well accident when my dad was 10. He had helped build the church in which we were married in the Becker Community near Kemp Texas. It and the old schoolhouse that they attended is sitting on the edge of our family land. My Dad donated a small piece for the schoolhouse to be moved and preserved. It now serves as the Becker Community Center. It echoes with silent stories, untold for a century.

Their mother, my grandmother, Mabel, supported them as a hairstylist during the Depression. I don't think I knew that when I was talked into giving it a try after finishing college. I heard several stories from those day....many times..and somewhere, I have a cassette tape of her telling some of them. I wish I could hear them again live. She later remarried, but that belongs in another story...or not.

Here's s one bit that might raise eyebrows. Right out of high school, young Gene Skinner went to Chicago to study this new thing called "Television." He built the very first television broadcasting and receiving set up in the southwestern US. I'll include a picture in this story and a Dallas Morning News story from 1937. He also wrote articles about this new phenomenon and speculated that one day, "you'll be able to watch the war from the front lines or watch your favorite plays in your own living room!" He couldn't have imagined "The Jerry Springer Show" or "Jackass." It's probably best.

In World War 2 he flew in the first official (and several unofficial) mission as a radar man. Ground radar would send a rough idea to his plane, and he would narrow the enemy plane's location. They did take a few down though often not. It was on one of these missions that he caught a chest full of flack metal that decades later caused his final heart attack and earned him the first Purple Heart awarded in WW2 and a listing in Who's Who. He also earned the earliest Air Medal with the Oak Leaf Cluster awarded in the European Theater.

In 1947, an army plane crashed into the Empire State Building. My dad, a pretty good photographer, happened to be right there on the street. Having press credentials, he grabbed his camera and was able to shoot photos inside at the crash site. A couple of them showed victims in the rubble. decades later, my mother watched a documentary of that crash and saw her husband walking around the scene taking pictures. She got footage from the news station and had copies made for all of us.

He retired as a Lt Col in the USAF in the early 60s and joined up with a fledgling company called Texas Instruments, Where he put to good use his Master's Degrees in Electrical Engineering acquired during his service years. He helped me with my 7th grade science fair project on Integrated Circuits. He brought home some silicon chips and mounts, which I put under a magnifying glass, and explained what they were all about. My teachers were flabbergasted. "WHAT IS THIS?? ALIEN TECHNOLOGY??" Oddly, he never owned one of T.I.'s calculators. He figured the costs would come down. He never imagined that they'd come free with magazine subscriptions or that they'd fit in your wallet. I've often said that either his mind would be blown by the tech we take for granted today or, more likely, he would have stayed on the cutting edge and would have been responsible for even more advancements. Sadly, we lost him at age 52 when I was 18. I never got to hear more about his experiences first hand.

He was a very smart man and he was also a good person. Every memory I have of him stood on good intentions. Even a couple of awkward attempts at joking around with me and my buddies. I recognize now, as a father, that it's difficult to play both sides of the father/friend field. I believe I've been at least as successful at that as he was because he was. Thanks, Dad.

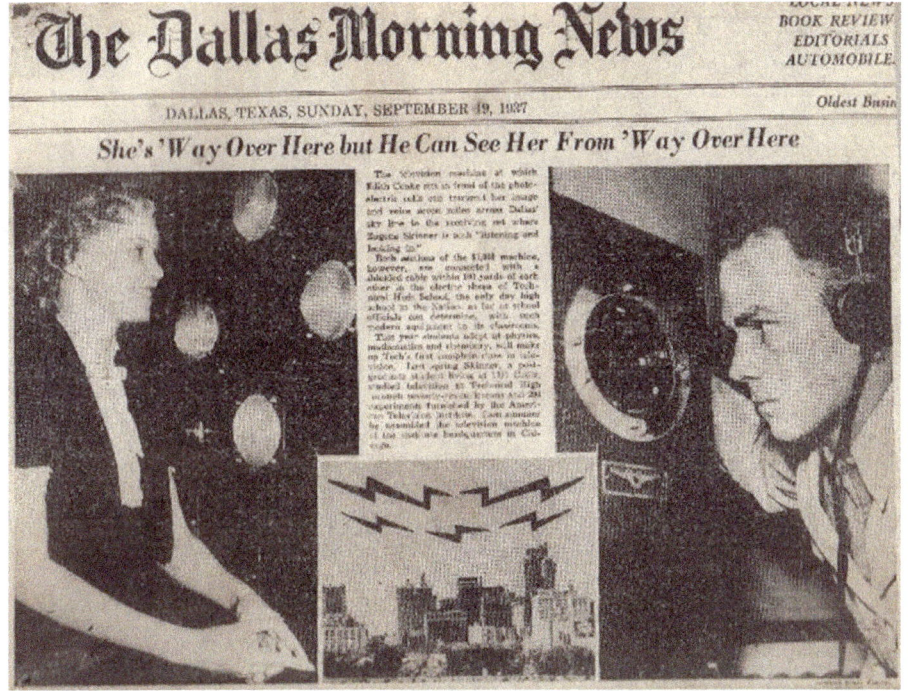

With television equipment
Constructed, 1937

Dallasite Recalls the Early Radar

Air Force Officer Established Some 'Europe' Firsts

The twin-engined Bristol Beaufighter rolled to a stop on a landing strip near Lincoln, north of London. An American radar man and a Canadian pilot piled out.

"Well, Yank," said a Britisher at the hangar. "You're at war now."

The American, an Army shavetail named Eugene Skinner, already had a dozen wartime missions behind him. He told the Britisher to go soak his crumpet.

Then the Britisher told him the Japanese had bombed Pearl Harbor.

That was a quarter of a century ago.

Radar was so new that nobody called it radar. It was "radio location" to Lt. Skinner and the others in those days. American sympathy for the British had run high since the start of the Battle of Britain. Some Americans had joined the Royal Canadian Flying Corps and other outfits. But U.S. forces weren't supposed to be fighting.

Skinner was.

An electrical engineering graduate of the University of Texas, Skinner had been assigned to the U.S. Signal Corps when he enlisted in July, 1941.

He volunteered to go to Great Britain to "study" radar techniques. He had arrived in November. After a few hours in a classroom, he was flying combat missions.

His first ride in a plane had been a lark in San Antonio. His second was a combat run in a Beaufighter.

It required an official wink at Skinner's formal status as "a neutral." But Great Britain was desperately trying to stop the German bombers which were switching from daylight to night raids.

"GROUND RADAR WOULD vector us to the general area of bombers, then I'd try to lock on them with the radar in our aircraft," Skinner recalled Saturday at his home, 4840 Nashwood Lane.

"More often than not, they got away."

But Skinner managed to nail a couple of German bombers.

And he established some military firsts. He flew the first combat mission by an American officer in Europe during World War II. He received the first Purple Heart awarded to a U.S. air officer in Europe. He owns the earliest dated Air Medal (with Oak Leaf Cluster) awarded in the European Theater. And he was the first American flier rotated back to the United States.

Rotation normally came after 25 missions. But Skinner, with his running start on the war, completed 27.

THE PURPLE HEART was for a chest full of flak metal he picked up during a raid over France. Twice he was aboard flights that landed at night in German-occupied France to pick up secret agents. He found the night landings "shaky situations" and the rescued agents uncommunicative.

Later, Skinner fought in the Aleutians and, still later, he served in the Korean War.

He retired from the Air Force as a lieutenant colonel four years ago. Returning to Dallas, his hometown, Skinner became manager of the communications and administrative services division at Texas Instruments.

Saturday he dug out some old flying goggles and his medals as he talked about the Battle of Britain. Kent Skinner, 13, and Barbara Skinner, 9, and Skinner's wife, Barbara, looked over the souvenirs as the retired officer talked about a 2-hour flight 25 years ago.

He went up a neutral and came down a combatant. —KENT BIFFLE.

—Dallas News Staff Photo by Bill Winfrey

Lieutenant Colonel and Mrs. Eugene Skinner and their children, Barbara and Kent, go through some souvenirs of Skinner's World War II service. He began fighting in Europe before any other U.S. air officer. Barbara is holding a model of a Bristol Beaufighter.

Good Friend and Cousin

It's been two years today that my good friend and cousin Steve Long left us. One thing I promised him was that I'd get his last book published. It's available on Amazon. It's titled "Confessions of a Psycho-Therapist: Essays From The Field"

Steve was a voracious reader and writer. He authored at least three books and dozens of songs and poems. He finished three cds of great, thoughtful and thought provoking songs, mostly in a Country/ Folk format. He was very intelligent but came off as modest and down to earth. He had a great sense of humor and was very self deprecating. This book is a fun and interesting read. He takes you from his youth, hippie days, traveling the US and Europe and through all the experiences that led him to being a good though unconventional psychotherapist working mostly with sometimes dangerous people referred by the justice system.

Going through his stuff was an adventure! So much paper and finished and unfinished work! It's been an honor.

For a few months before his passing, he had suffered from an ongoing respiratory problem that he believed to be pneumonia. He went to the doctor and fainted in the parking lot. When I picked him up from the hospital he told me that his body was riddled with tumors, his lungs, brain, liver....pretty much anywhere you can imagine. Needless to say, it was devastating. There really was nothing to be done. He called us one morning, incoherent and unaware of where he was. We figured out that he was in fact at home in front of his laptop. We got him into home hospice and just a few days later, he was gone.

He asked that we take a picture of him playing his guitar.

I am also grateful that I've gotten better acquainted with his two Stepdaughters, Melanie Ramos Goocher and Paige Holt and his good friend and collaborator Jed Harris.

Steve was very dear to our immediate family and was a regular Thanksgiving and Christmas attendee for years. I almost wrote "guest" but he wasn't a guest. He was family. One year we switched out the curried squash soup that he loved for a mushroom bisque. He commented "You know what this soup needs?....MORE SQUASH!!!" That next Thanksgiving after he was gone it was asked and replied "You know what this soup needs?....MORE STEVE!!!"

On his next birthday I was enjoying my coffee in one of his Coyote mugs when I remembered. I raised the cup and said "Happy Birthday Steve!"

Then in my head I heard him clearly say "It was yesterday." My jaw dropped until he continued "Gotcha!"

www.ingramcontent.com/pod-product-compliance
Lightning Source LLC
Chambersburg PA
CBHW061549120626
46550CB00004B/1418